Passionate Subjects/
Split Subjects
in Twentieth-Century
Literature in Chile

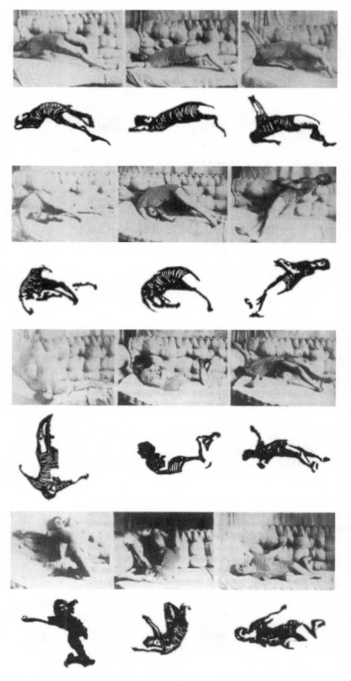

Images that combine ink stamps and oil paintings from the exhibitions "Declassified Salpêtrière, 1894–1998" and "Plague," Santiago, Chile, 2008. All images are by Chilean visual artist, Voluspa Jarpa.

Passionate Subjects/ Split Subjects in Twentieth-Century Literature in Chile

Brunet, Bombal, and Eltit

Bernardita Llanos M.

Lewisburg
Bucknell University Press

Associated University Presses
2010 Eastpark Boulevard
Cranbury, NJ 08512

The paper used in this publication meets the requirements of the American National Standard for Permanence of Paper for Printed Library Materials Z39.48-1984.

Library of Congress Cataloging-in-Publication Data

Llanos M., Bernadita, 1958–
    Passionate subjects/split subjects in twentieth-century literature in Chile : Brunet, Bombal, and Eltit / Bernadita Llanos.
        p.   cm.
    Includes bibliographical references and index.
    ISBN 978-0-8387-5733-8 (alk. paper)
    1. Chilean fiction—Women authors—History and criticism.   2. Brunet, Marta, 1901—Criticism and interpretation.   3. Bombal, María Luisa, 1910—Criticism and interpretation.   4. Eltit, Diamela, 1949—Criticism and interpretation.   5. Feminism and literature—Chile.   6. Literature and society—Chile.   I. Title.
    PQ7933.L56   2009
    863'.6099287'0982—dc22

                                                    2008045752

6/23/10 ✓

Contents

Acknowledgments

I WOULD LIKE TO EXPRESS MY GRATITUDE TO DENISON UNIVERSITY Research Foundation for supporting me in this project through an R. C. Good Fellowship and DURF funds.

My special thanks to the readers of my initial drafts: Eliana Ortega; Rodrigo Cánovas in Santiago, Chile; and my colleague, Gary Baker, in Granville, Ohio. My sincere appreciation goes to my women's studies colleague, Marlene Trump, who read one of the drafts of the introduction and made important comments.

I am especially grateful to Brenda Boyle, director of the Writing Center at Denison University, who read the entire manuscript in its various versions and did an extremely careful reading and editing work. Her aid was fundamental to bringing the book to completion in a clear and precise academic English. I am also grateful to my colleague in Spanish, Joanna Mitchell, for her thoughtful feedback on the last version of the introduction. My friend Ileana Rodríguez also read the introduction and posed important theoretical and political questions as I was in process of revising it.

I want to give a special thanks to Fernando Blanco and the numerous conversations we have had on Chilean literature and culture throughout these last four years. His company and support have been invaluable in the development of my ideas and this book.

I am thankful to Michael Sisson for his initial edition and help in translating some of the original works.

Also my thanks to go to Camilo Lorca at the Biblioteca Nacional in Chile for his initial assistance with the Archives with newspapers reviews on Brunet and Bombal; to two special members of AILCFH (Asociación Internacional de Literatura y Cultura Femenina Hispánica), Dianna Niebylski and Ksenija Bilbija, for their insightful suggestion to extend the scope of the book; to Cheryl Johnson at Denison University for her amazing patience and steady technical help; to Associate Provost Keith Boone for his ongoing support for my various projects; to Bev-

7

erly Herring for her unwavering bibliographic assistance; and to Mary Jo Myers for her inspiring presence when I most needed it.

I would also like to thank my friends and colleagues for their encouragement through these years and my son, Federico, for always keeping me on my toes.

Passionate Subjects/
Split Subjects
in Twentieth-Century
Literature in Chile

Introduction

THIS BOOK HAS DEVELOPED AS A RESULT OF MY DISCONTENT WITH the ways traditional gender roles shape subjectivity and their literary representations in the exclusively male canon of twentieth-century Chile. Furthermore, the masculine ideology that has shaped the canon and its reception is replicated in the historical context through a deliberately authoritarian exercise of power, particularly evident in dictatorial or military regimes. Paradoxically, female resistance literature becomes one of the most radical and persistent critiques of the twentieth century, as during Augusto Pinochet's dictatorship (1973–89), one of the most violent periods in Chilean history in the last century. While male writers were in exile writing about exile from a reductionist perspective of what had happened and had been lost, women whose citizenship had never been completed became active and defiant social actors.[1]

My selection of women's writing in this book is relevant today because their critique cannot be reduced to the experience of ideological militancy or external material circumstances but rather to the articulation of their opposition to a preexisting hegemony embodied in a patriarchal Catholic modernity. The authors question patriarchy, modernity, and the church during moments of social and political authoritarianism. That is why I have also reconsidered two other moments in the history of Chile during which there is a parallel between the literary historical reception of women's writing and the state's authoritarianism. I am particularly interested in the ways that modern subjectivity is constructed and the tensions and crises it undergoes. Moments or experiences of crisis, in my view, illuminate the hidden faces of modernity and what its rationalization means for subjectivities, particularly for those that are marginal and become the negative embodiment of the entire project of modernity and its ideal of progress and prosperity. My argument is thus against an economic approach, which is reductionist and Manichean, but it is not against modernity. I think that the imposition of one economic model (state capitalism, free-market neoliberalism) and one epistemological paradigm (Euro- or Anglocentric) to go along with it to modernize Latin American has invariably reedited colonialist and postcolonialist dependencies. The slighting of local realities and cultural contexts while social fragmentation and economic inequity become gruesome today alerts us to the contradictions that take place at a subjective level for those who are excluded.

Rereading these works, I have found there is a common thread I have defined as passion, which is not related to an aesthetic genre that privileges the author, or to gender readings that claim a political agenda that exhausts itself in the visibility of women. Instead what I argue is that these writings come close to the French psychoanalyst Luce Irigaray in her reading of Lacan and her discussion of the very structures of language and the construction of the feminine subject. Irigaray's challenging concept of mimicry shows that while women may imitate the patriarchal models of femininity they have learned, this does not reduce them to mere ventriloquists but rather enables them to subvert the mimesis of logocentrism.[2] These authors deliberately resort to the literary genre/gender system to disrupt the reproduction of a masculine ideology within the symbolic space of the canon. Following this line of thought, passion becomes a category that opposes the logos and where the subject constructs itself through the Lacanian or Freudian desire that precedes symbolic female representation, making meanings operate differently while liberating the process of signification from its conventional ties. Thus, when it is put into language, passion textualizes a singular and individual experience where the world is in a process of becoming rather than already completed.

Through the examination of the concept of passion and recovering its meaning from Greek pathos, as the Brazilian philosopher Marilena Chaui[3] traces its evolution in Western culture, my reading of three major Chilean writers, Marta Brunet (1897–1967), María Luisa Bombal (1910–80), and Diamela Eltit (b. 1949), presents subjectivity as an ethical tendency that expresses the subject's desire. Challenging the Christian patriarchal view of passion as sin and vice, on the one hand, and the economic definition of it as interest and calculation that modernity adds to it, the texts studied in this book represent passion against binary Western epistemology, moral judgment, and social usefulness. Passion is a form of knowledge, practice, and a language that defies social rules and legal contracts. These writers actually show that passion is embodied desire that makes self-reflection possible for women against the dictates of tradition and social norms. Passion, understood in this way, allows me to examine three historical moments of the Catholic authoritarian modernity in Chile and the ways this literature disputes it. In all three moments, literature denounces calculation, interest, and logical rationality as the tools for the reorientation of the passions or what is the same, the suppression of contestatory positions. This explains the fact that these writings and their authors have been considered ill (mentally, sexually, and socially) within medical and economic discourse.

Passion disrupts cultural organization by resisting the domesticating process that modernity unleashes and that inexorably reduces woman to a function in order to civilize and cure her of a constitutive animalism or irrationality. The modern views of the passions are indebted to Immanuel Kant's theory and his definition of them as "pathologies of the will." Kant reduces the complex discourse on the passions developed earlier and denies them any "role as a chief source of ethical action."[4] In contrast to Kant, ancient theory understood passion as pathos, that is, the inclination of individual character (ethos), which was modulated by the logos. Marilena Chaui argues that Christianity introduces a drastic change in these categories through the negativization of pathos. In this new framework, passion is linked to vice and opposes ethos in a binary system of moral judgments rather than ethical principles. Thus, the passions were to reason what virtue was to vice in a dislocation that drastically changed the epistemology of the pair ethos-pathos.[5] Furthermore, the passions always carried with them the risk of animalization. Chaui concludes that for modernity this risk is even greater because it is founded on reason as the guide of free will and passion against the danger of bestiality. However, modern reason soon realized that passion was constitutive of human nature in the form of "irrationality." This dislocation progressively takes the passions from the metaphysical, political, and ethical realms to that of medicine, to the clinic and to scientific psychology, as Michel Foucault's *Madness and Civilization: A History of Insanity in the Age of Reason* (1988) extensively discusses.[6] In his chapter titled "Passion and Delirium," the language of delirium is the organizing form of passion in the patient's mind within the scientific discourse on madness. Madness is beyond imagination but rooted in it since the mind erroneously gives total value and "absolute truth " to an image. Paradoxically, Foucault continues "the ultimate language of madness is reason," enveloped in the image, defined and limited by it but also unquestionably showing the "figures of logic."[7]

With this shift in paradigm, the bourgeois ideals of modernity uphold virtues against vices while making the former dependent on reason. Bourgeois morality suppresses the passions and exchanges them for values that preserve social order and institutions, particularly the family. The usefulness of the passions is a condition contributed by Adam Smith's theory with his addition of the economic and political concept of interest. In this framework, good passions are considered useful and may succeed over those that are destructive and detrimental to public and private interests. Interest in this line of thought secures self-preservation and the political stability of a contractual and consensual order. The notion of interest assimilates a mercantilist reason within its calculating rationality to achieve the desired goal. What is at stake is how to select and negotiate competing passions in order to combine public (state) and private benefit (individual wealth).[8]

My analysis has a different outlook, as mentioned earlier, by resorting to Irigaray's concept of mimicry as well as her concept of commodity, alongside Chaui's discussion on passion. As a result, I reclaim the ancient theory of the passions where pathos is the embodiment of desire in language. In her essay "Commodities amongst Themselves," Irigaray discusses the ways a patriarchal modern economy commodifies not only culture and nature, but specifically women's bodies. She points out that women, like signs, currency, and commodities, are exchanges among males in patriarchal societies. She further adds that the sociocultural order itself requires a homosexual organizing principle and that heterosexuality is basically the "assignment of economic roles." Men in this regime are the producer subjects and agents of exchange, whereas females as well as the earth are commodities to be exchanged. This process of commodification that modern culture extends to every aspect of social life and subjectivity is legislated through the law, in which gender inequity and class privileges predominate.[9] In this way, the libidinal economy that organizes the subjects has cancelled out the potential for liberation that the language of the passions carries with it.

In the literary practices I analyze passion defamiliarizes, in the formalist sense of the term, the linguistic system by establishing a play between subject and language that resignifies and reeroticizes the world, defying its libidinal economy. It also discusses the ways affects constitute imagination and representations of the female body as a source of radical and nontransferable experience. As a result, the force of the passions disclaims calculation, interest, or reason and instead perceives what is necessary and stronger, as Chaui argues.[10] From the perspective of the passions, culture becomes what is deadening of vital pulsations, particularly as it pertains to female identity. The language of the passions radically opposes the social pact of a patriarchal modernity in which diserotization becomes one of its overarching traits and a supragoal. The Peruvian psychoanalyst Kathya Araujo, following Foucault, asserts that in Latin America the forms of sexuality can be considered the very structure of social organization in different societies. In this way, sex; bodies, particularly women's; and their exchanges have been a field to control since their regulation is the basis for social ordering, the configuration of subjects and their relations. In the twentieth century, psychoanalysis, anthropology, and literature were the disciplines that contributed to the understanding of sexuality as a way to name the body's passions, which are interrelated with the ways bodies and subjects are constructed and regulated in a given society.[11] To this view, the Brazilian sociologist Claudia Bonan adds that during the process of modernity, despite the production of new forms of knowledge and rationalities through the idealization of modern citizenship, the Christian framework and its regulatory precepts toward family and marriage remained. The founders of the modern political debate on sexuality and reproduction did not establish an antagonistic dispute with traditional religious forces. On the contrary, the hierarchical power of the family, a fundamental element in the Judeo-Christian tradition, was instead displaced from the "divine order" to the "natural order." The latter was added directly from the laws of biology and was established as the basis for a rational social order in the discourse of positivist social thinking.[12] In this worldview, the Mexican anthropologist Marta Lamas argues that gender represents a threat to any fundamentalism because it questions the idea of the natural, which has been linked to the divine, and shows that it is cultural symbolization and not biology that establishes relative prescriptions to what is appropriate to each sex.[13]

In their texts, Brunet, Bombal, and Eltit deconstruct gender domination and fixed binary categories while also dismantling the cultural myths embedded in marriage, wifedom, and family. In most of these works, women are alienated and disenfranchised by a system in which the legal institutions (of marriage and family) and capitalist development validate the abuse of bodies (individual and collective).

Fear of the nation's effeminization constructs the male and patriotic literary canon, according to the Chilean critic Fernando Blanco, through the administration of a discourse on sexuality that guarantees the honor and public probity of the members of civil, religious, and military hierarchies. Blanco also asserts that the literary canon, as does the Chilean family, incorporates nonhegemonic sexualities only as long as they do not alter the class, ethnic, and ideological imperatives driving the national project. In this scenario, a Catholic/military sexual morality is guarded by the "presencia protectora de los códigos masculinos del honor conventual y el honor marcial" (the protective presence of the masculine monastic and martial honor codes).[14] Literature in the cultural context of the newly independent nation was supposed to educate and guide young Chileans and prevent them from becoming effeminate and lazy. The regulation of the Republic of the Letters and its narrative canon was clearly stated in 1843 by the eminent Venezuelan grammarian and jurist Andrés Bello, who not surprisingly would also write the Civil Code some years later. Blanco explains that for Bello the *logos* of science, the arts and letters, were in the service of progress and the consolidation of the republic through an "enlightened morality."[15]

Marta Brunet, María Luisa Bombal, and Diamela Eltit develop a counternarrative to the literary canon, in which cultural codes fall apart. From their perspective, hegemonic cultural discourse fails to include and recognize difference. Furthermore, it is plagued with flaws and fissures proper to a modernity founded on subordination. For Doris Sommer, romance is the cornerstone of the foundational narratives of nineteenth-century national projects in Latin America. My analysis looks at how these three Chilean women authors revisit and ultimately question these heterosexual narratives by representing the crisis of modernity through sexual and legal contracts in the twentieth century. The end of oligarchic political leadership in the thirties, forties, and fifties is the context I examine, and its legacy in the rural areas constitutes the cultural matrix of Bombal's and Brunet's writing. The development of a national industrialization project and its interclass alliance in the late fifties is also revised by Brunet in her later work, which shows its ideological shortcomings for female development. The total collapse of democracy and disenfranchiment of the popular classes after Pinochet's coup d'état and its aftermath are part of the social and cultural horizon of

Eltit's narrative. The advent of the Pinochet dictatorial regime and its dismantling of collective and social referents gave rise to a reign of terror sustained by military authoritarianism. The predominance of the military male and its counter female figure, the Virgin Mary (patron of the Chilean military), reshaped a national gender politics and public discourse in which Catholic ideology and militarism join. Institutional violence founded and shaped a new society in which dissidence was criminalized. As a result, the military state legitimized diverse forms of material and symbolic violence over civil society.

The liberal oligarchic paradigm prevalent in the last third of the nineteenth century and supported by the liberal governments in Chile collapsed in 1891, faced with the threat that the project of state modernization implied for the aristocratic elites. The liberal defeat resulted in the strengthening of hierarchical intersubjective relations and values, characteristics also found in the premodern modes of production and exploitation by the propertied class. Along with these facts, the extensive political influence of the oligarchy shaped the law and the regulations for the labor force. Within this model, gender relations are rooted in the same dominant-subordinate axis veiled by the perception of work as a modern means to reach social and individual happiness and where women are (re)productive bodies. We have to wait another forty years in order to see education as the vehicle for national development and cohesion as it had been characterized by the old and liberal enlightened values in which progress and civilization were intimately linked to education and language. The state project that carries on this idea is the patriarchal welfare state in which the state becomes the protector and warrantor of basic needs for the population, especially on behalf of new social actors: an organized working class, an emergent middle class, women, and children. Social benefits and social assistance through state programs are accompanied by industrial development through state protectionism. Class, however, predominates as a cultural marker in the private and public sphere as the examples of endogamous marriages within the oligarchy show in Bombal's works.

In different ways and with different perspectives, the writings of Marta Brunet, María Luisa Bombal, and Diamela Eltit critique modernity in Chile as a masculinist project that domesticates and uproots subaltern subjectivities. By presenting different and alternate subject positions in the margins of a national and dominant discourse, they confront the dominant masculine/heterosexual subjectivity. By doing so, they also question a literary canon and culture based on an authoritarian rationality.

Modernity is a cover-up of these negative and destructive effects, particularly as it affects women and others who have been excluded from it. In the twentieth century, literature written by these three women writers in Chile critiqued and questioned the hegemonic place of reason, particularly instrumental reason, in the project of modernity. For these authors, the prevalence of irrationality inside the process of modern rationalization is played out within conjugal and gender relations in which different manifestations of violence prevail.

The fact that Brunet and Bombal locate most of their narrative in a rural context reveals the different temporalities that constitute the dialectical process of Latin American modernity/modernization, and the ways that the disruption of time and space shapes a dislocated female subject. Eltit does this also but in the periphery of the city. The countryside and its inhabitants' reality appear to have been suspended in time in contrast to the relentless acceleration of history that modernity means, particularly in the metropolis. For Eltit's characters, temporality is a paradoxical transit between an industrial and service city (the center) and the periphery in the outskirts. The Argentine philosopher Nicolás Casullo has argued that modernity is the process of historical rationalization that in the West consummates and finalizes the disenchantment of the world instituted by religious, mythical, and sacred images. The progressive loss of religious representation, according to Casullo, creates a world that is dominated by the ideology of progress and the legitimation of scientific and technical reason.[16] In his essay "What Is Enlightenment?" Michel Foucault defines modernity within the history of philosophy through Kant's response to this question. For Kant modernity signals the entry into adulthood of humanity that is, European societies, through the possibility of choice and the use of reason. The great promise of the eighteenth century was that individuals learn to respect one another, freely abiding by the law of the despotic and enlightened monarchic state.[17] Foucault's thought shows the difficulties of Kant's text "What Is Enlightenment,?" as well as casting doubts on the mature adulthood of European societies in the twentieth century.[18] This Eurocentric paradigm of enlightened modernity is fraught with acute social tensions and cultural contradictions in the Latin American contexts where it is implemented in societies still struggling with a colonial past and its legacies.

Women's protest against a specifically patriarchal Catholic modernity is revealed in their search for meaning outside the confines of convention, as the literary worlds of these three writers show. The escape to the natural world together with the erotization of the landscape oppose the modern mastery and desacralization of nature. Vitality and sensuality in their texts take place by leaving the molds in which a masculine modernity places women and subaltern groups. In Brunet's case, eroticism is expressed in the public performance of her female character, whose appearance and behavior contradict gender ideology. Against the cold gaze of instrumental reason, Bombal's women give nature a mysterious and transcendental meaning of which their own subjectivity partakes, providing them with aliveness and emotional connectedness. This tendency represents Bombal's critique of social rationalization and her dissatisfaction with the predominance of a technological and scientific spirit as the only realm of knowledge and truth.

The female psychic and bodily fragmentation manifested in language is a negative stance in the literature of these three writers that finds in the body's dissolution a counterform to modern art, that is, a rejection of the canonical figurative shape of the female body. Since the nineteenth-century, the representation of female bodies in the visual arts has been created mostly for man's pleasure. Mary Ann Caws points out that in Western art the objectification of the female body has been monopolized by the male spectator's sexuality.[19] In European oil painting, as John Berger comments, feminine nudity has been a form of dress that responds to the male spectator rather than to the woman's sexuality. The female nude is displayed in a pose submissive to "the man looking at the picture," appealing to his sexuality and affirming his "monopoly" of passion.[20]

In the literature I discuss in this book, the female body and its linguistic representations become a contested symbolic arena. The political and sexual body of the female becomes a site in which power is exerted as an ideological and repressive force that prohibits and punishes desires and practices that are outside the confines established by a Catholic and state morality. The female body is inextricably linked to dominant moral notions of propriety, chastity, and spirituality. This bodyscape represents the last place to be claimed in a cultural grid where women are meant to be sacrificed to the nation's rationality and the continuation of the Chilean family. The mutilation and disintegration of the female body that Bombal and Eltit particularly resort to in their texts politicize it as a place of disjuncture that defies masculine and religious ideologies. In their writing, the female body resists appropriation by hegemonic constructions in its ability to metamorphosize into multiple and nonproductive shapes. Language plays a major role in the transformation of a female subject into a political individual even under oppressive conditions.

The subjects depicted in these texts confront the hegemonic reason instituted by a narrative that appropriates and vitiates the female body and vital passion of any significance. On the opposite end of this rationality belong close and intense attachments with mother, daughter, son, or lover forming the intersubjective web that counters prohibitions and imperative models of identity and sexuality as well as gender and class. In this context, marriage and the hacienda appear as two institutions in Latin America that historically legitimize the modern abuse of individual and collective bodies. In both institutions, the possession of the other's body is legitimated through economic and contractual agreements. The female body is in turn commodified for reproduction and labor. Profit becomes the overarching goal of all socioeconomic interactions. In the specific case of Eltit, the imaginary of the hacienda is still governing women's bodies, making them inseparable from the landscape of authoritarian and patriarchal regimes. The other two writers locate this body inside and outside the hacienda, midway between the country and the city, denouncing its appropriation and reduction. The process of regendering female bodies unleashed by modernity drives Brunet's character María Nadie out from the rural space and towards the North, to the modern city, with the hope of fitting in and finding a place for herself.

The impossibility of consuming the female body in the literary representations of these three Chilean writers reveals that the body is a territory in dispute. The phallic masculine ideals that modernity presents as self-evident and stable are questioned through the display of an experience that resists patriarchal representations. As Rita Felski argues in her book *The Gender of Modernity* (1995), the identification of modernity with masculinity may be seen in the key gendered symbols of the modern, particularly in the public sphere, the man of the crowd and the stranger. In this paradigm, women are situated outside history and embody an "atemporal authenticity seemingly untouched by the alienation and fragmentation of modern life."[21] Felski is here exclusively referring to an urban modernity in the Anglo-Eurocentric tradition, leaving out the wide range of peripheral modernities in which this paradigm is relativized and ultimately challenged.

Despite their peripheral position, women are not thoroughly contained or domesticated by the rigid enforcement of Catholic moral values and tradition. In spite of their subordination, females reveal a power that may suddenly and inadvertently disrupt normalcy and the hierarchies established by marriage and the family. Gender identities are dismantled and shown as not fixed but rather reaffirmed and redefined in specific contexts. Self-defense against male threats allows the canceling out of gender roles in situations under which life is in danger, as two of Brunet's women characters show. Strategy and ingenuity overshadow notions of propriety and femininity. Women are the depositories of violence in most of Brunet's narrative. Consequently, only the *pícara* and the old woman who understand the socioeconomic system and use all their resources are able to fight back and succeed. In Brunet's text the way out is always individual, and it depends on the courage and personal ability of females. In Bombal, the alternative is intellectual and is placed in the reflection of death, allowing woman to leave testimony of her life. Eltit, on the other hand, presents a revolutionary utopia requiring the transformation of alienation and the rage of workers into collective political action. Individual women together with other marginal citizens are condemned in a social system that excludes and commodifies them.

Since family and nation are intertwined in modernity and work toward the propagation of a model of citizenship and morality, they share the same gender division. Modernity makes the state as well as the nation its most productive machine of systematic social rationalization. This device economizes violence and creates an entire realm of domination in which the individual is completely normalized. The individual is indebted to the exclusive demands of this bureaucratic rationalization, as the Argentine philosopher Ricardo Forster suggests, in which reason has a central place.[22] The imagined nation, which the state embodies, represents shared values and norms that the state regulates. In a similar, hierarchical scheme, the state is to the nation what the father is to the family: that is, the seat of authority to which all must submit for the common good. His power is manifested and reinforced in the obedience and respect everyone in the household is expected to show. In the narratives analyzed, masculine authority appears in the patriarchal modern state, which is textualized in the different dominant economic gender positions.

In the texts I study, the word originates in the context of a metaphorical system and creates universes founded on imagination rather than logical relationships. In the writing of all three, we find the process of demystification of the myths governing an authoritarian Catholic modernity. These writers emphasize different aspects of this configuration while deconstructing its dominant images of the house, the family, and subjectivity through new passionate stories and theories of the world. They explain rather than duplicate history. Brunet, in her turn, renovates *criollismo,* the stereotypical representation of the countryside and its inhabitants, through a portrayal of a historic gender oppression. Her narrative exposes sexual abuses and reveals private secrets within the rural family (namely, rape and incest). She demystifies the countryside and shows its inhabitants within the web of hierarchical and abusive relations that the hacienda system sustains. Brunet's house is not a home nor a refuge but rather a temporal stop in which females are condemned to wait and age for a male. In many ways, this house resembles a labor and sexual camp in which women and children are the most exploited bodies. The house in this narrative is the seat of violence of a vertical and patriarchal order that severs familial ties and loyalties.

Bombal's poetic and surrealistic imagination conversely articulates an aesthetic that claims emotions and inner freedom as its places of enunciation. Within this imaginative and subjective paradigm, Bombal displays the process of the wife's alienation from within, revealing her consumption in a claustrophobic private space. The house is a place of confinement and isolation here, a kind of ivory tower that makes possible the imaginative process of writing and remembering. However, this space is also sterile and deadening in that it resembles a crypt, particularly for women. Bombal emphasizes the inner and psychological aspects of an imprisoned female who finds no place of confirmation other than in her imagination. Bombal's narrative also exposes the patriarchal model ruling the sexual contract through the different male figures. In it the landowner appears self-interested, indifferent, and cold, manipulating marriage from the outset.

Finally, Eltit's imagination demystifies the modern patriarchal and white mythology. Her texts show hostility and irrationality in extreme material conditions and under authoritarian and violent forms. Aggression and alienation in the city become embodied in the working-class man who abuses his dependents but also in the phallic mother who subjugates her children. In Eltit, houses are linked to emergency and precariousness. They are surrounded by instability, and a strong sense of crisis (of the family, the couple, the subject) defines them.

The literary genre/gender canon provides no space to recognize and analyze what these three authors do in their literary works since they are incorporated through *criollismo* (Brunet), surrealism (Bombal), and avant-garde (Eltit), erasing the gendered subject and the subjectivities that their literature presents. In consequence, they are written out as women and incorporated as (male) "writers" in accordance with the historical literary period of the time. When the "anomaly" of a literary work shows it to be evidently irregular or exceptional, the literary establishment makes its mission to close or halt that specific work. Blanco further adds that the discussion around the constitution of the canon in Chile is a "generational' one among fathers and sons who struggle to enforce their respective aesthetics in the national literary project.[23] Literature is understood as a homosocial space from which women are excluded, particularly in the 1930s and 1940s. Misogyny marks a masculine ideology that contains and controls the public access of women as well as their ability to write and publish. The fact that men could not accede equal rights to women without their own degradation as males is solved, according to the Chilean critic Rubí Carreño, by degrading what is considered "feminine."[24] Carreño further discusses in another essay on Diamela Eltit that she has been stigmatized by sectors of the literary media on the basis of sexism, a feature still prevalent in Chilean culture today.[25]

The writers present gender as a form of marginalization embedded in an authoritarian morality and law regulated by marriage and the family. In this context, female resistance irrupts and destabilizes the tight grip that a patriarchal hegemony sustains throughout domestic and private life. Female aggression and unconventional sexuality become a threat to patriarchal masculinity in the home, displaying an unforeseen possibility to alter and subvert it. This emphasis on the house and interpersonal relationships enables the presentation of a microcosm where passion transforms identities and positions that have been construed as fixed and unquestionable by social discourses. These narratives turn the house inside out, naming areas that have been ignored or devalued, highlighting the dynamics of authoritarianism, the points of resistance as well as rejection to offers and pacts. These disruptions undermine the entire system of compulsory heterosexuality, as Judith Butler has suggested in *Gender*

Trouble: Feminism and the Subversion of Identity (1990). The cultural alignment of sex, gender, and desire would have as its only product a single subjectivity (feminine or masculine) that fulfills social expectations.[26] What the works of Brunet, Bombal, and Eltit do is challenge the heterosexual cultural paradigm to the point that the Chilean canon in its initial reception naturalized gender in terms of an aesthetic genre.

The bleak and dire picture of marriage and family that is revealed in the texts studied illustrates subjectivity and gender relations still bound by patriarchal oligarchic values while a positivist ideology of modernity is being endorsed at the national and social levels. Intimate spaces and relationships are turned upside down, torn between the old and the new socioeconomic models while becoming the main sources of alienation and loss for women. In this way, the alienation of the modern subject not only is the result of anonymity and massification in the public sphere, as these narratives show, but also is embedded in the gender ideology that rules the private sphere. In rural areas Brunet and Bombal depict the persistence of feudal conditions of the social structure around the hacienda, in which the landowner is master and owner of people and things. The figure of the patriarch that he embodies is "the backbone of social and political life of the rural community in which he lives," as Jean Franco has asserted.[27] To escape his grip and alienation, women look to their inner world, to memory and passion. These become the last realms in which to claim individual freedom and respite from an oppressive order. Unless women accept the identity and double-edged security of marriage, their fate is "to be left by the train" or "dress saints." Both idiomatic expressions emphasize gender imperatives, on the one hand, and suggest modernity, on the other. The image of the train as the symbol of modernity and the negativity implicit in missing it in the case of women go hand in hand with spinsterhood represented in the unmodern duty of "dressing saints" as a demeaning and terrifying fate. Spinsters lack social identity and respect; they have no place in society other than what charity may provide.

Eltit's contemporary urban narratives remind us that as we move in time, female alienation increases, taking place inside and outside the individual, leaving fewer options for personal and collective freedom in the relentless and voracious expansion of capitalist modernity. Her aggressive familial and social environments leave us with decentered and socially unsheltered subjectivities. Her characters are expelled by the social order, left in the dark in a culture that discounts them. Evidently, the main difference between Eltit and Brunet, on the one hand, and Bombal, on the other, is that they understand marginalization and alienation as consequences of women's position in the economic and social order with specific historical and cultural ramifications. Bombal insists instead on gender position as the only explanation for female subordination. However, in all three writers, women are ruled by contracts that are regulated by sexual, legal, and national demands.

The creation of the bourgeois modern public sphere in the nation-state in the nineteenth century allows for the unprecedented public use of reason through public voice, as Jürgen Habermas shows in his philosophical discussion of modern subjects and public opinion.[28] The public sphere mediates between civil society (economy and labor), the family and the state. Joan B. Landes's feminist critique of Habermas's social claims of the universality of the public sphere shows that from the outset, masculine speech, objectivity, and reason were equated with truth and masked as a universal and abstract model. Women's discourse, she argues, was left out from the beginning and considered to focus on particular concerns that were deemed inappropriate for public debate.[29] In consequence, the public sphere was nonegalitarian and exclusionary in its conception of representation and power.

The ideal identities that modernity offers women push them to negotiate other subject positions that form a second system of gender identifications affiliated to the peripheral and different "styles" of modernization in Latin America, as Martin Hopenhayn argues.[30] Modernity in the Latin American context is a metanarrative imbued with the elements and ideals of the Enlightenment and its notion of history as an ever greater achievement of progress, rationality, and predictability. From the liberal economic model to the industrial state-sponsored model of development, modernity has been linked to modernization, to achieving the industrial utopias through a process of homogenization that has proved to be destructive, as Hopenhayn states, when referring to the state economic model as well as to the prescriptions of the neoliberal free market economy.

The belated Latin American modernity of the twentieth century shows this modern bourgeois sphere wrought with tensions and contradictions at the institutional as well as the symbolic private levels. The persistence of an old oligarchic worldview responds to what has been called a "baroque culture," which continues Hispanic colonial models in the hacienda. These cultural practices essentially conflict with the European rationality of the modern state that is incorporated into Latin America after the movements of independence.[31] As economic modernization was further advanced in the early twentieth century, the experience of modernity began to change. Unconditional faith in the ideal of progress and rationality was undermined in Europe, as Vivian Schelling has pointed out, giving birth to a restrictive view of progress as applied reason. In Latin America, "modernization theory" and developmentalism in the 1950s and 1960s became the privileged ways to disseminate entrepreneurship and a "scientific-instrumental rationality." From the 1980s onward, we see economic neoliberalism as the dominant paradigm in which "unfettered market forces" are turned into "the harbinger of progress."[32]

However, the persistence of a baroque culture within the project of modernity may be seen in premodern political practices that are gender- and ethnically marked. This previous culture, according to Jorge Larraín, develops during the modern project in Chile a tendency that is essentially authoritarian, unequal, and founded on dogma. In contrast, European modernity is constructed on the principles of liberal, revolutionary, and democratic ideals in which reason replaces dogma. The gap between European modernity and Chilean modernity and the relative belatedness of the latter with respect to the former leave an enduring mark in the social consciousness.[33] The elite's sense of being behind and of the need to be modern at whatever cost is an ongoing theme in Chilean history as in other regions of the continent.[34] This peripheral position makes Latin American modernity heterogeneous and multitemporal. In this line of thought, Schelling has traced the development of Latin American modernity, showing the increasing hegemonic role of a technocratic conception of modernity that has led to "a scattering, a deterritorialization of cultural forms and identities and their recombination in different contexts." The three moments that she identifies in the development of Latin American modernity (colonial, late nineteenth century and early twentieth, and the 1950s and 1960s) are determined by transformations that do not eradicate "feudal" and premodern social relations dating from colonial times. On the contrary, they acquire gender and ethnic significance.[35]

Hispanic and colonial cultural residues prevalent in the region, specifically in Chile, are tightly related to the latifundia system and its Catholic ideology, especially in the rural areas. A masculine power structure constituted by the father, the patron, and the clergy develops into a culture in which love and emotional feelings are excluded. The historian Maximiliano Salinas Campos shows that from colonial to republican times Chile is a hierarchical and seigniorial society that expresses itself in the culture of the hacienda. Love is absent as a discursive theme in a society that is sexually arranged according to a patriarchal and seigniorial theology. Marriage is seen as a way for men "to flee fornication" and lead a virtuous life in which Eros is substituted by Caritas. In hierarchical societies, popular sectors and women appear to defy this Catholic submission and resist the domestication of their sexuality.[36] Popular poetry, as Salinas Campos points out, reflects an alternative countersexuality to hegemonic models. The authors studied in this book also present a counterview to the identity models that sociohegemonic discourses affirm.

As a result of its colonial heritage, there is a double standard embedded in the separation of the public and private spheres in Chilean culture that allows each one to operate in isolation and with a different set of principles. The political ideals of progress and equality heralded by the nation-state disappear in the private domain where Catholic values reign and the male citizen defines informal contracts. His role as father and legislator of the private sphere reenacts the Catholic imaginary for females, on the one hand, and compensates his loss of power to the state in the public sphere, on the other. The Mexican writer Carlos Fuentes has described the dichotomy of Latin American identity in terms of legality and reality from colonial times to the present. He states that there always were two nations: one that was legal and consecrated in the Legislation of the Indies, and a real nation. The latter existed behind the façade of the law and could be found in the hacienda, the mine, and the small villages all the way from the Viceroyalty of New Spain to the Viceroyalty of Río de la Plata.[37]

One of the bedrocks for the institutionalization of Catholic modernity is marriage. In the Latin American context it becomes the only legitimate expression of sexual arrangement, obliterating multiple other forms that remain outside civil society and conflict with the modernization undergone by the public sphere in which women have been civilly recognized. Multiple sexual arrangements have historically characterized Latin American societies since colonial times (consensual unions, *la casa chica,* multiple partners, among others), despite the pressure of the church and the state. The Mexican historian Asunción Lavrín has extensively documented sexual behavior in colonial Latin America and how sexual agreements were shaped in tension with the notions of sin and honor in a society that was stratified by ethnic, cultural, and economic factors. Lavrín states that sexuality and sexual practices show a heterogeneous reality that is at odds with the politics of marriage and the social dictates of the Catholic Church and the state. According to her analysis, in the end the individual in colonial Latin America acted regardless of institutional or spiritual restrictions as the cultural artifact of *Casta* painting documents.[38] From an institutional stand, nevertheless, Lavrín remarks that the supervision and control of marriage had to do with the enforcement of a basic family order in a patriarchal society.[39] Moreover, Sergio Gatica Cortés explains that the institutionalization of the *dote* during colonial times reveals the powerlessness of women. It was a prerequisite in arranged marriages that commodified females by giving an assigned economic value to their bodies and reproductive powers. Despite the fact that gender norms in colonial Chile stated that women should consent to marriage, in general terms, Gatica Cortés asserts, it was a male matter. [40] María Emma Mannarelli has also discussed how hierarchical societies, in which the Catholic Church and the military work as tutelary institutions, have had their sexual life and family bonds affected. These areas have been founded on a gender hierarchy that establishes female subordination and obedience, and an unquestioning respect for authority (paternal authority, in particular).[41]

The institution of marriage is legislated in the Chilean Civil Code written by Andrés Bello in 1855 and put in practice in 1857. The main sources for the *Bello Code* were the French Civil Code Napoléon (1804), the Canonical Code, and the *Siete Partidas* laws of King Alfonso X, dating back to the thirteenth century. A diverse range of other European sources made up this code, which also incorporated commentaries of French jurists on the Code Napoléon. This hybrid compilation of laws was divided into four books, which established rights and obligations for people and property. Book 1 through its fifty-three articles addresses the issue of people and the question of marriage and family law. Marriage is defined in article 102 as a solemn contract by which a man and a woman were united indissolubly for life, with the goal of living together to procreate and help one another.

The enormous influence of the Chilean Civil Code in Latin America may be traced in the civil codes of many countries that adopted it almost without modifications (Ecuador, El Salvador, Nicaragua, Honduras, Colombia, and Panama) or wrote theirs with this model in mind (Brazil, Argentina, and Uruguay) throughout the nineteenth and twentieth centuries. However, since in Chile church and state were not separated until 1873, a fact ratified only in the Constitution of 1925, marriage legislation remained for a long time under both canon and civil law. Thus, despite the creation of a civil marriage law in 1884 as the culmination of the conflict between church and state, its application went hand in hand with the separation of church and state. This is the law that rules today with modifications introduced in the constitution of 1980 as well as the law that made divorce legal in 2004.[42] Nevertheless, the ambiguity and violent transit between the law and practice, public and private spheres, males and females, continue shaping social and intersubjective gender relations.

It is interesting to note the tension that the Enlightenment, its liberal ideals, institutions, and civil legislation, reveal in the context of a peripheric modernity in comparison to the metropolitan centers of cultural hegemony, France and its territories. The historian Isabel V. Hull shows that the Code Napoléon was an instrument of social reform that served as the modern model for civil society and social relations according to liberal "principles of legal equality and propertied ownership." Furthermore, it destroyed "feudal relations of subservience, restrictions of property holding and disposal, and on commerce."[43] However, Hull underscores that the code left married women at a disadvantage without legal and economic "personhood," since it gave all rights of marital property as well as sexual rights to the husband.[44] The Code Napoléon revolved around "the private and social status of the male citizen as family father and producer of wealth," giving him greater state-guaranteed rights.[45] The Civil Code in Chile similarly discriminates against women and wives in tandem with the sexism embedded in Catholic ideology that shaped the Canonical Code. Subjectivity is here marked by gender and cultural imperatives that operate in conjunction with a national enterprise that ultimately fails to guarantee equity and progress to all citizens. Brunet, Bombal, and Eltit write as intellectuals from the interstices of modernity, from those places where the flaws and weaknesses of this project reveal its contradictions, imbalances, and violence. One of these problems is sexual difference, which in the modern protocol is resolved in marriage through a pact that proclaims male protection in exchange for unconditional female obedience. As a consequence, a female's status and social identity result from being her husband's wife and mother of his progeny.

This contradiction is based on a conflict of interests in the hierarchical relationship between a man and a woman that marriage implies by having female subordination as its basis. In the erasure of identity that the marriage contract imposes on women violence is naturalized.

Subordination of difference becomes the overarching feature guiding modernity and development in Chilean society. In it women are civilly dead, childlike, and dependent on their husbands' protection and authority. Throughout the twentieth century, a married woman appeared to owe her husband traditional duties such as housekeeping and sex, similar to what has been demanded of wifehood in other cultural contexts in the Western world, as Marylyn Yalom comments in *A History of the Wife* (2001).

In the thirties and forties of the twentieth century, women's writings presented new visions that questioned the dominant oligarchic views from within and without this model. The erosion of the oligarchic cultural and political models enabled the emergence of new voices and social agents that proposed new ways of configuring the nation and the state as a consequence of the democratization of education. As the book *Modernidad en otro tono: Escritura de mujeres latinoamericanas: 1920–1950 (Modernity in Another Tone: Latin American Women's Writing: 1920–1950)* (2004) clearly shows, women's integration into the labor force alongside other economic, political, and social changes taking place made visible new subjectivities. The entrance into the public field allowed Latin American women to face the challenges posited by modernity in a cultural and historical context, where the old and dominant ideologies were giving way to other political and social alternatives. Women writers openly questioned the "ideology of domesticity" and gender that had prevailed and began to define a discursive modality that presented specific and nonhegemonic perspectives about modernity.[46] Grínor Rojo has pointed out that during the last decades of the nineteenth century, particularly in upper and oligarchic classes, females were physically secluded. In this cultural context, marriage and motherhood were the cornerstone of all classes for social reproduction and production. In contrast, the first three decades of the twentieth century showed "women leaving the house" during what Rojo calls "the second stage of modernity in Latin America." [47]

The first half of the twentieth century gave birth to a modern conceptualization of womanhood in the "new woman," an image that combined the old ideals of self-sacrifice and sensibility with a sense of gender equality with men, as Asunción Lavrín asserts. Simultaneously, for example, Latin American feminism succeeded in giving a social meaning to the ascriptions of femininity and womanhood. As a result, motherhood within feminist discourse became a social function in which women provided the state with lives and human resources. [48] The new modern woman in Latin American culture faced many of the challenges and restlessness produced by the abandonment of domesticity that women confronted in the United States and Europe. The weakening of dominant ideals of femininity and domesticity is acutely portrayed in the literary representations of women writers that emphasize the absence of equality and the deadening of identity. In contrast, the counterattack of conservatives, particularly the church in Chile, serves as an ongoing reminder of the glories of being a wife and a mother and the unnaturalness of any other options. Women from all walks of life equally faced a strong Catholic and civil patriarchal tradition that made it almost impossible to redefine the conjugal model and change the law. Asunción Lavrín states that until the early part of the twentieth century, marital codes ensured the husband's "right to control his wife's actions," and female "submission" was "carefully delineated" in the law. Moreover, Lavrín underscores that "the legal restrictions on married men and women imposed by the church" were "sealed by Civil Codes" in Chile, thus providing legal responsibilities with "canonical foundations." The *Patria Potestad* ensured that the husband's power became a father's privilege, providing him with the rights over minors and their property.[49]

However, women's increasing employment in urban areas made these codes harder to enforce with married working women. Economically independent women, as Lavrín shows, posited new legal challenges to legislation and social life. Women's civil equality and suffrage became a political issue from the mid-1910s onward. The need to reform the Civil Code to allow married women to administer their property and a bill "to enfranchise women" proposed by conservatives reflected the extent to which political and civil rights were an increasingly significant issue across the board. Despite this social reality, Lavrín emphasizes that in the Southern Cone, no legislator supported radical gender change in behavior in- or outside the family. None of the changes that were proposed altered gender relations, either. Reform was seen rather as strengthening women's faculties as mothers without undermining the husbands' right and authority "as head of the family." In consequence, gender hierarchy and men's legal authority within the family were preserved despite minor reforms and shallow changes.[50] While this took place in public history, in literary history women writers were accusing legislators and revealing the consequences of this state of affairs.

Questioning patriarchal views of motherhood and wifehood is a predominant trait of the three literary worlds studied in this book and may also be found in the works of other female writers of their times. In the literary arena, the crisis of the traditional and hierarchical marriage is a reiterated topic that highlights dire consequences, particularly to women and the family unit. Maternity and wifedom, specifically in the works of Brunet, Bombal, and Eltit, are presented as institutions that stifle identity on behalf of a social order organized by class hierarchy and gender privilege. The official blissful views of motherhood and of woman as the "queen of the house" are substituted in these texts by contradictory and dense bodily and psychic experiences that contrast with the unconditional acceptance and complicity required of mothers from a patriarchal order, as Patricia Rubio has pointed out in her reading of Chilean women authors.[51]

Gender identity in this context is acquired exclusively and only through a vicious rite of passage from the father to the husband. In this vertical order, the family is a close space that reproduces endogamous bonds that are not only social but also sexual. The husband becomes a substitute for previous blood-related males, who restricts female identity to the role defined by the marriage contract. This institution becomes the major source of power that grants or denies identity to adult women. Signing the marriage contract and the sexual pact that it legitimizes represents for women the entry into the social as well as the dominant cultural model of identity that entraps while it defines subjectivity. From one prison (family) to another that is social (marriage), woman is considered an exchangeable good. As a consequence, women become gendered subjects through exclusion (and seclusion) from a rationality that discounts them from the start. Carole Pateman lucidly shows in her book *The Sexual Contract* (1988) how modern patriarchy is based on an original contract that hides its sexual nature, one that guarantees all men the law of sex right over women through marriage. The story of "the sexual contract is about the genesis of political right," according to Pateman, in a social order in which only men are considered individuals. Women do not have a part in the original contract, but they are incorporated into it via the sexual contract that puts them into a sphere (the private sphere) that is and is not within civil society.[52]

Clearly, there is a connection between the Enlightenment project
and modernity in relation to the social contract in which freedom
is conceived as a masculine civil right. National projects in Latin
America inherit this legacy and condemn women to subordination in the private sphere as the "servants" of the fatherland.

Females are secluded in the household as reproductive bodies
and left in the margins of a national project that identifies masculine reason and progress as the only valid venues of subjectivity
and power. Women who have been denied their citizenship are
made part of the nation through the identification with "the Virgin Mother" of that same nation.[53] In her book *Madres y huachos:
Alegorías del mestizaje chileno* (*Mothers and Huachos: Allegories
of Chilean Mestizaje*) (1991), the anthropologist Sonia Montecino
takes the mother out of the private sphere and shows the different meanings attached to the Virgin Mother in Chilean culture.
She embodies two ethnic and social images as the *Virgen mestiza*
of the poor and the Europeanized *Virgen blanca* of the military
and the elites. In authoritarian and military regimes, the Virgin
Mother image has been particularly used to signal "la patria"
while man becomes the hero/defender of the Chilean nation/fam-
ily. In this Catholic version of modernity, as we can see, the passions and their bodily prohibitions have all been used to make the
sign "woman" equivalent to a holy mother who is bodiless and
selfless.

The narratives I discuss present a wide array of cultural regulations that script the forms of femininity that may be acquired
and what female experience means in these constraining conditions. Through emotional relationships, marriage, and family,
women characters are confronted with gender asymmetry, power
inequity, or outright violence. Gender oppression is textualized
as an unresolved and continuing conflict that cuts across class
and economic lines, cultural values, and geographical locations. It
is also portrayed as the relation that sustains all other forms of
social and sexual oppression. In this context, masculinity is acquired through the rejection of the feminine, making the heterosexual male the model, the object of cultural desire, and the ideal
norm.

More significant is that universality and development are
shown to be gender and class bound, defining a nation founded
on the sexual and social privileges of heterosexual males. Gender
also cuts across class in urban and rural settings to secure masculine power through a cultural discourse and practice where, once
again, women are exchangeable and disposable. Against the Cath-

olic ideal of womanhood propagated through *marianismo,* these texts portray female characters restlessly facing the power of patriarchal figures (embodied in parental and conjugal authority), as mentioned.[54] Maleness is defined in contrast and direct opposition to all these features, making virility and aggression its salient features.

Sonia Montecino introduces a different interpretation of *marianismo* by making it not only a key concept in the Latin American imaginary but also a founding narrative of origin that may be liberating as well as oppressive through different historical periods. For Montecino, the myth of the Virgin Mary is the result of the religious syncretism of diverse cultures and peoples who through a common *mater* find a place of recognition. From a gender perspective, she interprets the myth of Mary as a cultural frame constituted by the story of a single mother and her son, underscoring the absence of the (Spanish) father. Here lies a foundational historical tension that is solved through sublimation. The emptiness that this dyad reflects is evident in the absence of the father and sexual identities in the mother and the son. This lack tends to be filled with the phenomenon of *machismo* while sexuality is embedded in the complex relation between a mother and son through a symbolic incest, perversion, and transgression of the social order.[55] Additionally, Sergio Gatica Cortés explains that *marianismo* in Chile institutes the relationships among the imaginary, ideology, and power in which religion reinforces the domination of women through the mother goddess figure. He adds that during colonial times the behavior patterns that *marianismo* promotes served to establish a class difference among women. The structure of the family was preserved by women from the elite who became the reproducers of the dominant regime through marriage while lower-class women had freedoms that were socially devalued.[56]

The persistence of this ideology is also present in the Chilean patriarchal welfare state of the 1930s that promoted the incorporation of women in the public sphere while keeping the ideology of "gender complementariness," as Carreño accurately notes.[57] Women were supposed to do in the public sphere the things they did in the private realm, namely, take care of the home and children while being strictly subordinated to the husband in all matters. Thus, the process of secularization and democratization that modernity predicated through the incorporation of women in the public sphere, mainly through education and work in urban areas, did not eliminate the cultural phenomena of *marianismo* and *machismo*. The ideology of gender differentiation and female subordination allowed for greater freedom (work and education for women) as long as they were "resources" for the husband. Sexism here shows the tension that modernity introduces with its different economic and cultural discourses in a peripheral culture that has hierarchical gender norms and models of identities. The crisis that these traditional values, institutions, and subjectivities undergo with the arrival of the new forms introduced by a Eurocentric and Anglocentric modernity is manifested as a threat to cultural and national identity in which gender and sexuality play a major role. In a contradictory and mixed fashion, a modern woman in Chile became someone who had won the right to vote in municipal elections in the 1930s but whose main social responsibilities were in the privacy of her house. Consequently, as Carreño states, the public sphere became a domain to legitimate these traditional gender and family values in a country that feared the obliteration of gender differentiation once women left the household.[58]

A peculiar feature of the economic modernization carried on by the state in the decades of the 1930s and 1940s in Chile, then, is the ideal of this modern woman who is incorporated in the public sphere quantitatively but is not liberated. Her Chilean version is expressed in the works of the eminent feminist Amanda Labarca (1886–1975), one of the most outspoken educators who wanted to change the legal status of women during the 1940s claiming a "feminism of equivalences." In her book *Feminismo contemporáneo (Contemporary Feminism)* (1947), she states that women who were born after the 1930s found a very different world from their foremothers. "Neofeminists," according to Labarca, were not belligerent and did not feel inferior to men as women in the past had, since they were respected and admired as equal partners with them. They made their demands to "collaborate in the house, the country and humanity" in accordance with their abilities, "emphasizing" their womanhood without rejecting their femininity from Labarca's perspective.[59] For this educator, neofeminists combined traditional qualities of housewife and mother with work outside the home representing a "feminism of equivalences" that enabled them to balance marriage and work successfully. Labarca saw no antagonism between the expansion of women's rights and the fulfillment of a maternal mission. Lavrín correctly points out that rights and protection for women would be an ongoing aspiration that "satisfied the quest for modernity."[60] According to Labarca, women's new social roles and identities were those of mothers, teachers, philanthropists, or cultural reproducers. Alejandra Castillo shows in her book *La república masculina y la promesa igualitaria* (*The Masculine Republic and the Igalitarian Promise*) (2005) that Labarca tried to combine two antagonistic areas by having feminism replace the mother. Thus in her thinking the inclusion of women in public life meant a continuation of maternal duties—such as the education of children, tending the sick and the poor—across the nation.[61] In fact, the Chilean literary Nobel Gabriela Mistral (1889–1957) assumed a public persona between the identities of mother and teacher that enabled her to act publicly as a writer.[62]

In her book *De lo social a lo politico: La acción de las mujeres latinoamericanas* (*From the Social to the Political: Latin American Women's Action*) (2000), the feminist sociologist Teresa Valdés gives a thorough overview of the social and political incorporation of women in public life in Latin American countries throughout the twentieth century and draws interesting parallels along class lines and feminist issues. She contends that working-class women's organization had a class and gender awareness dating to the late nineteenth century, and that their journals and publications clearly expressed it. Women from the middle classes, on the other hand, were mainly involved with areas of culture as a result of their access to education. On one end of the spectrum were upper-class women who were greatly influenced by Catholic discourse on the duty for women to assist others through charity.[63] However, the fight for women's citizenship as the twentieth century progresses cuts across class and ideological lines, uniting women's rights with feminist concerns. Feminists were the ones responsible for moving forward other legal reforms in search of equity as well as founding feminist parties in Chile, Brazil, México, and Uruguay. However, suffrage was restricted to the cities and to educated women, since the right to vote did not include illiterate women or peasants. Dictatorships and military coups d'état, as Valdés suggests, constituted another serious restriction to the newly acquired female citizenship.[64]

In contrast to public discourse, the writings of Brunet, Bombal, and Eltit contest the idealization of the private sphere and show the house as a surveilled space, an uncertain and potentially destructive place in which protection is based on subordination. From the perspective of female protagonists, domestic space resembles a prison ward in which each family member performs specific roles while being governed by an authoritarian order. Rewards and discipline are applied to women according to their successful gender performance. Femininity for daughters, wives, and mothers means following the stipulations of the law set by the marriage contract through its legal and religious formalization. Within a patriarchal family structure, the father is the head, while the wife and children are his dependents. Gender, age, social class, and landownership establish power and authority between husband and wife. The patron/father becomes the sole owner, following the pattern set by the hacienda. This form of private ruling was implemented by the military projects of the nineteenth century that equated national and family values. Diamela Eltit's narratives best represent this symbolic conflation within the Chilean imaginary.

In the case of females, deviation from assigned gender identities and socially expected behaviors yields chastisement or criminalization. Within this coercive model of power, alienation and insubordination of females are recurrent motifs. In such a regimented and vertical order, transgression becomes a frequent and reiterative theme in the lives of women. This specific version of Chilean *machismo* has been linked to the Conquest and the right to conquer that Spanish conquistadors were granted for their participation in this enterprise. Consequently, the family was symbolically constituted by a violent (military) father, who became a founding figure in Chilean cultural identity. He is portrayed as an omnipotent and arbitrary male who enforces his will through violence. In the history of Chile, this male identity became embodied in the national figures and conservative role of the military and the landowner, both powerful and feared men. The mother, on the other hand, is dichotomized through the Virgin Mary and the fallen and impoverished Indian woman. She is idealized in the Virgin Mary while becoming a disembodied and ahistorical figure. Her indigenous ancestry is rejected from the start while her inferiority is forever manifested in her tainted and sinful nature (marked by gender and ethnicity). In this family story, male offspring identify with the powerful and aggressive father and adopt some of his traits: primarily aggression and violence against women and other subordinate groups. Jorge Larraín explains that an important cultural aspect of Chilean society has been authoritarianism; this feature has persisted in political action, in the administration of both public and private organizations, and in family life. Chilean culture gives a primary role to authority and the respect for patriarchal authority is especially considered essential. In this value system, men are at the center of society controlling all power in the political, economic, and social arenas. Women, on the other hand, are relegated to secondary positions and are discriminated against in all types of activities.[65] The Pinochet dictatorship took full advantage of this cultural trait and systematically widened gender, social, and economic gaps, together with ethnic differences, in its institutional and public programs.[66]

The law has defined a series of sexual crimes against "the order of the family and public morality." Under this category sexual difference becomes the ground for the construction of deviant behaviors and crimes in the Civil Code. The law creates the crime in a strategic plan of social regulation, as Lorena Fries and Verónica Matus argue. There has been a historical continuation of the patriarchal system in which the law has been a fundamental instrument for the preservation and reproduction of a gender system. As one of the normative systems that regulate and discipline men and women, the law perpetuates gender discrimination. Consequently, the law defines and confirms a specific identity for women, circumscribing them to roles (primarily biological and social motherhood) and places (the private sphere) that are specific and different from males'.[67] Deviation inexorably criminalizes women when they assert sexual and reproductive individual rights. The phallogocentric view of the Civil Code in Chile results in the sexual control of woman by the (male) head of the household and the assigned roles of wives/mothers as reproducers within the family.[68]

In the narratives analyzed in this book, the effectiveness and desirability of marriage and family are challenged through the display of failed intimate relationships and the crisis of identity. From their marginal position, women manifest a wide range of diseases when faced with the oppressive grid of the house under the rule of fathers and husbands. Physical and verbal aggression permeates conjugal and rural family relations in the hacienda system depicted by Marta Brunet. In this culture, education itself is violent and is used to control women and children. With *María Nadie (María Nobody)* (1957), Brunet's second literary period crystallizes in the capital city/rural town antimony in which past themes and women's issues are revised through the coexistence of a phallic matriarchy within modernity. This trend is revisited in her urban novel, *Amasijo (Hybrid)* (1962), in which maternity takes a central role in the formation of masculine subjectivity. Here the son's gender and sexuality are denied and claimed by the mother, revealing her omnipotent power and its oppressive consequences. In Bombal, female altered states, self-effacement, and rage contrast with the impersonality and coldness of oligarchic husbands. In both authors, marriage and the hacienda sustain outright abuse of subaltern bodies, making women and popular sectors particularly vulnerable. Diamela Eltit rearticulates and politicizes all forms of exclusion under the neoliberal conditions imposed by the Pinochet dictatorship. The dictatorship embodies an ultraversion of authoritarian modernity in which oppression achieves its most extreme expression of impunity.

Traditionally, the discourse of domesticity in Chile has included the household and women on similar terms in that it considers them subjective, marginal, and lacking in rationality. The literary critic Ana Pizarro has pointed out that the discourse of the house is what is expected from females, marking the boundaries of their movement and language. Meanwhile public discourse or street discourse is legitimate because it is about history and society and has a (male) subject that speaks from the center of enunciation.[69]

The separation of the public and private spheres that liberal modernity introduced to Chile and the principles of the marriage contract that the Civil Code applied clearly appear to favor males of the propertied class, leaving women civilly dependent. Furthermore, the Hispanic heritage and Catholic influence provide their own modalities to civil institutions, giving form to an uneven cultural heterogeneity and "diversely situated 'rationalisms'" that are constitutive of it, as the sociologist José Joaquín Brunner claims.[70] As a consequence, despite the dominant changes in economic models and modernizations that the late nineteenth and early twentieth centuries implemented, this colonial legacy with its patriarchal and religious imprints provides a distinctive and differentiated cultural imaginary to Latin American modernities, especially in Chile.

Paradoxically, the shift from the liberal oligarchic paradigm to the patriarchal welfare state arises from two different authoritarian political movements—the first, to the civil war after the liberal president José Manuel Balmaceda's suicide, and the second, to the coup d'état by the military leader Carlos Ibañez del Campo in 1924 and his later elected authoritarian nationalist government (1927–31) that rejected liberal democracy. Ibañez's second campaign in the 1950s reiterates the identification of national and public values with the family and domesticity, as the image of the broom succinctly exemplifies.[71] The broom became the symbol for national order and cleanliness paralleling in the administration of the state what housewives did in their house-holds. Starting with Ibañez's political project, the nation is equated with the family with all the implications that this has for the female subject and the public and private realms, as we can clearly see in Brunet's and Bombal's literature. In contrast, El-tit's ideological position affiliates its claims with those raised by the working-class women's social movements of the 1920s and 1930s.

Forty years later, another military coup d'état in 1973 iniati-ated a third moment of authoritarianism during Augusto Pino-chet's dictatorship and the implementation of neoliberalism in the economic realm. With Pinochet's return to the foundational authoritarian Portalian constitution of the nation dating back to 1833, he sweeps away the liberal and welfare advances and im-poses a regime ruled by political repression and a free-market economy. While the state abdicates sovereignty for national de-velopment, privatization and the market are regulators of social life. The state is reduced and freed from any social responsibility and instead assigns them to the institution of the family. In this scenario, gender inequity and social disparity drastically in-crease, together with human rights violations and rampant con-sumerism, as Eltit's literature reflects.

As the discourse of modernity moves closer to the present, it is increasingly contaminated with economics and authoritarianism. In the case of Chile, as in other Southern Cone countries, the dic-tatorships maintained a hierarchical and repressive social order for the implementation of a free-market ideology, military doc-trine, and religious traditionalism. These three elements, accord-ing to Brunner, are essential components of the authoritarian view of the world that the dictatorship upheld. Brunner rightly argues that the capitalist refoundation of Chile that the Pinochet regime embarked upon could not be accomplished under a demo-cratic regime. In his book *The Untimely Present: Postdictatorial Latin American Fiction and the Task of Mourning* (1999) the Bra-zilian critic Idelber Avelar further considers the epochal paradox of what he calls the "quasi religious form of cultural moderniza-tion that Southern Cone dictatorships took," making it the "ines-capable horizon for Latin America" while doing away with any illusions of social liberation. This explains why after the experi-ence of the dictatorships, modernization in the region has meant aggressive integration into the global economy.[72] In his cultural analysis of the transition from the state to the market, Avelar ar-gues that commodification negates memory since the market needs to replace previous commodities and promote a sense of perpetual present according to "a substitutive, metaphorical logic in which the past must be relegated to obsolescence."[73] Eltit's writing makes a similar critique of market ideology and its erasure of the past and historical memory for the oppressed and marginalized voices. Brunet and Bombal are from the liberal bourgeois world, and their imaginary, in contrast to Eltit's, responds to and contests those ideals with lesser or greater tension and according to different generational discourses.

The writing projects studied here articulate identity as a resisting position and challenge the hegemonic and heterosexual models, in this case, the patriarchal literary canon. They stand on the opposite side of the socioimaginary base institutionalized by the national discourse of modern rationality reproduced by the literary reception of a paternalist group of intellectuals. Since Andrés Bello's foundational talk in 1843 in the Universidad de Chile on the enlightened and moral role of literature and higher education in the republic, male intellectuals have wanted to make the literary canon fit with educational and national values of progress and ideals of citizenship. Brunet and Eltit in their writings critique Catholic gender ideology and modernity, understanding the latter as a modernization that abandons rural regions as if they belonged to the past or were in fact the past of the nation. In this version of modernity, the past is conceived as being rural or a hybrid urban temporality in a rural utopian space where new subjectivities are condemned to the alleged backwardness of the old. This same sense of datedness and uselessness is what Eltit's characters confront in an authoritarian city that has become the terrifying embodiment of a disciplinary and globalized neoliberal society.

A gendered reading of Chilean modernity shows its embodiment in marginal social subjects who face instrumental reason across the twentieth century and that the dictatorship takes to its starkest and most fearful expression. The neoliberal economic model that the Pinochet regime instituted birthed a culture oriented toward consumption in which civil rights became equated with purchasing power in a simulacrum of democracy that has continued during the postdictatorship period. A critique of democracy and its "citizenship market narrations" has also been integral to artists' and writers' work in Chile today. Among them, Pedro Lemebel's performance and urban chronicles and Voluspa Jarpa's painting question not only a peripheral modernity but also its dominant systems of representation while critiquing the official aesthetic paradigm.[74]

Finally, in my reading the tensions between the passions and modernity generate three female psychic landscapes. Brunet's writing takes a realistic and social outlook on the plight of women from the peasantry, the landowning class, and the emergent middle class. In her stories, gender is a social construct tied to class and other forms of discrimination. Though domestic life and emotional relationships are fundamental in this world, they are part of a larger universe ruled by authoritarianism and the virtual absence of the welfare state. National development and the impact of the industrial state are hardly seen in the rural areas but are always posed as a forthcoming threat by males. The provinces and rural regions have become the periphery of the nation, reproducing the same axis of power and development that the international capitalist economy develops throughout the continent. In this context, experience for women is defined by premodern social relations that reproduce the oligarchic authoritarian model established by the hacienda.

Bombal's phantasmagoric females and dreamy landscapes of private lives also unfold in the hacienda but reflect the absence of affects and eroticism within oligarchic marriages. This literary world is characterized by the irrelevance and ultimate obliteration of history from the view of the characters who live entombed in the household. Life is an isolated and solitary matter that is aestheticized by the flight from a constraining and lifeless reality. These women are torn by an existential void and an increasing sense of meaninglessness. Underneath their apparent indolence, dreams and passions surface, giving evidence of the personal price of accepting conventions and staying in unwanted marriages. Bombal's novels poignantly present female erotic desire and estrangement in a deadening, conjugal world from the perspective of the wife. Life for her protagonists is mediocre and depleted by social demands in which gender is fate. Learning and growth are only attainable in a shroud, in an afterlife state in which thoughts and feelings are still in conflict. The life of the living, as Bombal's second novel portrays it, is the endless repetition of senseless acts that leave no room for engaged or real attachments. Amid a lifeless oligarchic milieu, women are haunted by obsession and unfulfilled desire. Inadequacy and an extreme sense of lack shape a sensibility that fluctuates between total withdrawal (depression) and extravagant acting out (omnipotence). Bombal's disembodied females are enclosed in the private domain, and their passions arise directly from the Catholic imaginary of Chilean modernity. They construct themselves against guilt and sin as defining and restricting obstacles that they transgress through sexuality. However, they succeed only by negating the other and claiming self-identity through autoeroticism.

In the culture of this rural context, females are supposed to be submissive and blindly follow their fathers' commands. Speaking up and acting independently are seen as transgressions against an immemorial and almost divine masculine authority. This order is based on the uncontested power of the husband and father. Incest, virtual or real, is part of a masculinist power that controls women's sexualities and keeps them in their subaltern position. Sexual and domestic violence, as well as emotional pain, characterize Brunet's rural tales of battered wives, fierce grandmothers, and defiant daughters in this coercive order. Female deviation and rebellion are punished verbally and physically. Abuse rather than love from fathers and husbands appears as an ongoing motif in Brunet's family stories. The house is a metaphor for the nation in its crudest and most abrasive sense (physically, economically, socially), where the strongest dominates. This premodern worldview and experience dramatically challenge the project of modernity and its "civilizing" influence over the nation and its citizens.

Within the dictatorship and postdictatorship periods, Eltit's antirepresentational novels emphasize the place and subjectivity of popular urban women in equally controlled public and private spaces. Here power is experienced as all-encompassing, leaving no place or identity outside its domain. The urban landscape is a wasteland, as the postcoup city displays in its social and physical decay. Modernity reveals the totalitarianism of its enlightened values, particularly through the instrumentalization of reason and its domination of people and nature, as Theodor W. Adorno and Max Horkheimer explain in *Dialectic of Enlightenment* (1972). These negative features seem to outweigh the successes and promises of freedom and prosperity in an increasing alienation and a complete disenchantment with the world.[75] This negativity of the Enlightenment carried on by the project of modernity is significantly worsened and further dislocated in Latin American societies that have become, at different historical junctures, the proving grounds to implement numerous colonial and neocolonial economic and cultural enterprises. As a consequence, negativity becomes consubstantial with the forms that modernization takes in Latin America because of internal contradictions that are greater than any possible gain. The portrayal of the postmodern/urban space as a nightmarish spoil and ruin is an heir to this legacy of negativity.[76]

Eltit's women characters transgress the public and private spheres; in this way they are the most radical of the females who are represented in this literature. They politicize gender and sexuality and use them against the oppressive structures in their world. They fight against power at large, be it within the household, the street, or culture. This political consciousness results directly from Eltit's intentions and the social and political role she attributes to discursive and symbolic practices. Whereas in Bombal, the politics behind her texts have to be deduced, in Eltit there is a clear awareness of class, the conditions of production, circulation, and reception, as well as the political coefficient of the literary field. What distinguishes her work from the literature of Bombal and Brunet is her critique of modern ideals and the high social price paid by those who have been silenced or excluded from them. Her literary work can be read as manifestos in which politics and aesthetics join to denounce a state of violence and social crisis as the signs of contemporary culture.

From the most contemporary perspective, Eltit's resistance unfolds in cultural and symbolic margins that are inhabited by strange and eccentric figures who live in inhospitable and oppressive conditions within cityscapes. Uncertainty and disjuncture delineate a neo-avant-garde refractoriness and its linkage to an oppressed imaginary still present in postdictatorial Chile. Disenchantment and dissidence characterize Eltit's critique of a market economy and globalization. In the new Chilean democracy, consensual politics appear to contain opposition, whitewash memory, and subsume resistance in a citizenry numbed by frantic consumerism. In this period, according to the philosopher Olga Grau, the family is the subject of political interest, together with marriage and divorce.[77] The hyperrepresentation and symbolic presence of the family in public discourse in Chile, Grau argues, reveal its replacement of the modern state as a unifying element of social life. With the weakening and withdrawal of the state from the public sphere, the family becomes the sign that represents social cohesion. As a result, family and state form an alliance that is enforced by the Catholic Church and its religious discourse. Thus, in the neoliberal economic model, the family is supposed to fill the gaps in the system without really having resources to confront social disintegration.[78]

Eltit's writing fractures the pillars of phallogocentric discourse by proclaiming the absence of the military hero. In the crisis of hegemonic models of identities, Eltit substitutes this national epic figure with woman's historical intimacy. Eltit and Brunet reflect on the memory that is embodied by predominantly rural peasant, middle-class, and lower-class women and their bodies, alongside other popular subjects. In their novels, modernity is located in the margins of the socioeconomic model and in the borders of official culture. Bombal's class choice confronts this issue in her novels from a liberal bourgeois perspective and not the collective one that Brunet and Eltit present.

Chapter 1 examines Marta Brunet's *Aguas abajo* (*Down River*) and the dynamics of violence and betrayal that develop within the patriarchal family. Family ties and romantic ideals are shattered in these three rural stories, in which passion and power determine gender relations and family interaction. Positions and loyalties are in flux in a world governed by patriarchal authoritarianism and irrepressible passions. As a result, unprecedented events take place in the house with the family members' silent acquiescence. In "Piedra callada," ("Silent Stone"), after a submissive wife is killed in childbirth and from her husband's beatings, the grandmother becomes the avenging killer of the man. A daughter turns out to be a mother's worst rival in "Aguas abajo" ("Down River"), usurping her place in the house and the bedroom. The perfect wife turns into a wild and fierce being in "Soledad de la sangre" ("Solitude of Blood") in order to defend her most prized possession against her husband's appropriation. These powerful stories display how an apparently immutable rural order may be dramatically shaken by women.

Chapter 2 centers on Brunet's novel *María Nadie* (*María Nobody*), and the negative aspects of independence for a single woman. María is the embodiment of modernity and one of Brunet's few characters freed from the legal and cultural bindings of marriage and family. She embodies the new woman who earns her living and lives by herself while also becoming a kind of fallen virgin. The very fact that she cannot be labeled (as wife and mother) makes her socially inadequate. Maternity is central to this novel, and it represents a double-edged sword for women. It becomes a trap for most females in the small rural town of Colloco, who endure it by sacrificing. On the other hand, maternity also signals liberation when it is the result of choice. Nonetheless, this possibility is socially punished with exclusion since single motherhood does not abide by the institutionalized forms of maternity, as María's fallen state embodies. She is stigmatized and socially marginalized by the ideology of womanhood. Brunet presents subjectivity within and outside the social and sexual pact, underscoring the ways patriarchal laws manifest in both public and private space. María remains displaced and rejected in a social and cultural context in which her modernity is devalued.

Chapter 3 analyzes María Luisa Bombal's *La última niebla* (*The Final Mist*) and the alienating role of the oligarchic wife and how she survives through her imagination. Her search for passion develops into an imagined romance that blurs the distinctions between reality and fiction for some time. Writing and imagination intertwine in the protagonist's existence to privilege inner life, ceaselessly disengaging her from social experience. Gender difference in her case is lived as an insurmountable rift from the husband, where psychic death becomes the only foreseeable alternative. This novel also textualizes the crisis of values undergone by women in the oligarchy. The protagonist goes from playing a role to having a sense of subjecthood to playing a role once again in a context in which modernity has vanished.

Chapter 4 focuses on *La amortajada (The Shrouded Woman)*, in which Bombal returns to the imprisoned wife of the landowning class to reveal that she has literally died to keep the marriage contract and the identity it provides. Set in an afterlife temporality, the narration focuses on the protagonist's psyche, still entangled in resentments. Ana María intensely recalls how she ages and devitalizes in the path from childhood and adolescence to wifehood. Her erotic quest is left unresolved by marriage and unfulfilled by a virtual adultery. In both relations, Ana María maintains her place as an oligarchic lady, as a social good in the patriarchal economic system of classes. In exchange for this she gives up her vitality and sacrifices her passion. As a consequence, we are in the presence of courtly love and a sadomasochistic lady who accepts the pacts that culture and its love discourse provide her. Without life, she becomes a kind of inverted virgin, to be admired and honored. In a shroud, Ana María reflects on her past life and becomes aware of the contractual nature of her relationship with men and her own identity.

Chapter 5 examines Diamela Eltit's *El cuarto mundo (The Fourth World)* through the struggle for identity and domination within the family. Eltit's novel turns binary oppositions, particularly self and other, upside down by textualizing the struggle of twins—male and female—for assertion and nurturance from their very conception and development in the womb. Two gender views organize two narrations that trace the conflicts of sexual identity, separation and connection between the siblings and lovers. Against idealizing values, Eltit's textual womb is not a blissful place but rather the crucible of chaotic and organic power of the maternal body. The female body is represented in its power to disrupt, posing the greatest threat to human survival, and most acutely to the male. The father in this narrative is not the founder of what is being created since he has been replaced by the mother. In this universe, symbolic culture is within the female body, more precisely, the mother's body. The incest motif is reiterated in this novel as a sign of the insubordination of the symbolic prohibition that founds Western culture and that the patriarchal family maintains. Eltit looks at the premodern (endogamic) kingship family as well as the patriarchal modern (exogamic) family to find that neither structures work. The desacralization of the mother as well as the family reveals the crisis of institutions and contemporary sexual identity.

Chapter 6 revisits the family structure, now constituted by a mother and her disabled son, in Eltit's *Los vigilantes (Custody of the Eyes)*. Letter writing is here a genre defined by the narrator's seclusion and altered states that range from paranoia to phobia and psychosis. The letters written to an absent yet all-powerful man become the narrator's way of coping with relentless harassment and surveillance. Being systematically watched and forbidden to leave the house is a political allegory of a panoptic power that has taken over life in its entirety. Through a web of intrigues, the husband and the mother-in-law become agents of the surveillance and censorship that rule civil society. The strange dyad constituted by the destitute mother and her son signals their banishment from a modern patriarchal order and the death of humanity with their final loss of language.

As these chapters reveal, the texts dispute the place of the feminine in sociomasculine cultural discourses. They deconstruct how power operates over subjectivity and the female body through physical and symbolic forces. The authors explore what gender difference implies in a rationality that homogenizes a national culture while creating separate spheres of social life that attach opposite gender and subordinate imperatives to them. The passions here run counter to a masculinist rationality, enabling the rethinking of bodies and subjects politically as they have been excluded from modern patriarchy. A passionate word and gender perspective illuminate wifedom, motherhood, singleness, and other contemporary female experiences with an array of new images and significations.

1

Marta Brunet and the Outrageous Text

MARTA BRUNET (1897–1967)[1] WAS BORN IN CHILLÁN, A SMALL RURAL town in southern Chile. This locality and its gender ideology presented Brunet with restrictions on what becoming a professional writer entailed. When she announced her literary vocation, her parents accepted it, provided their only child would write while living at home.[2] Her parents, who belonged to a wealthy rural family of Spanish descent, earned their living through commerce and provided their daughter with all the comforts and education they could afford. Marta Brunet's education was in the hands of governesses and private tutors who taught her in her home. From 1911 to 1914, her parents took her on a three-year journey in Europe during which she visited Spain, Italy, Switzerland, France, Belgium, England, Germany, and Portugal. She also traveled in South America in Argentina, Uruguay, and Brazil. The trip was interrupted by the conflicts arising from the outbreak of the First World War, forcing the family's return to Chile.[3] This ritual journey finished Brunet's gender and class education, as the critic Haydée Ahumada Peña points out.[4] The parents' morals and expectations opposed their daughter's desire first to become a doctor and later a dancer, but strangely allowed her literary vocation to develop inside the home. In this way, they permitted her to have an intellectual identity in the private space and preserved her from public exposure and dishonor. Through her social skills and aesthetic refinement, she would become a perfect wife for the men of the elite. In consequence, Brunet increased her symbolic value as female merchandise in search of a husband. However, the trip to Europe also had an added benefit for the young Brunet in that it provided her with a different cultural and social context for women. This experience gave the future writer a diverse set of cultural and gender modalities as well as the possibility to compare women from Europe to those in the agrarian Chilean province. In the European cities she visited, Brunet probably saw and met women who had jobs, were educated, and played roles other than those assigned by tradition, particularly rural tradition.

In an autobiographical account, Brunet relates the shortcomings of her success in the context of her small town when her first novel, *Montaña adentro (Mountain In)*, was published in 1923: "Cuando salió la novela, las señoras beatas de Chillán, armaron un lío tremendo, acusándome de inmoral y de hereje. Las niñas de las familias bien, recibieron orden de quitarme el saludo"[5] (When my novel came out, the pious ladies of Chillán put up quite a commotion, accusing me of being immoral and a heretic. The girls of the better families were given orders not to greet me).

Social rejection within a small community was an experience that Brunet would return to in her literary work, particularly in the ways it undermined creativity and self-expression in female characters. The reception of Brunet's novel was paradoxical: it was surrounded by scandal, mostly around moral and class issues, while also receiving praise and recognition from critics in a literary scene dominated by men.[6] Hernán Díaz Arrieta (pseudonym *Alone*), one of the most influential literary critics of the twentieth century in Chile, characterized Brunet's writing as having all the "right attributes," namely, clarity, audacity, brevity, and strength. According to him, her first novel surprised the male literary establishment, which expected a "señorita's novel" and instead got a "solid and strong work."[7] Furthermore, this powerful critic compared Brunet's narrative "perfection" to the consecrated *criollista* writer, Baldomero Lillo, and to Guy de Maupassant in her "virile freedom."[8] Brunet's gaze is defined as male since her passionate pulsation has the female body as its object. She sees from the perspective of power, but without identifying with the places and subjects invested with it. On the contrary, her point of view feminizes the landscape and the land and privileges the feminine in ways similar to Mistral. Coincidently, in both cases, canonical readings manifest the same process of virilization that veils and normalizes not only lesbian desire but any other form of exclusion.

To add to his appraisal, Alone reiterated in his book, *Panorama de la literatura chilena del siglo XX (Panorama of Chilean Literature in the Twentieth Century)* (1931), what the editor of the prestigious Editorial Nascimento had said about Mistral and Brunet: namely, that they were the only writers in Chile. In a curious gender reversal, all other Chilean writers were considered to be women writers by this editor and, presumably, by Alone. In regard to Mistral and Brunet, Alone adds: "En realidad, ambas muestran un vigor raro y se diría viril, si los hombres poseyeran siempre esa cualidad" (In truth, both show a rare vigor that could be called virile if men always were to possess this quality).[9] With this definition of writing as an essentially masculine talent that lends itself to travestism as the works of Mistral and Brunet show, their place in the canon was forever secured.

Brunet's career as a twenty-six-year-old writer was launched with the outstanding distinction and official support of the male literary critics. This approval by the literary establishment provided Brunet, as well as Mistral, with a symbolic veil that recognized her as a writer, allowing her to stay single and respected. Consequently, Brunet's literary commitment persisted in spite of the opposition she met within her family and social circles. Around 1931 she explored acting and formed part of an amateur theatrical company directed by Luis Pizarro Espoz, among whose members was María Luisa Bombal, who had recently arrived from Paris.[10] Brunet's unwavering success made her the recipient of the National Literary Award in 1961, only the second woman to receive it after Gabriela Mistral. Her diverse experience in writing, journalism, and teaching shows versatility and competence in a wide range of work. As with Mistral, Brunet's numerous diplomatic positions in Argentina, Brazil, and Uruguay also gave her a degree of independence that was unusual for a woman.

From 1934 to 1939 Brunet directed the magazine *Familia,* a publication geared to urban middle-class women, their concerns and aspirations. In a contradictory fashion, the magazine encouraged women to participate in the public world while also trying to quiet the anxieties brought about by this very inclusion. Brunet contributed under the pseudonym *Isabel de Santillana,* providing "feminine" advice on how to balance home, culture, and work. *Familia* endorsed a traditional and hierarchical view of gender while telling females to become modern and go out into the public sphere. It aimed at being a guide for modern women inside and outside the house, trying to respond to the new ideals as well as safeguarding the institution of marriage. Brunet's literature, as I will show, drastically contrasts the hegemonic and stereotypical discourse on women found in the magazine *Familia.* In regard to Brunet's awareness of the cultural relevance of the media, the critic Rubí Carreño has noted its impact (particularly that of magazines, radio soaps, and films) in domestic life and women's experience in several of Brunet's literary works, such as *Bienvenido* (Welcome) (1929), "Piedra callada" ("Silent Stone") (1943), and "Soledad de la sangre" ("Solitude of Blood") (1943).[11] Brunet's more ambiguous and challenging feminine subjectivities are literary representations endowed with qualities and values that dispute male hegemony. Brunet's literature moves away from traditional and reproductive sociosymbolic paradigms and creates an imaginary where the female body eroticizes natural and symbolic spaces.

With Brunet's highly successful publication of *Montaña adentro,* her work was forced into the *criollista* literary tradition together with the rest of her novels. Consequently, she enters the canon as a writer of national identity set in a geographical and linguistic landscape. Brunet's early work was especially conflated with *criollismo,* the regionalist school that equated the mimetic portrayal of localisms with a national literature. The main exponents in Chile of this tradition were Mariano Latorre (1886–1955), Baldomero Lillo (1867–1923), Federico Gana (1867–1926), and the systematically excluded Francisco Coloane (1910–2004).

Brunet's virtual disappearance from the Latin American and Chilean literary canon, despite her success,[12] may be related to the anti-*criollista* position held by the Boom in the 1960s, as Kemy Oyarzún has pointed out. Paradoxically, Brunet always kept her place as a public figure and a prestigious intellectual. The Boom's refoundational concern with Latin America, however, silenced Brunet's political claim against women's systemic abuse. This literary perspective virtually effaced everything that had preceded it and saw Brunet as a "transitional *criollista* writer,"[13] further reinforcing the view of her texts as local and descriptive. Nevertheless, Brunet's creation of Colloco in *María Nadie (María Nobody)* (1957) as an oppressive rural town anticipates and parallels Donoso's El Olivo in *El lugar sin límites* (1966) (published in 1972 as *Hell Has No Limits*), as microcosms of Chile's most conservative and hierarchical latifundia enclaves.

In my view, the *criollista* category used by the Boom writers as well as others was a cover-up that makes Brunet's vast literary production disappear. Nobody saw the relevance of sexual identity in her texts as a significant literary aspect of Latin American identity. The lack of publications and critical attention she received after the Boom, despite the growing number of publications and translations of other Latin American authors, also contributed to Brunet's marginalization.

Brunet alters the regime of signs used by *criollismo* by moving its point of signification. Instead of making her characters products of nature and the geographical space they live in as in *criollismo,* she subjectifies the landscape, providing a multiplicity of signs that cannot be reduced to one interpretation. Thus, her narrative constitutes a system of signs opened to interpretation and signification.[14] In this way, the rural world she depicts is not closed as in the logos of *criollismo* that organized it according to the assumption that the character of a people is determined by the environment. In contrast, Brunet presents men and women in terms of their subjectivities and an array of relationships with the world and others. Furthermore, her gaze constructs a space and a landscape in which what is feminine is in the center of signification.

Brunet's work was thus pigeonholed and made to fit the national identity endorsed by *criollismo*. This ideological view imposed a mimetic paradigm in which national reality was represented in the documentation of peasant life, its habits and "battle against natural barbarism," as Latorre asserted.[15] In this way, it silenced Brunet's critical perspective by catering to the needs of a national literary canon. This dominant view may be traced in the works of well-known critics such as Alone, Fernando Alegría, and Raúl Silva Castro, who coincide in defining Brunet as a *criollista* writer.[16] Another segment of the literary establishment considered Brunet's novels "universal" from the publication of *Humo hacia el Sur* (*Smoke to the South*) (1946) onward, emphasing its psychological and existential conflicts. Among the critics who have supported this tendency is José Promis in his book *La novela chilena actual (Orígenes y desarrollo)* (*The Present Chilean Novel [Origins and Development]*) (1977). Most of these interpretations share the omission of gender and the significance of female experience in Brunet's literature. This reductionism has been embedded in the official reading of Brunet's texts throughout the years and, in some cases, has gone hand in hand with a gender consideration of her talent. In 1926 the critic Pedro N. Cruz for example, noted with the publication of *Bestia Dañina,* (Damaging Beast) that in the literary realm woman "was competing with man" to signal that Brunet wrote like a man.[17] To this reiterative assertion, Brunet responded with a clear awareness of the gender ideology operating in the literary field:

> A mí no me halaga eso, ni entiendo que tal cosa pueda ser un elogio. Decir que una mujer escribe como un hombre parecería querer significar que el talento literario es cosa privativa, exclusiva del sexo fuerte y que lo contrario es la excepción. Y dígame usted si eso no es exagerada petulancia por parte del hombre.[18]

> [I do not feel complimented, and I do not understand this to be a compliment. To say that a woman writes like a man would seem to

imply that literary talent is something exclusive to the strong sex and that the contrary is an exception. And tell me if it is not an exaggerated arrogance on the part of man . . .]

Brunet was among the first writers to make a public statement about the ways gender worked to discriminate against and discredit women writers to prevent them from entering the field of literature.

Most of Brunet's critical reception continued in the 1980s along the lines of *criollismo* or existentialism. Among critics, feminist Lucía Guerra excluded Brunet's narrative, particularly its early novels, from what she considered the "feminine novel" in Chile because Brunet adopted "the dominant masculine tradition."[19] Guerra's analysis dismisses Brunet's writing as "masculine," echoing what traditional criticism had said for different reasons. Guerra's approach to the novel written by women discounts how difference and the coexistence of alternatives are not reducible to one form, as critic Márgara Russotto has rightly argued. Brunet's materialist and concrete thematization is a discursive strategy that is adjacent to María Luisa Bombal's and other modes of female expression. These different modalities are united by what Russotto calls "the secret and the unsaid." The fact that the literature of Bombal and Brunet remained separated must be attributed to the cultural differences in ideological position, class, and literary affiliation.[20]

During the 1980s, Guerra's perspective was challenged by critics such as Gabriela Mora and Marjorie Agosín, who consider Brunet a pioneer in the field of women's writing.[21] Mora questioned the validity of the reiterative view of Brunet's work made by critics that divides her production into *criollista* (the first part) and superrealist (the second half) and highlights Angel Rama's break with this cliché.[22] In 1989, Brunet's story "Solitude of Blood" ("Soledad de la sangre") first appeared in English in the collection of short fiction *Landscapes of a New Land: Short Fiction by Latin American Women*, edited by Marjorie Agosín.[23] In 1995, "Down River" ("Aguas abajo") was published in a Chilean collection of short stories written by women titled *What Is Secret: Stories of Chilean Women,* also edited by Agosín.[24] These translations put Brunet's writing in circulation in the United States within the context of Latin American and Chilean women's letters.

Brunet's valorization from a gender and feminist perspective developed in Chile in the mid-1990s with the creation of the

Centro de Estudios de Género in 1995 at the Universidad de Chile. The works of the critics Kemy Oyarzún, Rubí Carreño, and Berta López Morales (from the Universidad de Bío Bío) and the writer Diamela Eltit[25] contributed to the establishment of a gendered reading of Brunet's literary production. In the United States, Sonia Riquelme and Cecilia Ojeda wrote from a gender perspective in the 1990s as well, establishing a dialogue with the contributions of literary scholars in Chile. In 2001 the journal *Nomadías* published an issue in which the poet Carmen Berenguer and the critic Fernando Blanco featured an anthology of poetry and narrative[26] that emphasized difference and how the canon normalized it, mirroring society. Among the texts cited by Blanco was Brunet's last novel, *Amasijo,* as an example in his discussion on cultural politics and narratives that propose new subjectivities. Also in 2001, Juan Pablo Sutherland's *A corazón abierto: Geografía literaria de la homosexualidad en Chile (Open Heart: Literary Geography of Homosexuality in Chile)* mentions Brunet's literature, and particularly *Amasijo,* as an example of gay/lesbian narrative within his discussion of identity politics.[27]

My own understanding of Brunet takes into account this debate in Chile but articulates a different line of argument by posing a concept of passion defined as an individual's ethics that prevents the subject from becoming normalized through repressive discourses of sin, pathology, or the common good that have served to sacrifice women. This politics of passion, then, opposes patriarchal reason and its authoritarian imperatives.

Angel Rama once asserted that Brunet's work discontinued old patterns and stretched the limits of Chilean narrative much in the way women poets, namely, Gabriela Mistral and Juana de Ibarbourou, had in South America. Rama's reading of Brunet remains perceptive and pertinent, particularly in his realization that hers was a new gender perspective that looked at the world against patriarchal traditions. In Rama's reading of Brunet, culture stopped being exclusively masculine and recognized women as coparticipants and creators.[28] Her concern with cultural practices across gender and class lines fractured the monolithic literary establishment. Brunet's narrative project rejected sentimentality and instead depicted intense social and psychic conflicts in which gender subordination and violence were prominent. Ultimately, she demystified the countryside and rural life together with the national ideals attached to them by an urban and lettered elite.

Marta Brunet became a journalist and cultural reproducer,

combining two of the allowed female public identities. However, her texts, like those of Mistral, show a persistent and passionate estranging quality of language that the literary establishment slighted from the beginning in its domesticating reception. Brunet's political aesthetics creates different types of women that cannot be reduced to one or to a series despite the fact that the social and cultural dynamic they are immersed in might be the same.

RITUALS OF DOMINATION AND VIOLENCE IN *AGUAS ABAJO*

At the level of content, Brunet makes a public denunciation of women's domestic abuse while discursively she creates strong women by giving them an option to break away from victimization. Furthermore, her narrative presents spaces crossed by intersubjective tensions and by what Kemy Oyarzún terms a desiring economy that creates a defamiliarization of what has traditionally been familiar or loved.[29]

The trilogy *Aguas abajo* (1943) gathers a story of a crime, another one of rivalry and betrayal, and a third on surviving within marriage that have female protagonists struggling within the binary heterosexual system of domination. These women show the extreme choices they make in order to empower themselves in a patriarchal order in which gender, class, and male sexual desire organize all social and subjective relationships. Their actions respond to their historical condition as subordinated and plundered bodies and minds. In these three stories, "Piedra callada," "Aguas abajo," and "Soledad de la sangre," women's oppression becomes violence in erotic, familial, and conjugal relations while subjectivities are singularized in each specific context.

Brunet emphasizes how power is both an exterior and an interior force that shapes consciousness through social relations. The subordination of women to men is the ground that sustains all other forms of power throughout this rural trilogy. Women become the depositories of masculine aggression or its masculinized female version acted out by women themselves. The stories are appropriately told from the standpoint of females in their different hierarchical and patriarchal roles.

The three stories that compose the collection highlight the problem of domination within the family and how it shapes gender, sexual, and social identity. In this cultural system, gender dichotomy is integral to its patriarchal forms of subordination

and definitions of femininity and masculinity. Sexuality is organized according to the expectations of reproduction, of an heterosexual economic matrix where the female body as well as other
material conditions and ways of living within modernity maintain
and reproduce the capitalist system. From a *criollista* reading,
this has been seen as a picture of typical rural life. In this view,
the stereotype of the peasantry justifies the dynamic between the
characters. This worldview romanticizes the peasant as a noble
savage who needs to be known and redeemed through progress.
Furthermore, *criollismo* defines literature as integral to the configuration of national identity, as a "picture of the popular man
and his environment," following Tolstoi's advice: "Describe your
village and you will be universal."[30] In time *criollismo* makes of
this idealist vision an epic in which man struggles against nature
displaying his courage, strength, and willpower. Brunet fractures
this representation by moving the struggle to gender relations
and subjectivity, undermining the idealist and epic frame within
a system of domination and outright violence.

"Piedra Callada" ("Silent Stone"),[31] "Aguas abajo" ("Down
River"),[32] and "Soledad de la sangre" ("Solitude of Blood")[33]
link male omnipotence (in its psychic and social implications) to
the enactment of dominance and submission. The house becomes the stage of a master-slave dynamic that is enacted in diverse cultural practices ranging from sex to domestic tasks and
roles showing features that connect it to the brothel. The critic
Rodrigo Cánovas has read the brothel as a metaphor to understand the interrelations between sexuality and culture in Latin
American literature. He claims that in several Latin American
novels and Chilean *criollista* narrative as well as novels of the
Boom, the brothel embodies the rituals of exclusion of the nation. These national allegories give shape to the infernal world
of subjugation and desire that has been unleashed by modernity
and that the social space of the brothel stages.[34]

RETRIBUTION AS JUSTICE IN "PIEDRA CALLADA"

"Piedra callada" is the most descriptive of the three stories and
perhaps the one most indebted to a *criollista* rhetoric in its use of
rural sociolect and linguistic transparency to depict the rural
frame in which the characters and their actions develop. In fact,
the point of view of Eufrasia, an older woman, is the one that predominates in the narrative in order to protect her daughter

Esperanza, who has been raised as "a flower" despite being "una huasita" (35), a little peasant, fabricating the embodiment of the rural woman. But a closer reading reveals in the landscape the uncanny and sensual elements that destabilize the rural depiction.

Privileging the old woman's perspective in this story changes the point of signification for Brunet's poetic semiotics and makes her passion the driving force against the destructive power of her son-in-law. Besides the incorporation of rural language in the dialogues, Brunet resorts to a transparent language to describe and denounce the criminal and his crime. Bernabé is here the abuser, the product of years of colonial domination and a patriarchal rural culture that condones sexual and physical aggression. Thus, what is important in this text are the signs that constitute his crime as they are presented in the story to show that there is a discriminatory and deadly legality against women mostly represented in the consuetudinary sex right of "derecho de pernada."[35] This male sexual right allowed *patrones* and *inquilinos* unrestricted sexual access to the females they chose. This legality operates in the story through the *patron*'s consent when he allows Esperanza to marry against her mother's wishes. This colonial legacy reenacts the role and power of the *patrón* in all personal as well as economic matters within his hacienda and his staff. *Criollista* depictions surface again in the candid testimonies of Esperanza's children, who reveal the truth of her abuse as firsthand eyewitnesses. In their revelations there is no subjectivity but rather an almost *costumbrista* or portrait of manners in which everything is explicit—their father raped and beat their mother and them while he buried numerous stillborns. This depiction shows the countryside as a ruthless place dominated by a violent masculinity, drastically questioning the essentialist paradigm of the *criollista* hero. The language here serves the purpose of rendering the crime as clearly as possible to pave the way for Eufrasia's unflinching action and ethical accountability.

Brunet emphasizes the old woman's power, her monumental vitality, and her courage to exert retribution in a context of inequality. Eufrasia is also the one who articulates meaning since her fears of her daughter's fate and Bernabe's crime are announced from the beginning. In this way, Brunet takes advantage of the transparency of *criollista* language in order to justify what Eufrasia does at the end with a clear mind and intent, embodying a feminine passionate ethics. As a result, the entire *criollista* regime is reinterpreted through the figure of Eufrasia, showing that power establishes relations in a hacienda that was an *enco-mienda,* and not the alleged purity or character of the people, as *criollismo* would have it.

In Brunet's rendition, we find a revision of the Judeo-Christian myth of David and Goliath in which the young David is replaced by the old grandmother, and the warrior Goliath by the huge and brutal Bernabé. In this context, Brunet makes gender oppression and age the obstacles Eufrasia has to struggle against to save her grandchildren. Her final victory parallels David's in that the weakest opponent wins over the strongest and, as he does, Eufrasia fights and kills on behalf of others. Contrary to stereotypical and patriarchal views, the powerless grandmother becomes a heroine of mythical dimensions in Brunet's fiction, a woman who fights against patriarchal violence. In a way, her success and retribution can be read not only as her sole victory but also as that of women who face abusive forms of power. The final instauration of a matriarchal power headed by Eufrasia sheds light not only on a different way of understanding power but also on subjectivity. This feminine subjectivity appears to be mainly relational and founded on passion.

Violence embodied in any subject maintains authority and differentiation. Abuse becomes the bedrock of an entire society and intertwines with gender discipline within the family, especially of daughters, who learn to fear and obey so that they may become proper wives and mothers in the future. Pierre Bourdieu points out that the social order works as a great symbolic machine that tends to ratify the masculine domination that supports it. The sexual division of labor, the existence of specific spaces and times reserved to males and females, are all part of an applied social program of perception. The social world constructs the body as a sexual reality and as a recipient of the visions and division of sexualized subjects.[36] Thus, masculine domination reinforces the need to keep females under control so that they do not drift away from submission, first to their parents, and later to their husbands.[37] Brunet's focus on violence in the family and marriage is a literary operation that links eroticism with power and destruction. Her texts present *machismo* as a perverted cultural system in rural society that determines relationships and establishes hegemony through aggression. Brunet explores what it means to be masculine and feminine in a society where emotional attachments and interrelationships are patriarchal and abusive.[38]

FEMININE ETHICS

"Piedra callada" tells of the effect of marriage through the story of Esperanza, who, despite her name, is inexorably transformed from a spirited and strong-willed female to a voiceless and battered wife. Eufrasia's authoritarian opposition to Esperanza's suitors discloses the hierarchy that structures the patriarchal family. She scolds, slaps, and punishes her daughter for disobeying her. Her mother's warning against the fatal consequence of marrying a "brute," which represents the risk of symbolic and material death in the countryside, is dismissed by the rebellious daughter. Once married, Esperanza is coerced into intercourse and forced into sexual servitude. The (grand)mother's prophecy is thus confirmed by the grandchildren's account after their mother's death. Marriage became a trap and a curse that killed Esperanza. She was tortured and abused by her husband, Bernabé, becoming a victim of his sexual and physical violence. The hope of freedom is fatally shattered in a masculinized universe as brutal as the one the mother probably experienced herself.

The husband's desire and aggression, on the other hand, remain uncurbed within the family while the wife withstands abuse and beatings in a self-sacrificial position. Violence prevails in this world and its predominant site is the female body, which submits through physical pain. Esperanza is repeatedly raped by her husband and impregnated numerous times. In her case, marriage is an endless cycle of aggression, torture, and degradation. The absence of consent in conjugal sex reveals not only female objectification but also male sex right as the foundation of the sexual contract. Ultimately, the crisis of marriage and the patriarchal family it preserves is enacted in the vulnerability of a female subject who is threatened by annihilation as part of the contract. Furthermore, rape, as José Bengoa has discussed, is symbolically embedded in the foundation of the state in Chile, which is conceived as an act of force. Thus social discrimination and sexual attraction would be the bedrocks of the interrelationship between power and masculinity in an essentially authoritarian culture.[39]

According to historical studies, the fact that abuse in marriage was permitted and socially tolerated to discipline a rebellious or deviant wife reveals the subordinate and dependent situation of married women. Violence against women was so prevalent in the rural areas that women who were alone, whether single or married, were at risk of being raped, robbed, or battered in the countryside. As rural oral histories have also shown, husbands used coercion and violence everytime their wives did not comply with their sexual and reproductive demands. Lack of employment for rural women and the responsibility for their children prevented them from leaving abusive husbands or from going to the police.[40] Furthermore, the isolation that the wives of small farmers lived in made them easy targets, particularly those who were tenants on the *latifundia*. They were subject to a hierarchical structure, economically dependent, and forced to accept the strict control of fathers and husbands. Women suffered frequent sexual violence, which occurred in diverse circumstances, according to the historian Catalina Arteaga.[41] Brunet's Pascuala in "Don Florisondo" (1926) is raped and becomes pregnant by a migrant worker while her husband is away working. In *María Rosa, flor del Quillén* (*María Rosa, the Quillén Flower*) (1927), the protagonist escapes being raped through her swift reaction and timely self-defense. María Rosa, despite remaining the entire day on her own, does not follow the norm of becoming an easy victim to her assailant. She belongs to Brunet's repertoire of *pícaras* like Eufrasia whose sharpness and ingenuity succeed over male deception and abuse. In her case, female honor is preserved in the image of the faithful wife despite an extramarital affair. In order to keep her reputation intact she fabricates a story in which she has been not only seduced but abused by a rapist. Her story is also a means of self-retribution, as she has been used and lied to by the man she loved.

Esperanza's tragic fate, on the other hand, shows what happens to inexperienced and disciplined women. Her marriage discloses what marrying the wrong man in rural society entails. For Brunet, sexual violence and rape are possible within marriage as a regulation of the contract, whether in the form of a threat, punishment, or rule, as this narration displays.

Rape here represents the transgression of the boundaries between life and death. It implies a fundamental break and crossing of limits in its starkest expression.[42] For the submissive female subject, as Jessica Benjamin has shown, violation breaks physical as well as psychic limits of the self. In submission to erotic domination, we can see the paradox in which the individual tries to achieve freedom through slavery, release through submission to control.[43] This sadomasochist relationship expresses an extreme form of erotic life where differentiation gives way to absolute control of the female slave by the male master. The masochist subjectivity is constructed in a way that echoes the colonial subject for whom domination is also constitutive. As the colonized may never deny his/her previous condition even after becoming independent, the masochist cannot forgo his/her previous enslavement when he/she hears the voice of the master.[44] In this instance, empowerment is entangled with subordination in a process of identification with the other that leaves almost no room for separation and self-assertion. In this way, by assuming the dominant model of femininity, Esperanza is trapped in the erotic patriarchal fantasy that culture has provided to her.

Esperanza embodies the mistreated wife whose existence is progressively destroyed. Her pain and silence underscore how deeply gender domination is embedded in the social and cultural system of the hacienda. Her mother's fear of Bernabé, on the other hand, represents a woman's experience in the countryside, later confirmed by Esperanza's death. This fact makes her mother, now a grandmother, recover her self-identity as an abused woman who protects the new generation (particularly her granddaughter) and decides to stop the abuser.

Masculinity in this context appears subject to aggression, sexual aggression in particular, and a tendency toward destruction (of self and others). Brunet's story suggests that the *latifundia* economic and cultural system enhances this violence in *patrón* and peons alike who reproduce hierarchies and abuses. Bengoa shows a similar understanding of agrarian culture in Chile and how relationships of power maintain it. The *patrón* is the one who possesses and is also the father, while he establishes his dominion over a territory he commands with force. This is the dominant model for masculine identity in the hacienda cultural system, where subordination to authority is imperative. Bernabé as a peon and tenant takes these reproductive aspects of the sexual contract to the extreme form in order to realize his fantasy of domination and economic improvement. In his view, marriage is a productive process of labor force in which woman becomes a commodity that produces children. In this economic trade-off, the female body becomes the source of capital. Consequently, Bernabé never constitutes a family but rather an economic business that validates his power. Esperanza's body is presented as something owned by Bernabé, who uses it at will, equating sexual activity with sexual violence. He is unable to understand his own role in her tragic end; being basically blind to his responsibility, he asserts:

> La verdad era que los chiquillos lo habían arruinado todo. Porque la culpa de la enfermedad de la Esperanza la tenían los chiquillos, tantos chiquillos. Parir y parir. ¡Pobrecita! (49)

[The truth is it was the children that had ruined everything. Esperanza's sickness was the children's fault, so many children. Having
babies and more babies. Poor thing!]

Through Bernabe's inner monologue, we access his sexist and
abusive thoughts and feelings for Esperanza and the children.
For him his wife's death is due to her body's inability to withstand having children. Later he complains that she was not
woman enough because of her incapacity to have as many children as nature provided her. "Porque él necesitaba mujer para
ayuntarse y tener hijos" (Because he needed a woman to mate
and have children) summarizes his attitude toward Esperanza's
"failure" to meet his expectations (57). Masculinity is expressed
through the animalization of sexuality in a world where the male
dominates the female in order to procreate. The underlying assumption is that the phallus concentrates all collective as well as
individual fantasies of fecundation.[45]

Mother and daughter encapsulate contrasting aspects of femininity in this patriarchal rural order: Eufrasia is accustomed to
dominating while Esperanza is a strong-willed daughter who
wants to escape her mother's control. In order to do this, she mis-
takenly marries a violent man who makes her subservient. She is
literally dispossessed of her body and integrity as her psyche and
body disintegrate. Rape is here a deliberate and violent act of possession and degradation that reduces her to an object. It becomes
a purposeful annihilation that enacts debasement through sexual
violence.[46] Esperanza surrenders her sense of self while her husband remains in control of her until her death. Rape is a male
prerogative and, as Susan Brownmiller has pointed out, "a conscious process of intimidation" to keep women and children in "a
state of fear." The dependency established through the family
further weakens the "victim's resistance" and "confounds her
will."[47] Esperanza's progressive self-effacement and powerlessness as wife are highlighted by her silence toward the middle of
the story. The husband's unrestricted power in the domestic universe lasts until his mother-in-law arrives, sent by the landowner, the source of seigniorial power.

In the peasant marriage the rights of man are not restricted,
turning the contract for the woman into exploitation. The only
option for females is to choose the right husband, that is, one who
is a good patrón. Bernabé instead acts as an ill-willed master who
uses threats or actual physical force to control his wife and family. Moreover, his sense of maleness is designed to instill fear and

obedience.[48] Brunet's representation of family life within a rural context shows the virtual absence of the state, leaving each individual to fend for himself or herself.

Dominance is again asserted in Bernabé's sense of possession when Eufrasia wants to take the children away. For this husband, his late wife and his children are property. His language shows orality and dialecticism as central in Brunet's depiction of a world that has been left virtually untouched by a lettered modernity.

> Y aquella vieja que le quería quitar los chiquillos. ¿Por qué, si eran suyos? Intrusa. . . . Los chiquillos eran suyos, para que él hiciera con ellos lo que le diera la gana. Todos. Los chiquillos y la Venancia. Para apalearlos si se le antojaba. Para dejarlos sin comer. Iba a aprender la condenada vieja aquella. (57)

> (And that old woman who wanted to take away his little ones. Why? They were his, weren't they? The old meddler. . . . The little ones were his, to do what he liked with. All of them. The little ones and Venancia. To beat them if he felt like it. To let them go hungry. He was going to teach that damned old woman.]

Eufrasia's attempt fails in the face of Bernarbé's aggressive language and outbursts. Violence fills him and compels him to verbal and physical abuse. Furthermore, connected to the father's power is his daughter Venancia, who physically resembles her mother. This is a recurrent motif in Brunet, where women are seen as copies of one another, signaling their exchangeability as sexual and economic objects in the hacienda culture. *Aguas abajo* reiterates women's disidentity by turning them into copies and doubles of each other. The father's comments when he looks at Venancia reveal his incestuous desire and her quality as replica (59). The (virtual) incest between father and daughter appears as a perversion that exalts individual omnipotence over social taboo. It also signals that the foundations of Western culture not only are challenged in this context but may be shattered at any moment.

After learning the incriminating evidence, Eufrasia decides to avenge her daughter and secretly plans Bernabé's end. This decision puts patriarchal morality and its servitude into question. The marriage contract is thus revealed as an oppressive reality conducive to crimes that may disappear into the identity of the wife as Esperanza's fate illustrates. The prestige of the patriarch in the vertical culture of the hacienda takes on a seigniorial virility, according to María Emma Mannarelli. His dominion finds few limits over those it subordinates. Patriarchy is thus this personal power inside the home, and it develops through personal dependency and obedience. In this kind of authoritarianism, the father remains a figure who is not accountable to a written law sanctioned by a public or state institution.[49] The virtual absence of the law shows that women like Eufrasia have to resort to retribution with their own hands with the *patron's* silent acquiescence to her deed.

Through an impersonal and matter-of-fact account, Bernabe's silent and sudden death with a stone ends the reign of terror of the brutal master. Most significant is that the identity of the murderer is not revealed until the very end, when the grandmother claims her successful revenge (64). Cunning and strategy prove to be more valuable and effective in defeating an enemy than mere force. The grandmother's social disempowerment as an old widow is cleverly overcome by the accurate use of the slingshot. This surprising turn of events illustrates the "knockout" effect[50] that many of Brunet's short stories have, leaving the reader astonished. In "Piedra callada," Eufrasia reinstates her power by a carefully planned action in which she takes the law into her own hands. Her decision is an example of Brunet's torsion of the *criollista* narrative, showing the extent of women's will to live and protect the young in a patriarchal universe.

THE BETRAYAL OF THE MOTHER IN "AGUAS ABAJO"

"Aguas abajo" opens with a man building a house with rocks and mud set against the backdrop of an enormous rural landscape. Here the mountains, the crevices in the rocks, and the river are open signs that constitute a bodyscape that is not only subjectivized but eroticized. Through the creation of an aesthetic landscape that reappears in several of her rural settings, Brunet departs from *criollismo,* rejecting the illustration of a national character, a Chilean landscape, and the profitable exchange value of landownership. The signs here are ordered through a female gaze, creating a feminized space that encompasses all of nature as well as the family's history and interrelations. In contrast, the *criollista*/male gaze attempts to depict an idea of the nation in a closed regime of signification where the landscape and the characters are immutable and heroic in their fight against the forces of nature. This explains the sense of *costumbrismo* and outdated picturesque depiction that many of the *criollista* narratives share.

In contrast, in "Aguas abajo" the openness and vastness of nature are drastically opposed to the man-built house, which is a closed and asphyxiating space that has been marked by the male and his will. Furthermore, the appearance of the young and sensual female while the man is penetrating the wood with his hatchet becomes a sign and point of inflexion in a larger and complex discursive system. The text has an interpellative function that calls for the reader's interpretation of polysemic signs. Brunet's aesthetic operation is not in the rural speech of the characters' dialogues, which has been identified as her *criollista* signature, but rather in the subjectivation of both natural and cultural spaces. The result of this hybrid discursive system is an aesthetic tension expressed in a modern subjectivity in which the founding principle is feminine and the gaze is female. As a consequence, the representation of the countryside does not reproduce the project of an urban national modernity but rather opposes it.

Brunet's awry gaze sees from the stance of an urban and lettered modernity those subaltern subjectivities that resist modernization and through them invents new myths. In contrast, the *criollista*'s literary representation replaces the countryside with a picture of the national landscape that not only fits a masculine modernity but also proves its success. This is why in their texts male characters are always heroic while the male body is epically depicted in its struggle with and mastery of an indomitable nature. In the *criollista* texts, there is a national iconography that sustains the signification of the landscape through the romanticization of man and nature. The latter is construed according to a naturalist-scientific framework in which the native species of flora and fauna are identified according to a specific geographical region. In Brunet's stories, however, there is nothing epic, heroic, or scientific in the representation of the rural world. Instead, we find a fictive and imaginative landscape and people that are closer to a mythical expressionism where the senses and the passions shape their world. As a result, hyperesthesia governs nature, alerting the reader to the fact that anything may happen in a game of multiple signification. This awry perspective that organizes Brunet's text makes it suspicious rather than transparent, deploying signs that move, clash, or explode conventional meanings and, particularly, *criollista* readings.

Furthermore, the Greco-Latin myths and their female protagonists are revisited within a family drama that produces new subjectivities in this story. Maclovia, the daughter in "Aguas abajo," is a kind of Electra who betrays her mother and symbolically kills her to be free to pursue her passion. In the classical narratives the characters were responsible for bringing about a tragic destiny that was closer to pathos, whereas in Brunet's version, they are subjects of passion. They express a singularized vitality and an ethical tendency proper to the realm of desire against social and cultural norms.

In this second story of the trilogy, Brunet goes further in her exploration of the taboos that founded Western patriarchal culture by depicting the constitution of new transgressions to sexual morality. We read the inversion of the classical Greek myth of incest in the daughter's seduction of the stepfather. In this way, Brunet contrasts the alterations and prohibitions around sexuality and the masculine principle that organizes them. As a consequence, Judeo-Christian morality is changed in the text through the daughter's transgression and the inability of the mother to interdict her. In this world, familial relations take a wide range of forms, making women interchange positions while the patriarch keeps his place and authority.

Brunet also confronts us with a paradoxical view of the constitution of female identity through the conflictual mother/daughter relationship. Maclovia, the fifteen-year-old female, resents her mother and her authority in a similar way to Esperanza in the previous short story. Without her real father in the home, she is only subject to her mother, who is unable to impose limits or rules. The mother's absorption with her husband dictates family relations and sexual morality. Brunet explores here what happens within the family when there are no prohibitions. According to Freud, the persistence of taboos, which are set up by parental or social authority, shows that the "original pleasure to do the forbidden still continues" in the unconscious.[51] The possibility of bringing about a new order in which nature and culture are transformed, as Lévi-Strauss notes on incest, makes this rule embrace what is most foreign to society and also what will surpass nature. In this way, society prohibits what is most likely related to a rule that is social in that it is a rule, and presocial in its universality and the kinds of relationships in which it is imposed.[52] Brunet's story dwells on the absence of the incest taboo and the disastrous consequences it has, particularly for the mother/ daughter bond. The transgression of the prohibition takes a turn in that it underscores the decline of the father's authority and the mother's inability to exert power over and establish rules for her daughter.

Maclovia learns the value of her young body and is willing to use it to escape her mother's power and affirm herself. The image of a ripe fruit highlights her sexuality and her body's ability to attract others.

Within the first paragraph, Brunet establishes the precariousness of the house and the consequences for the rural family. Promiscuity and lack of privacy determine the physical and psychic conditions of the members: the grandmother pretends to pray while the children sleep and the couple has sex. There is no separation of spaces or distance between family members, who are forced to participate in everyone's actions, particularly at night. As a precedent to the transgression of incest, Maclovia's sexual arousal manifests as her mother and her "husband" are having sex:

> Pero a veces un gemido más agudo inquietaba el sueño de la muchacha, la ponía al borde del desvelo, cuando no la despertaba de golpe, anhelante, sabedora de lo que pasaba allí, viéndolo sin verlo, trasudando angustia, con los pechos repentinamente doloridos y los muslos temblorosos, uno contra otro, apretados. (70)

> [But sometimes a more penetrating moan disturbed the girl's sleep and put her on the verge of waking, if it didn't wake her completely. The girl was left yearning, aware of what was going on there, seeing it without seeing it, sweating in torment, her breasts suddenly aching and her thighs trembling, one pressed against the other.] (144)

This erotic twist in the representation of the girl's arousal and body presents another instance of Brunet's awry and female gaze. The narrator's view organizes the signs in a way that Maclovia's sensuality coexists with the emotional loss of her childhood. Her adolescent psyche becomes overexcited by a series of stimuli that she cannot control. Her organic reaction as she hears her mother's moans is depicted in the passage, underscoring the sexual energy that circulates through this space and the bodies. Freud points out that for the child the person who cares for him is the source of continuous sexual satisfaction and excitement. The mother is the person who directs the feeling that originates from sexual life: she is the one who kisses, caresses, and cradles the child. Sexual pulsations organize during childhood and transform in adolescence. Freud has also shown that sexual energy during this period becomes essentially genital, changing from its previ-

ous autoeroticism. Shame, disgust, compassion, social moral constructions, and authority circumscribe the orientation of sexual
pulsations.[53] The lack of limits in Maclovia's upbringing and the
confluence of material and psychic spaces confuse the positions of
mother and daughter.

Maclovia's corporeal presence, on the other hand, is moved to
the foreground of the narration as the result of the sexual violence to which she is subjected. We can assume that sexuality has
been imposed on her life from an early age and that this scene has
been repeated over time. There is a psychic continuum between
mother and daughter in the episode described, in that they are
both sexually excited by the same man. This sexual energy results
in the daughter's frustration at not getting what she wants: that
is, to have the mother's rights and privileges.

The narrator's gaze is highly erotic and interchangeable with
those of the other inhabitants of the house. In this voyeuristic
and orgiastic scene, we hear the couple's sexual negotiations, the
grandmother's prayer interrupted by what she hears, and
Maclovia's bodily reactions. The girl awakens with her mother's
sexual climax as she probably has other times. In this sense, we
can say that they all share the same bed without distinctions of
role, identity, or consanguinity. From the sexual rituals of her
mother, Maclovia has learned that bonds and affect do not restrict individual actions and desires. Through the mother's unrestrained sexual behavior, the ground is prepared for the
daughter's rebellion. The fight for power takes an unforeseen
turn by making mother and daughter rivals for sexual power. In
this phallic context, the mother is unable to impose the incest
prohibition that will finally strip her of all authority.

Amid material dispossession, raw power and passions intertwine, turning each family member into a potential enemy. Brunet's rural stories literally turn bourgeois and Catholic morality
upside down. Within this social order, relations and positions inside the house change and anyone may become the other in the
threesome. The house as a sacred Catholic and private refuge is
here replaced with an insecure and aggressive space in which primal feelings are at play. The woman's sexual practices in the
presence of everyone erase the mother figure, leaving her place
empty. Maclovia's adolescent arousal transgresses conventional
notions of femininity as well as family and sexual morals. Moreover, her arousal manifests within the family structure, molding
itself after her mother's sexual practices. The man, on the other
hand, appears to be oblivious to others in the room, conscious of

his sex rights as head of the household. The next episode shows the encounter between Maclovia and the man, emphasizing masculine sexual desire for the young female. The girl has been sent by her mother to call her husband. Maclovia unwillingly obeys and follows the sounds of his ax in order to find him. When she finds him, she sees his virile and strong body, exuding sexual prowess in a reiteration of the sex scene. The passage also evokes and recreates the girl's sexual fantasies, which have been made conscious. Maclovia has seen him possessing her mother, who is now absent, leaving the road free. Desire takes hold of the man upon seeing the girl as a sexual object. His sight travels upward over Maclovia's body, symbolically standing above him as a kind of wild virgin. Sexuality envelops nature here through the image of the elements that highlight primitive forces opposing culture and its prohibitions:

> Y los ojos se le soldaron a la figura alzada allí, viéndola desde abajo, con las piernas desnudas y el vientre apenas combo y las puntas de los senos altos, y arriba la barbilla y todo el rostro echado hacia atrás, deformado y desconocido, con las crenchas despeinadas por la mano del viento, mano como de hombre que la quisiera y la acariciara. (72)
> . . . Súbitamente pegó la frente a sus piernas, alzó las manos y las pegó a las piernas. Y un momento se quedaron así, como parte del paisaje, sin pensar en nada, sintiendo tan solo la tremenda vida instintiva que los galvanizaba. (73)

> [And his eyes fastened upon the figure above him there, viewing her from below, with her bare legs and her gently rounded stomach and the tips of her upraised breasts, and above them her chin and her whole face thrown back, distorted and unfamiliar, with her hair disheveled by the hand of the wind, a hand like a man's, desiring and caressing her.
> . . . Suddenly he pressed his forehead to her legs. He raised his hands and pressed them to her legs. And for a moment, they stayed that way, like part of the landscape, unthinking, feeling only the tremendous instinctive life that fused them together]. (146)

The man experiences desire as an extreme power that possesses him. It goes out to the girl and encompasses the landscape, eroticizing all of nature. Desire here is part of an uncontrollable force that transgresses social laws and taboos. Since the mother is not present, there is no control (neither Catholic nor civil). As a consequence, the man pursues his desire without concern for civilized consequences, for what this will do to his wife or to

Maclovia. The girl, on the other hand, lets him touch her but walks away, still resisting. What is interesting is the ventriloquism at play here in the gaze toward Maclovia which feminizes and eroticizes the entire universe surrounding her. This female gaze then masquerades behind the voice of the weaver to speak from the perspective of a female who desires a female body.

The next episode, sometime after, succinctly describes the mother's devastated state after discovering the betrayal. She recognizes her new position and what she has lost. Her sense of impotence and dispossession inexorably foreshadows her fate in the house. Maclovia's last act of defiance clearly shows that something has changed. The mother's reality is shattered after finding her husband and her daughter embracing.

As the taboo is contravened, the family restructures under the new sexual bond. Most significant is that the man keeps his place as head and authority while mother and daughter exchange positions and duties. The daughter becomes the sexual partner and housewife with all the privileges that these identities entail. She takes her new place without visible signs of confusion or discomfort. Maclovia not only has won independence from her mother but also devours her.

In a world that enforces rivalry and competition among women, loyalties and blood ties are easily undermined for a man's attention. The quickest and most intense way to achieve this is through sex. Since in this patriarchal setting power can only be accessed through a man, women fight to be the chosen object of his desire. Man grants privileges and status to women based on the services they provide him in the house. This is the privilege of the husband as he coldly reveals to his wife that Maclovia is now his woman. On the other hand, it is also the lesson taught by the mother to her daughter: that a man is object and vehicle for female identity.

The older woman is humiliated and replaced by Maclovia, the young and sexually available female. The need to reject the mother's power holds the promise of freedom for the daughter, as Jessica Benjamin explains.[54] Independence for Maclovia means being beyond her mother's control and becoming the woman of the house. The power struggle between mother and daughter is settled with the mother's final debunking. Maclovia takes control of everything in the house. At the same time, the mother loses her daughter as Maclovia had lost her mother in the past. She asserts her autonomy by moving up in the gender and sexual hierarchy in order to become the man's sexual object. In this way, she rejects and denies her mother's authority and her bonds as daughter. From a feminist psychoanalytic interpretation, the daughter who wants to separate in the preoedipal stage struggles to differentiate, "to tear herself from the attachment to mother." This disidentification with the mother is expressed in the need to find a subject who represents independence and desire. The father becomes the ideal figure in the "identificatory love" that develops between daughters and fathers. He stands as the model for ideal love and recognition, as Jessica Benjamin has shown.[55]

Brunet inserts incest (stepdaughter/stepfather) as another possibility in the sexual contract, more so when it is based on a pure agreement (since the woman was probably not married to the weaver). Brunet also presents the dire consequences of this virtual incest for relationships and identities within the family. This may be especially seen in this story, in which older women are discarded.

The substitution of the mother is made possible by the patriarchal order that structures the family and privileges the husband. His incestuous desire affirms his masculinity, on the one hand, and his dominance in his personal world, on the other. In the domestic sphere, as the story dramatically shows, his power is exercised without limitations. The interchangeability and reassignment of functions and positions among the different members do not affect the structure of the family. The man remains the sole authority with unlimited control to contravene taboos. As the head and authority figure, the weaver establishes rules and prohibitions. The image of the household as a kingdom ruled by the incestuous father is also pertinent here. All other family members are largely silent and powerless to curb his abuse. Conjugal and parental authority are thus embodied in the male, while the mother is completely silenced and marginalized. Historical studies of the rural household in Chile have shown that the man was the "king of the house." He exerted unchecked autonomy and authority and exercised a role that went beyond that of breadwinner, according to Heidi Tinsman. The image of the *huaso* best conveys rural masculinity, in which strength, independence, irreverence, and sexual prowess are distinctive features.[56] His language and ideology are the focal points of Brunet's narrative exploration and how they impact feminine subjectivities.

The depth of the intrafamilial conflict in the story is encapsulated in the mother's pain at seeing her daughter as rival and usurper. As a consequence, the mother/daughter relationship is violently shattered by setting one woman against the other. The daughter has learned to scorn and ultimately betray the mother. The mother, in turn, is demoted in the sexual division of labor by having her role reduced to insignificant domestic tasks. Old age leaves women powerless, as abandoned copies of one another whose usefulness (for men) has ceased. The awareness of this cruel reality is portrayed in the torn monologue of the abandoned mother who accepts that she has become "la vieja" and thus is forced to relinquish her place. She sees Maclovia taking away her entire life, symbolized by having a man, a home, and the responsibility and authority of being the housewife. The blind grandmother, the weakest member of the family, advises acceptance and resignation.

As the mother's new reality takes shape, thoughts of death and suicide cross her mind. She thinks of various ways of ending her life—the river, the cliff, the rocks—to see her husband and daughter riven by remorse. Surprisingly, she holds on to a thread of hope and decides to wait for the man to have a change of heart. In her mind, "waiting" and putting up "a good front" of sustained self-effacement will win him back. Thus the prospect of a simulated submissive act becomes a chance to regain the man. Self-delusion is her last resort for denying that she has lost her power. This same fantasy perpetuates her sense of identity only through a man, a lesson she engrains in Maclovia. Brunet's critique here sheds light on the ways women may trap themselves into perpetuating *machismo* and patriarchal forms of gender identity.

In staying on to play a more demeaning role, the woman's subordination deepens. In the process, she has become a bodiless silhouette (like the grandmother), who remains subordinate to the very man who controls her and her daughter's destinies. The woman's inability to leave underscores the depth of her dependency and her difficulty in living without a man.

Brunet's narrative announces the decline of the father and, as a consequence, the lack of interdiction for culture. Paradoxically, modernity brands these disrupted worlds with its own rationality, introducing acute contradictions in the forms of organization of the private sphere.

THE WOUNDED SPHINX IN "SOLEDAD DE LA SANGRE"

Subjectivation plays a major role in the story of confinement and loneliness of an educated wife who shares a similar imaginary to the landowner's wife in "Piedra callada." For the former, music and for the latter, radio soap operas constitute the modern mass culture that the elite may have access to in the rural areas. Both women make of these cultural products fetishes of modernity that relate to their fantasies and solitary enjoyment.

The gramophone in "Soledad de la sangre" introduces a totally modern relationship with objects that alters perceptions and relations by creating a subjective space for the protagonist. The gramophone is the point of explanation for the last third of the narrative, revealing the woman's subjectivity, memory, and sensuality. What is important is that her subjectification of the gramophone and what it does for her reassembles an otherwise split self. Thus, this modern object provides a mode of subjectivity in the rural area that counters the premodern cultural and subjective modes operating there that have oppressed the wife.

The extension of hearing that the gramophone allows recreates the woman's own fetishistic enjoyment through a modernity that contrasts the earthly and submissive image of the plain that her husband and marriage impose on her. Language in this story does not reproduce any sociolectical idioms resembling peasant or rural speech, as in the dialogues of the previous two stories. Since memory predominates in this instance, a subjective point of view is used to reveal the protagonist's passions and sense of loss.

Eroticization is also a salient feature of this regime of signs, particularly in the descriptions of the woman's appearance and body. When the narrative voice describes the protagonist's youth and looks, her physical body and sensuality are highlighted. Her lips, her height, and her tan skin in the present constitute a sensual presence that reveals the erotic narrative perspective toward the female body. In contrast, the husband seems a stone figure, rigid and taciturn under the lamp. In less than two hundred words, Brunet emphasizes the significance of the lamp, the first article bought by the wife, as a product of modernity that illuminates both the couple's distance and the comfort of their home, thanks to the wife's labor. As a result, the lamp and the gramophone also reveal the plight of the wife and the dire existence she has settled for with a man she never loved. In this story, objects are subjectified and eroticized through the wife's perspective and her relationship to the world.

The corporality of her body is again heightened in the fight with the two men who attempt to touch and take her gramophone. Her bites and kicks as well as her offensive words give us evidence of her untamed body and subjectivity. Finally, when she is wounded, her body is also moved to the foreground to reiterate its physicality in the extreme struggle between life and death. In this critical moment, the natural imagery of undercurrents and waters insists on the woman's sexuality and how she has sublimated her desire in order to bear a life of order and conformity. Being wounded in this context forces her to see what she has tried to deny. Thus, the signs are once again placed within an expressionist framework in which blood and pain illuminate the existence of premodern forms of subjectivity that clash with modern ones. From this perspective, the opening description of the husband, who seems to have been chiseled in wood, speaks of other subjectivities and the ways they signify the world. The wife has remained blind in order to preserve her marriage and lead the life she was brought up to live. However, the experience of being wounded changes the woman's point of signification, allowing her to see her husband as undeserving and repulsive. By denying her sight, she had privileged hearing and established her own solitary pastime and solace. After the wound, she is able to see what her life has been. These changes of perception and understanding are represented through a pattern of signs in which embodiment is central to achieving awareness of reality.

Additionally, "Soledad de la sangre" reiterates names and natural sites that reveal the creation of an incipient fictive rural region in the collection *Aguas abajo*. Don Valladares's death, for example, is mentioned in "Soledad de la sangre" by the protagonist's husband, who craves his land. Don Valladares also appeared in "Piedra callada" as he oversaw the *hijuela* where Bernabé and Esperanza lived. Thus certain characters, motifs, and particularly landscapes delineate a fictive world that not only is cited by Brunet herself but can be recognized by the reader. The creation of this fictional world in 1943 is a precedent to Rulfo's Comala (*Pedro Páramo,* 1955); García Márquez's Macondo (*Cien años de soledad; (One Hundred Years of Solitude),* 1967; as well as Brunet's own Colloco in *María Nadie* (1957), showing another very significant departure from the *criollista* aesthetic mode.

"Soledad de la sangre" is the longest and most subjective narration in the trilogy. It marks a shift in Brunet's literary view in that it introduces psychic and emotional life as a fundamental aspect of female identity. Hence the life of the protagonist's mind and her inner conflict represent the core of the narrative. How the wife feels, desires, and remembers her youth are integral to her understanding of the present and the way she faces it. The loveless relationship with her husband displays submissiveness and disappointment as central elements. The marriage had been arranged by the protagonist's father, who chose an older, prosperous suitor who owned land.

The story is told from the perspective of an "emotionally battered" wife, who feels lonely and hopeless.[57] Her experience of marriage echoes that of Bombal's protagonists. She has no name and also shows the emotional numbness and limitations that male omnipotence has imposed on her through the marriage contract. Marriage actually destroys what the woman could have been through an asymmetry expressed between her fantasy and daily life. She is an object within the transaction that marriage implies and is reproduced in every single act signed by the exchange. The wife's sublimated passion in the story contrasts with the economic interests that rule marriage.[58] In this scenario the wife becomes a submissive other who performs the duties demanded by tradition. She turns into an object of the husband's desire, confirming him with minimal resistance, following the transaction signed by her father and her husband. She becomes a good exchanged from one man to another, transforming herself into what she is permitted. Angel Rama has pointed out that individual freedom in this story is conceived as the only uniquely human sphere: hence the irreconcilable opposition it represents to the bourgeois economic structure that marriage supports and that threatens to annihilate the woman.[59]

The anonymous protagonist's upbringing paves the way for her passive obedience. The narrative voice discloses that "nunca había podido sobreponerse a una obscura sumisión instintiva de hembra a macho, que antaño se humillaba al padre y ogaño al marido." (89) (she had never been able to prevail over a dark, instinctive submissiveness . . . who in former years humiliated herself to her father and in the present, to her husband.") (64). Obedience and gender submission keep her bound first as daughter, later as wife.

The highly scripted and circumscribed life that she has lived for eighteen years is encapsulated in the anticipation of the Saturday night rituals. The schedules and repetitiveness of her existence are bracketed once a week when she is allowed to stay up late, listening to records on her phonograph all by herself. Her tension and anxiety prior to actually putting the music on revolve around her husband's falling asleep so that she can be at peace by herself.

An important aspect of the marriage contract is revealed through the protagonist's success selling her knitted work locally. The money she earns is reflected in the things she has purchased for the house. As she recalls, the husband had told her she had to have a business to take care of her expenses. His control over the money she makes and what she does with it is reiterated in several examples. The most significant is the time he lent her money to buy wool to start knitting. Later, when she succeeds, the husband demands to have the money back and spends her earnings on the household. His actions reveal the economic and capitalist foundation of marriage, where profit is the bedrock. According to the husband's pragmatic and utilitarian rationality, her work is "time that is useful" because it earns money. Earning money in this story does not procure equality within marriage, since the husband yields the private space but does it only as long as it is an investment. For Brunet, economic autonomy does not give a wife independence either, because the husband's authority still binds her.

On the other hand, money also allows another logic of capitalism to satisfy or replace the wife's emptiness by fetishizing objects, among them the phonograph, which is the most significant. The fetish here has its traditional significance, in which the object acquires its own powers. In this case, the phonograph evokes and restitutes the protagonist's past. It heals her suffering by providing her with something sacred that completes her. This transformation contrasts with her sense of inner split between what she is (a wife) and what she was (a young and virgin female). The phonograph becomes a sacred object that enables the reconfiguration of her identity.

Through a series of flashbacks, her youth unfolds as she listens to the music and reclaims herself through memories of the past. The sharp contrast with the past is obvious in her confined and solitary life in the present. Gabriela Mora has pointed out the parallels and oppositions that her immersion in the past shows through the brilliant and intense colors associated with the laughter and light of her adolescence. Silence and darkness, on the other hand, characterize her present after eighteen years of order, immobility, and repetitive gestures.[60]

Marriage in this story is modeled on cultural and gender hierarchies. The protagonist's indifferent acceptance of the arranged marriage is soon succeeded by feelings of fear and oppression during the wedding, as her evocation shows. The "uncomfortable" dress, the "oppressive" garland, and her fear of tearing the veil (68) highlight her fear of losing her virginity. More significantly, these images also foreshadow the loveless marriage and the rejection that characterizes the bond with the husband.[61]

The present in the protagonist's consciousness is shaped by the repression and sublimation of her deepest desires. Her social performance as a sphinx underlines the split between inner and outer selves. The sphinx symbolizes the monster (part woman, part lion, and part bird) who gave Oedipus riddles, among them the one of the two sisters. One sister gives birth to the other and she in turn gives birth to the first. The inextricable union of a two-faced process is expressed in this riddle.[62] It also highlights duality as an integral part of life and nature. In the same way, Brunet's protagonist is defined by the duality of her consciousness as she experiences being a wife (imposed from the outside) in dramatic contrast to her sense of wholeness provided by her virginity and youth. The music she plays on the phonograph recalls memories of a different, young, and joyful self. Music represents solace in the barren loneliness of her married life.[63] Her tension before these solitary moments underscores a secret inner life that is protected from the husband. Listening to music becomes the pathway to carefully kept memories of friendship and love. Her aesthetic sensibility finds in music a medium to formalize her repressed desire and fantasies.

The woman's hidden adolescent love unfolds as the most treasured memory. The initial march takes her back to her friends and her days back in the north. While listening to a waltz, love and the desire she has kept within emerge in the evocation of a green-eyed man and how he eroticized her:

> ¿Qué mirada iba a tener esa magia? ¿Ese quemar que le ardía adentro, no sabía dónde, como anhelante espera de no sabía que dicha? ¿Su nombre? . . . Enrique . . . Juan . . . José . . . Humberto . . . . . . No importaba. Ella lo quería siempre, con cualquier nombre. . . . Lo quería. . . . Quererlo. . . . Quererlo como quiere una mujer, porque ella ya lo era y sus quince años le maduraban en sus pequeños pezones, mulliendo zonas íntimas y dando a su voz un súbito trémolo obscuro. Quererlo siempre. (93)

> [What gaze was going to hold that magic for her? That burning that raged within her, she did not know where, as if waiting longingly for some unknown happiness. His name? . . . Enrique . . . Juan . . . José . . . Humberto . . . . . . It did not matter. She would always love him, whatever his name was. . . . She loved him. . . . Love him. . . . Love him the way a woman loves, because she already was a woman and her fifteen years were ripening in her budding breast, bringing a

downy softness to her intimate zones. . . . She would love him for-
ever]. (67)

This green-eyed man stands as the recurrent reminder of the
woman's first and only romantic fantasy. This evocation is embodied in the woman's eroticism and body, which bring to mind
Maclovia's portrayal. Brunet's queer perspective surfaces here in
the eroticization of the wife's body and the subjectifation of her
memory and fantasy. For the mere fact of desiring the young
man, she supposes that her desire is reciprocated. She is only fif-
teen and falls in love with a stranger she sees from time to time.
Her equation of passion with magic is crushed the day the man
vanishes without ever having spoken to her. Her friends confirm
her love, however, and the man's disappearance through the
myth of "la calchona." This mythic figure embodies alternatively
a female who takes away unfaithful men or, through metonymy,
female genitalia with identical consequences. Devastated by this
loss, the young woman accepts betrothal to a rich man for whom
she becomes the perfect wife, a sphinx without expression.

Historical studies in Chile have shown that in the upper and
middle classes, the model for the Catholic wife was the sphinx.
She had to hide her emotions and feelings in order to perform socially without ever complaining; she had to be prudent and self-
controlled and "the soul of her house."[64] Female consciousness in
this cultural context is thus divided between duties and feelings.
This is precisely the condition of the wife in "Soledad de la sangre," who embodies this social script and prescribed identity. As
this behavior is bound by the sexual contract, Brunet recreates
the protagonist's inner drama and her longings for a different
identity.

Brunet's writing technique changes significantly in this text,
which shows a double movement: one from the countryside to the
"casa patronal" and another from rural females to an educated
woman from the bourgeoisie. This story displays the real rules of
marriage as an arranged bourgeois contract. As a consequence,
language also changes in that Brunet always historicizes subjectivities.[65]

The sense of time wasted in an unsatisfying marriage is kept
inside by the protagonist. Her unexpressive eyes and demureness
are ways to hide what she feels. From her perspective, the husband is like a patient "vulture," ready to swoop and feed, reiterating a predatory image. This perception echoes Bombal's
characters, who see men as hunters in search of victims or crea-

tures of whom to take advantage. Through the narrative voice in Brunet, we get a series of details and examples of how the couple spent the wife's money, and how they saved and invested mostly in land. Their marriage stands as a metaphor for bourgeois order and its ethics of productivity, managed and controlled by the husband.

During a business dinner in which he is eager to make a deal selling pigs, the wife cooks and serves food for him and his guest. As the dinner progresses, her solicitousness and apparent calm give way to an increasing irritation with the guest, who wants to play her phonograph. The woman's exterior poise is abruptly halted and replaced by a sudden hate boiling inside her. The tension among the three escalates as the woman denies the guest's request to listen to the phonograph. For the first time, she says "no" to a male, expressing what she feels to the other. The drunken guest, however, persists and finally touches her sacred object. At this point, the husband joins in with the guest to snatch the phonograph. The wife is beside herself, completely transformed by the power of anger. She kicks, screams, and punches to prevent the men from reaching the most valued possession. Her mysterious aura has turned into concrete violence in which she bites and hits both men without fear.

This final loss of control reveals a new aspect of the protagonist's identity. The sphinxlike wife is taken over by an enraged woman who eschews manners and propriety. Quite the opposite, she uses her entire body and physical strength to defend the phonograph. She attacks to guard what makes her whole, that which means a life that is all possibilities. Through physical aggression, she tears away the cultural demands that have encaged and contained her. Here subjectivity appears to be defined by profound and unconscious forces. Within the wife there is an untamed side, which is embodied in her aggression to fight and survive.

This episode ends with the woman fleeing the house, wounded by the broken records she has struggled for. This painful yet cathartic moment is accompanied by her weeping, screaming, and howling out on the plains. However, experiencing physical pain paradoxically provides a new awareness and clearness. For the first time the protagonist is not split and is able to integrate her consciousness.

While bleeding almost to death, the woman reviews her life and how it would be without her husband. She sees the resentment and disgust for him vanishing if she stops living. Nevertheless, death would end not only an unfulfilling marriage but also the

romantic memories from her youth. More importantly, she realizes that death would mean the cessation of everything she is.
Letting herself die means not only getting rid of an unwanted
husband, but more fundamentally, stopping being. This is the
reason she chooses to live because it implies being. The future remains open to the choices she might make. Her final decision to
return to the house leaves the reader with an open ending. We do
not know whether she goes back to being a wife or whether she
walks out. However, from her perspective, her oppression remains individual, with no awareness of its collective and social
character.

2

María Nadie, or the Fallen Virgin

MARÍA NADIE (1957) IS CONSIDERED BRUNET'S BEST NOVEL, PART OF Chile's national literature. In his prologue to the novel's 1996 edition, the critic Hugo Montes states that it is a breaking point in Brunet's literary project. He especially highlights Brunet's use of psychological characterization, humor, and autobiographical confessions. Furthermore, in this novel she portrays the lives of men and women of little social importance, anticipating the literary realism of Manuel Rojas (1896–1973) and his generation in Chile.[1] From the canonical point of view, then, *María Nadie* represents the epitome of a new existentialist turn in Brunet's aesthetic in which localism has been passed.[2] Hence, existence for María is the enactment of authentic and inauthentic forms of behavior, as José Promis suggests. The interplay of these opposing forces is interpreted as what constitutes the inner image and understanding of the character.[3] Critic Berta López Morales has been among the few, with Kemy Oyarzún, who have pointed out the contradictions that the literary establishment showed in evaluating Brunet's long writing trajectory. Another critic, Raúl Silva Castro, as López Morales notes, commented with great surprise that Brunet, who had a "manly" talent, had provided the first example of "feminine" Chilean literature with *María Nadie.*[4]

In my view, this novel is a phenomenon much more complex than these patriarchal readings have suggested for the formation of the canon. Brunet's work critiques and discusses epistemological categories of gender and modernity through the process of modernization of a rural and traditional culture, creating a world in which the old symbolic regime persists within the new urban institutionalization. *María Nadie* constitutes a departure from previous literary history, gender identities, and types of modernity in which these relations take place.

This novel culminates the second period of Brunet's literary paradigm, as critics have pointed out, a trend some see already present in *Humo hacia el sur* (*Smoke to the South*) (1946).[5] In this sense, the novel represents both a break from and a continuation of Brunet's literary trajectory as she focuses on how modern female subjects are formed amid an ongoing process of modernization and the impact of institutionalized cultural forms. Critic Cecilia Ojeda finds that the dismantling of bourgeois female stereotypes is a common feature of this novel and *María Nadie*. In *Humo hacia el sur,* Doña Batilde, the embodiment of the authoritarian and powerful woman, is contrasted with herself as the young Tilde whose romantic hopes were crushed in marriage. For Ojeda, *María Nadie* goes a step further by revealing María's difficult independence, social marginality, and unattainable ideal of authenticity.[6] Though this is certainly true, I think that *María Nadie* represents Brunet's redefinition of subjectivity in a world where the separation of moral, religious, and scientific spheres has not completely taken place. Under these conditions, women's independence and autonomy seem untenable. Heterosexual family, patriarchal/rural modernity, and Catholic marriage are the three aspects of a constraining triangle for feminine identification in the passage from the private to the public sphere. Maternity plays a major role in this novel, defining women's identities as well as their possibilities for autonomy and subjection in a traditional cultural context.

The narrative structure of the novel is divided into two distinct sections that textualize the social and cultural spaces that Brunet's favorite female protagonist, María, confronts.[7] This character shares the Virgin's name but represents her opposite in a parody of the biblical narrative. She has lost her virginity before marrying and has a romantic sexual relationship with a man without being his wife. Moreover, rather than delivering a child, she has a miscarriage. Brunet's María López stands against tradition, representing the challenges of a modern and independent woman. The first section, "The Town," describes the early development of a rural town named Colloco[8] and its daily life through the polyphonic narration of its inhabitants. In the second section of the novel, titled "Woman," María López narrates her past and present life, giving a testimony of her failures.

THE LANGUAGE OF DELIRIUM

The first half of the novel reiterates the same fictive landscape that Brunet recreated in other narratives and that we saw in

Aguas abajo. The gorge, the river, the mountain are natural elements of a landscape that has been dislocated from the *criollista* aesthetic while becoming a feminine or a childhood space in Brunet's poetics. In the novel *María Nadie,* she resorts much less often to a rural imaginary, focusing more on what life means for the inhabitants of the town of Colloco. The characters are presented as incomplete outlines that speak halfway because María's presence interferes in their sense of identity and desire.

Women undergo all sorts of linguistic, animallike metamorphoses that range from being a *burra,* (donkey), to refer to Ernestina's sexual potency, to a *lagartija eléctrica* (electric lizard), to signal Reinaldo's lover. All these markers reiterate, however, the male fear of castration and masculine anxiety.[9] Faced with sexually powerful females who possess men instead of being passively possessed by them, men not only are threatened but progressively lose their private and public presence and a sense of identity with the modernization of their world.

Petaca is another powerful female in Colloco whose authority is encapsulated in an anger that turns her into a *basilisco irresistible* (irresistible basilisk) who imposes her will and ability to work on the entire town. She manages a restaurant, her suppliers and customers, her son and husband, and she does it all alone. She owes her restaurant to her former *patrón's* loan, reiterating the connection between the creation of Colloco and the old hacienda regime. Furthermore, Petaca's economic success is contrasted with the fate of men who talk about leaving Colloco, going away to the city to find better jobs and more opportunities. Many have moved but have returned after finding only poverty in the city's crowed slums. Generational differences also surface through the younger men who are more politically aware than the older ones. Petaca's husband, representing the older generation who have been displaced, fantasizes about blonde prostitutes, reproducing the male gaze that mass culture has popularized through cinematic depictions of male fantasy.[10] In this way, modernity has drastically altered gender relations, and, while it has given more opportunities to women, it has also eroded not only intersubjective relations but feminine and masculine subjectivities.

María is very different from the women in Colloco because she has a critical perspective and embraces an enlightened modernity rather than an economic one that perverts relationships and identities. Her life is governed by reason and art (namely, music and literature) as creators of the world instead of capital. María's imaginary belongs to a lettered culture in which reading and the representation of passions of all sorts are central. Her exposure to abjection and passions that have been excluded or censored by sexual morality shows her resistance to mass culture as well as to tradition. In this aspect, María is similar to the woman in "Soledad de la sangre" who also saw music as noncommodifiable. For them the limit of capital is located in the sociosymbolic space, which also alters subjectivity. In Brunet's narrative, we can say, then, that the relationship between nature and passion is what changes the world and our understanding of it.

The system of signs governing the second part of the novel is triggered by María's delirium due to a fever and scandal instigated by her coworker, Melecia. The sign woman and particularly the mother take center stage in this monologue in which María tries to know who she is. As she does this, the memories and images of her mother move to the foreground as she tries to figure out her irresistible and ultimately destructive power. From the perspective of subjectivities, this second part of the novel revolves around damaged subjectivities within a capitalist culture in which the middle-class family, headed by a public official (María's father), cannot keep up with its own consumption and expectations. The mother in this instance is a kind of cyborg that functions in the system reproducing the economic and social demands within the private sphere, despite her family's detrimental fate. Brunet here shows how the family is annexed by capitalism through women like María's mother who, despite not having capital, maintain the system through their children and their consumption. In her case, we have a feminine subjectivity that is a capitalist agent within a family whose energies and vitality are used to acquire and consume in order to have a sense of social identity.

María's own psychic split is intimately tied to the process of identification and disidentification with her progenitors. This second portion of the novel, therefore, focuses exclusively on María, her family background, her parents, her romance, and her work, all experiences that shape who she is. Despite the fact that María responds to the model of the modern woman in the public sphere, her subjectivity has been shaped by her family's stories and scandals. Here Brunet develops a framework in which parents play a major role in the development of their children's identities. They basically provide the models for gender identity and sexuality within the process of identity formation and have a major impact. Revisiting the past, María examines under a very critical light both her parents, and especially her mother. According to María, her mother is obsessed with social success and money, forcing the family to live with financial deficit and debts. Furthermore, she is a seductress who used her physical attractiveness to get what she wanted (a salary raise for her husband, a promotion, a change of location). The mother's expectations were evidently above her husband's income, but this did not deter her from spending and playing the patriarchal games that modernity provided by becoming the lover of influential local men. In this scenario, the father becomes a *garfio movedizo* (movable hook), dehumanized and barely surviving. However, as her daughter shows, he lacked the strength to stand up to his wife and turn things around. His subservient position to the wife's whims and power made him a diminished man who spent his life asking for financial extensions and moving from town to town.

The mother, from María's stance, is a negative force, unscrupulous and completely self-centered. Furthermore, she is dominated by the logic of consumption and what a capitalist modernity offers to women without a salary: to sexually attract men and use sex to gain influence, status, and a social identity. Furthermore, María describes her as the "queen" of parties, dashingly attractive and always at center stage. In her physical description, María recreates the same erotic attraction her mother's body produced in others. She notices her splendor and erotic power, even as she parodies it in the image of a circuslike queen with her court of admirers.

The mother's overwhelming power goes even further and transforms María's father into a listless puppet in the way a ventriloquist does his dummy. The mother moves him around according to her desire and ambition, using his male voice to say what a woman cannot say publicly. In this way, she strips him of social and personal identity, effacing his sense of self in a relation she dominates. As a result of this sadomasochist arrangement, she is the one seen, admired, and desired by everyone while the husband is barely visible. This reversal of roles foreshadows and confirms Colloco's modern gender and sexual arrangements within marriage and how women gain public power at the price of perverting intersubjective relationships.

María defines herself against this maternal and feminine model, identifying instead with the father whose humiliation and powerlessness overshadowed his emotional qualities. In contrast to her mother, María rejects the objectification of herself and others and works to become financially independent. However, she cannot escape her family's past and becomes for the women in

Colloco what she rejected about her own mother. Her sensuality and nontraditional behavior are read as signs of her sexual immorality verging on scandal.

María's expulsion from Colloco, then, is related to her being a social pariah of sorts who has no social bonds or community. Furthermore, the marker Nadie that Melecia gives her highlights this uprootedness as well as her identification with her father, who was unable to become somebody in the relationship with his wife.

In this sense, María's condemned subjectivity, having no friends, distrusting people, and being critical, shows that she cannot produce herself alone autonomously, as modernity demands, since despite the fact that she is part of the capitalist model and functional to it publicly, she is not in the private sphere. Psychically she feels split, rejected and ostracized. However, as Ivonne Cuadra claims, María López is clearly an enunciating subject who has narrative authority within a cultural context in which the religious pattern of femininity is deeply rooted. As Cuadra rightly asserts, María's social plight is linked to her lacking a defined social and gendered position and thus being caught between the ideal of the sacred woman (the Virgin) and the nonexistent female (stressed by her Nadie)[11] that modernity provides.

In my reading of the main character, María embodies a passionate understanding of life experiences, among which maternity becomes a form of preserving life rather than the social order. Brunet seems to claim a different rationality through the exploration of María's passion in the context of two antagonistic cultural understandings of motherhood. On the one hand, her modern vitality eroticizes the Western imaginary of maternity and its institutionalized forms. However, María goes against it as well by resisting the established rules and dominant identity models. In contrast to her passionate position, we see the townwomen and the ways the sexual contract is enacted in a kind of phallic matriarchy founded on a Western ideal of an emasculating maternity in which a masculine panic of castration is revisited. Reinaldo's fear and rejection of his wife's body, for instance, reveal the panic of being devoured by a harmless and semiasleep female who is turned into a *vagina dentata,* showing the anxiety produced by the modern male's public decline. At night he sees Ernestina as an animalized body ready to devour him: "Ese cuerpo que estaba ahí, tendido con una especie de laxitud, quieto como una alimaña en espera de presa. . . . El cuerpo de Ernestina parecía crecer, avanzar a tocar el suyo" (30) (That body that was there, lying with a type of laxity, still like an animal waiting for the prey. . . . Ernestina's body seemed to grow, advancing to touch his).

Reinaldo's defensive and patriarchal perspective splits Ernestina into the efficient daytime wife and mother and the night animal ready to possess him. This duality is finally resolved through abstinence and the avoidance of physical contact with Ernestina, who in turn becomes a model housewife and mother. As a result, both spouses achieve the gender patterns established by a modernity whose cultural base is both traditional and patriarchal.

In a parallel story, María is presented with the power to eroticize the world and constitute an attachment with two children, Conejo (Petaca' son) and Cacho (Ernestina's son), who give her pleasure and especially confirmation. They are the only humans with whom she willingly spends time in Colloco. Childhood is here seen as the state of freedom and imagination. In the children's fantasy world, María becomes the blonde princess who joins them in their secret hideout in the mountains. She meets and plays with them, sharing their stories and dreams. No questions about her identity are ever asked, in a pact in which role playing becomes the only significant practice. The world of Conejo and Cacho resembles that of the girl Solita in *Humo hacia el sur,* in which nature and imaginative fiction predominate. The boys become María's only friends, who accept and value her as a magical character. In this agreement, María finds a refuge, as in music and literature, in the world of imagination. This realm offers multiple identity positions that oppose her fate as a female.

María represents the modern in a gendered modernity in which the ambiguities surrounding the sign "woman" range from the femme fatale to competitive mother and businesswoman. The feminist critic Rita Felski has not only pointed out that the figure of woman embodies the dangers and promises of the modern age, but also shown the connections that exist between femininity and modernity in the social imaginary. The way this intersection develops in specific sociohistorical contexts reveals its differential character.[12] In the Chilean context, for instance, women's social and emancipatory movements had already gained recognition in the areas of education and labor. However, most of them fought for equality, leaving untouched Catholic and bourgeois gender ideology.[13] Contrary to this, *María Nadie* unfolds the intersection of a peripheral and contradictory modernity with a Catholic and phallic model of femininity embodied in Colloco's females. María López opposes this model and makes a different claim by cancel-

ing the family and the state's national values. By critically looking at her parents, she is demythifying the family as a Chilean
ideal: "Ese es el axioma en el cual se basa el equilibrio familiar.
Lo maravilloso es poder juzgarlos y hallar en ellos sólo virtudes,
modelo para calcar nuestra propia personalidad" (112) (That is
the axiom in which family equilibrium is based. What is marvel-
ous is to be allowed to judge them and find only virtues, a model
to copy our own personality).

In a culture in which the family is the executive arm of state
morality, the main character's rejection represents a radical and
dangerous position. As Antigone, she defies patriarchal law by
turning away from its institutions and claiming as a right what is
considered a crime. Judith Butler has shown that Antigone portrays the resistance to the universality of the state and its legality.[14] María, however, does not defy the state itself but the family
and the patriarchal tradition that orders it.

The double and contradictory spectrum of modernity is evident
in this character's freedom (from family and marriage), as well as
in her sense of anonymity and constraint. When she lived in the
city of Santiago, seat of modern urban culture, she lived in a pen-
sion with little money. Her work as a telegrapher in an urban setting already foreshadowed the negativity of automatization and
the absence of meaning for the worker as the following quotation
makes clear:

> Tomada a veces por el pavor de no ser si no parte de un aparato
> mecánico, un grotesco ser hecho de madera y metales, de hilo y cau-
> cho. Y creánlo ustedes, los que me dicen orgullosa, diez años pueden
> pasar en ese trabajo embrutecedor. Diez años que la dejan a una al
> otro lado de la treintena, mirándose en el espejo los ojos fatigados, las
> comisuras de la boca que tienden a desplomarse. (113)

> [Sometimes taken over by the fear of not being but a part of a me-
> chanical machine, a grotesque being made of wood and metals, of
> thread and rubber. And believe me, the ones who call me proud
> should spend ten years in this stultifying job. Ten years that leave you
> in the thirties, looking at the mirror with tired eyes, the corners of
> the mouth falling in.]

Here María is acutely aware of the cost for being a (state)
worker and the specific demands gender places on salaried bodies.
Furthermore, she recognizes the goal of modernity in the workplace as it affects women, which men have already experienced.
Being reflective, María is aware that the new economic system

has turned her into an object, "a nothing" who sells her productive capacity.

More significantly, she embodies a number of civil rights within a gendered order in which reproductive rights and sexual citizenship anticipate feminist claims and new models of subjection.

María's return to an economically changing rural locality confirms that there is a process of economic modernization in which women have taken on productive roles and men's roles as breadwinners and providers have declined. Men in Colloco have fallen behind as a result of the new economic role of women; females in turn are forced to enter into a game of substitutions in which they libidinize money. Women's incorporation into the public world, as the novel shows, reduces male public power. This novel evidences that modernity has provided women with the possibility of contesting masculine omnipotence and authority through the libidinization of economic power, but also through the sacrifice of their sexuality. With their diserotization, motherhood becomes a redemptive identity in which the formation of a new masculinity is at stake.

Humo hacia el sur revealed libidinization with the *cacica,* Doña Batilde, whose passion for power is identified with the seigniorial stratification in which she is the landowner. Ironically, several female characters in Brunet's literature become powerful through their misidentification with the phallic principle that rules the overlapping of the public sphere and the social contract. The centrality of women in *María Nadie,* inherited from the culture of an indigenous peasantry in which female work was essential, is now relocated in the private sphere as well as in the public realm. The presence of a social organization based on a gender divide is also found in the *mapuche clans* who practiced polygamy in the context of a patriarchal and warrior society. Brunet's first novel, *Montaña adentro* (1923), *Montain In,* represents and emphasizes rural women's work at home as a multifaceted endeavor that ranges from cooking and cleaning to making textiles. The story "Aguas abajo" ("Down River") reiterates female work as something constitutive of gender as well as of the cultural identity for the peasantry. "Piedra callada" ("Silent Stone") extends these female tasks to the hacienda and the landholding structure where the grandmother, Eufrasia, cares for the animals besides doing domestic labor for the landowner.

In *María Nadie,* women's productive labor has changed, and rather than complementing the domestic budget, it becomes the sole income. In this way, a private business is turned into a public one, as in the case of Petaca, who is able to support her entire family with her restaurant. However, competition between females and males in the public arena results in men's withdrawal and disempowerment. In this scenario, women embody the strong and efficient individual proper of modernity's ideal and in which feminists have seen the seeds of domination.[15]

In the face of this new social form, María seems uninterested in economic success and unwilling to give up her vitality. Her body provides her with unlimited possibilities for identification. Through the gaze of others, we see a sexualized María, a femme fatale, a girl, a princess, as well as an erotic woman. This is the result of María's rejection of the heterosexual family as the primary and only regulatory source of the social imaginary. In its place, art in the form of literature and music becomes her cognitive and ethical systems. María asserts, "Yo vivía en parte desmaterializada en la música. Pero vivía también en los hechos que la lectura entrega, amalgamada con cuanta pasión puede agitar al ser humano: de la más celestial a la más abyecta. Nada me era extraño" (117) (I lived in part dematerialized in music. But I also lived in the facts that reading provides, mixed with every passion that may shake a human: from the most celestial to the most abject. Nothing was strange to me). Even more, María declares, "nunca sentí deseo. Eso que se llama "deseo." Esa vaga o imperiosa urgencia que hace presente el sexo" (117) (I never felt desire. That which is called desire. That vague and pressing urgency that makes sex present). This rationalization, nevertheless, crumbles when she falls in love with Gabriel, "the young god" who infantilizes her through children's stories and fairy tales in which she becomes "the little chicken who wanted to marry" or the "Nordic princess." As if enchanted, María falls into this magical narrative that evolves from the story of Adam and Eve as the first lovers to her becoming the emblem of a blonde and detached beauty. As the magic fades, she is ultimately transformed by Gabriel into a "crazy witch," who is seduced without any obvious resistance. He, on the other hand, personifies a virile and athletic god, a kind of celestial creature as his name *Arcángel* reveals (124). However, this enchantment of sorts that the experience of love means for María is undone when she gets pregnant and Gabriel harshly reminds her of their different social positions. The annunciation of life that María awaits, in her fantasy as the mother of God's son, is transformed into a hopeless and tragic awakening. The biblical story goes back and reinstates the Old Testament God who punishes rather than loves. In this way, the figure of the Latin lover is substituted with that of a hegemonic male. Gabriel represents this masculine principle within heterosexual and class imperatives. He becomes the modern example of the traditional bourgeois identity taken on by European immigrants (Italian, in his case) in the first half of the twentieth century in Latin America. Marriage, for the first generation born in Chile particularly, allowed upward mobility in a rigidly stratified society. By marrying someone from his class or above, Gabriel's social ascent and power within Chilean society could be secured. In this social context, María would never be considered marriageable or "un buen partido" (a good deal).

As a consequence, the romance abruptly comes to a halt with Gabriel's rejection of his paternity in contrast to María's claim of her maternity. María represents a fallen virgin of sorts in this romance as she finally is stigmatized for her nontraditional actions and declared guilty by the very man she loves. The story with Gabriel inverts the biblical annunciation and instead reveals class prejudices and hierarchical social relations consecrated by the Judeo-Christian tradition. An open and free consensual relationship with a woman is dismissed in contrast to marriage and legitimate paternity. Gabriel's rejection of his child with María by identifying him as a *guacho* (132) points to marriage (civil and religious) as the only legitimate sexual contract, one that endorses class hegemony and masculine rights.[16] He accuses María of intentionally becoming pregnant to force him to marry her. Moreover, he foreshadows a future of hardships in which María is condemned for being a single mother.

As María recounts this story to a cat, we learn about Gabriel and the impact he had in her life. Through a retrospective perspective, María highlights how she felt when she was in love. Revisiting their relationship, she underscores her restless state of waiting. Her life during this time was wrapped around Gabriel as she found herself entirely devoted to him and completely dependent.

Her helplessness progressively increases as Gabriel asserts his autonomy. The early enchantment wanes as the asymmetry of the relation slips in. His freedom to come and go drastically contrasts with María's progressive anxiety at not seeing him regularly. María's life loses importance as she becomes entangled in her expectations and fears around love:

Mis días de entonces no tienen otro sentido: esperar. El método en mi departamento, las horas de levantarse, de comer, de dormir, el día que se lava, el que se plancha, los domingos ociosos, las idas a los conciertos, al cine, las largas horas de lectura en la biblioteca, las caminatas bajo los árboles teñidos de los múltiples tonos que traen consigo las estaciones, nada de esto existe. Yo soy nada más que una mujer que espera. (125)

[My days back then have no other meaning: waiting. Putting my apartment in order, what time I got up, ate, slept, laundry day, ironing day, lazy Sundays, going to concerts, movies, long hours of reading in the library, walks beneath the trees which the seasons colored with their various hues, none of this exists. I am nothing more than a woman who waits.]

María's life, as this passage poignantly reveals, becomes increasingly ruled by her fantasies and uncertainties about Gabriel. Love and emotional dependency strip her of autonomy and the power to act independently. In this case, the Other robs her of freedom and objectifies her in the relationship. Brunet shows the power and extent of traditional female expectations about love and their impact on identity. Even in the case of a modern woman who defines herself against tradition, the discourse of love takes away her ability to think and act independently. The lack of alternative models and stories of how to act in the romantic plot is revealed in the feelings of lifelessness and entrapment that resonate with Carolyn Heilbrun's argument. As she points out, the absence of other forms of representation imprisons female characters in sacrificial and powerless positions.[17] We can suspect that María's literary education is played out in her actions and reactions, reminding us of Madame Bovary's readings and their effects. Rita Felski has noted that the French heroine reads and dreams of love and that all her energy is channeled through the erotic script. Felski concludes that gender affects in different ways how we read and the meanings we construct. Bovary's example as a female reader shows romance as a substitute for action and a drab and impoverished existence. Moreover, the romantic script underlines the need for intense passions and the active role of male lovers in order to succeed.[18] However, María shows a reflective attitude that prevents her from being totally absorbed by any narrative. Her lack of romantic experience is, in my view, what disables her analytic abilities to evaluate a situation governed by unknown and overwhelming feelings. Having broken away from tradition, she is struggling alone about how to make sense of her gender and sexual identity outside the margins of convention.

In this way, María confuses her expectations about Gabriel without realizing that what they have is an affair rather than a formal and committed relationship. In reality, she does not have what she wants, and that in turn destabilizes and undermines her:

> Y se iba o no se iba. Yo tenía los nervios rotos, con la falta de sueño, de descanso, con la tensión del trabajo, con la pregunta de dónde estará que no viene, y que está aquí y debo irme, y que ha llegado, y que si lo habrá visto alguien llegar, y que se ha ido, y que si alguien se habrá cruzado con él, y que dónde echará las horas que no está conmigo, y que si en verdad yo soy tan sólo la comodidad de una mujer enamorada que se aviene a todo, y que si en su vida habrá otra mujer, otras mujeres a cuya casa también llega sonriente. (128)

> [And he would leave or not leave. My nerves were frayed from lack of sleep, lack of rest, with tension at work, with wondering where he would be that he hasn't come, and that he's arrived and did anyone see him arrive, and did anyone pass him on the street, and where must he be spending the time he's not with me, and if I am really just a convenience, a woman in love who'll do anything, and if there might be another woman in his life, other women, whose houses he smilingly visits.]

Traditional gender differences and expectations undermine María's confidence and sense of identity. Her isolation and lack of friends serve to trap her in the relationship. Brunet makes her most independent character face what Heilbrun and Felski term the erotic plot that leads to failure. As a result, María experiences what living the traditional demands of romance implies and what it means to have a man as "life's absolute and only center."[19] The protagonist's sentimental involvement confronts her with the sexual contract in the bourgeois heterosexual paradigm.

Being alone creates feelings of angst and acute disappointment for Brunet's main character. The emotional and economic security that marriage and family stood for in the past has been replaced by a sense of anonymity and nothingness.[20] María longs for company and inner peace but cannot find it in her work or personal life.

Thus, only when María leaves sentimentality and passivity does she regain the strength to move on. She is offered a new job and moves out of the city, hoping to find the utopia of a simple and peaceful life in the country. As we already know before finishing the second part of the novel, this utopia is also crushed with disappointment and a cruel reality.

MATERNITY AS THE UNDERLYING TEXT

That being alone remains unresolved for María makes her fall into the cultural web of maternity. She becomes trapped as a result of the fantasy of reproducing herself in a child and having to acknowlegde that the sexual contract of marriage is still mandatory. Though she embodies the modern woman, she cannot go against a social model in which civic and religious spheres overlap. Hence, having a miscarriage in this context is a way out of a maternity that cannot be lived as choice, a privilege reserved for a few. The pregnant cat that María talks to in her autobiographical account signals precisely the cancellation of this natural path for a modern femininity that is culturally ruled by a Catholic and patriarchal paradigm.

María stands as an essentially refractory and uprooted subject[21] in a closed and authoritarian modernity. Her literary precedents may be found in the Bible and in the romantic melodrama *María* (1867) by the Colombian writer Jorge Isaac (1837–95). As Doris Sommer suggests, this novel is a narrative in which the romantic story between Efraín and María founds the Colombian nation. As with Isaac's María, this María does not belong to the landed class, and so her social origins as well as her identity are unclear from the viewpoint of established society. However, there are also significant differences in terms of what female identity and autonomy mean in the context of Latin American modernization. Brunet's character highlights gender oppression despite her job and relative economic autonomy. Sexual difference in a cultural context governed by the dichotomy of collective representations puts María outside the limits of social identity despite having a job.

In an unprecedented fashion in literary history, María breaks away from her family and social background to start a life for herself. Rather than following other female literary figures and gender imperatives, María's actions, before falling in love, resonate with those of marginal male protagonists in the Chilean tradition who leave home and town to carve out a life of their own. María is closer to the urban and marginal male, the antiheroic protagonist depicted by Mariano Latorre (1866–1955), Joaquín Edwards Bello (1887–1968), and Manuel Rojas who is essentially undetermined, nonreligious, and anarchistic, as José Promis points out.[22] Keeping this in mind, we can say that María López is the representation of the female antiheroine in the Chilean novel who transcends the city and country divide only to find the persistence of a semifeudal, patriarchal culture.

Ironically, María moves from the Chilean capital to an unknown town, escaping from the romantic disappointment with Gabriel. She ignores what this journey to a presumably calm life in a small town will bring. As María's experience reveals, Colloco turns out to be the opposite of her romantic expectations of rural life and culture. It is a town eminently hostile to outsiders, in particular to unconventional and unattached women like her who lack social connections. José Donoso's (1924–96) infernal and ruined town, El Olivo, where *El lugar sin límites* develops, finds its precedent in Colloco. As are many towns in rural Chile they are both created by oligarchic interests and hierarchical values.

The opening description of Colloco as a miniature town, with little painted houses where life is always the same, underscores the picturesque as a façade that hides oppressive cultural structures. The endless reproduction of Catholic morality is what defines Colloco and binds its inhabitants. Belonging to the town means upholding values and social distinctions based on class and gender that have become naturalized over time. Moreover, Colloco's origins are tied to the landed class and its foundational enterprises in the South of Chile. As other southern towns were, Colloco was conceived as a copy of others that responded to the economic and political interests of the oligarchy. It was built as all rural towns were, with social, economic, and educational institutions that replicated the oligarchic model. As a consequence, the internal social life of a modernizing rural town reproduces the hierarchical pattern of the hacienda from which it evolved. Its culture, as the first part of the novel manifests, is founded on the exclusion of all forms of diversity. Its identity is determined by sameness, expressed in a monolithic and homogeneous discourse enunciated by the chorus of women for whom the "common sense" of gender roles dictates political life. They hold official morality and gender as absolutes that provide certainty and continuity to their private and public lives. In this context, María's arrival uncovers the inversion of gender roles and modernity in Colloco. She encounters a town where everyone has sacrificed a part of his or her sexual and social identity, becoming a modern "male town" of *marimachos* and *maricuecas*.[23] Here money has acquired a symbolic value in which it becomes a fetish to produce

more. Women as *marimachos* take men in order to enter into the
game that capitalist modernity has procured. Petaca, for instance, grows bigger and powerful as a penis while her husband
drinks himself away. Ernestina, *la burra de mujer,* has turned
into the perfect and efficient housewife and mother in order to
avoid sex and pregnancy. Finally, Melicia desexualizes herself
to have power and social status as a religious widow and public
servant. Men, on the contrary, are feminized and made passive
maricuecas, displaced by women from the productive side of capitalism. Thus for these *marimachos* and *maricuecas* sexual desire
has been relativized and replaced by a libidinal attitude toward
economic exchange and surplus. Gender here is shown to be vari-
able, depending on the economy, while the heterosexual system
seems another product of the imagination.

The intricate connections between gender and social status in
Colloco's society are further reiterated by the role of men in the
novel. They have lost legitimacy and protagonism by becoming
passive followers. Social habits and the power of convention have
killed valid forms of assertion for males. They are alienated by
the requirements that marriage demands of them. Their resistance is expressed individually through alcoholism and spending
time with male friends in bars (Don Lindor) or through numerous extramarital affairs (Reinaldo). These appear as the only venues for asserting a degree of freedom in the face of conflict-ridden
marriages. Men in general are portrayed as weak and dominated
by their spouses. María's father stands as an extreme precedent
for husbands in which weakness and acquiescence to the wife undermine assertion. Others are aggressive and self-centered, im-
posing their will on the women they want (Gabriel and Reinaldo).
In the economic modernization of Colloco, males have been relocated to a secondary role in which they have lost authority as a
result of their wives' more competent and competitive labor.
Lindor, for example, wastes away drinking while his wife, Petaca,
restlessly works in her restaurant business, trying to improve it
and make it more profitable.

María's separation from and criticism of her mother and father
represent a paradigmatic example of a subjectivity that denies
love attachments and dependence. She detaches herself from the
sentimentality ascribed to women and in particular from the unconditional love and obedience expected of daughters. Her disap-
proval of her parents forces María to withdraw, while witnessing
endless family scandals. Her critique encompasses not only marriage but also the bourgeois family in Chilean culture, where a

weak father appears to be ruled by a phallic mother. In this novel, Brunet's feminism is linked to a social critique of the family and the marginal position occupied by María.[24]

María represents an aspect of modern autonomy by breaking away from family ties and traditions. Her job as a telegrapher also highlights the newly available positions for women in the workforce at the end of the 1950s in Chile.[25] María embodies the "new woman" who is the result of personal effort and independence, as Simone de Beauvoir described in her influential book *The Second Sex* (1949).[26] This new condition, however, engenders feeling divided and an inability to have inner balance, due to the renunciation of being a "feminine" object. Brunet here concurs with Beauvoir in that the independent woman is forced to live simultaneously as man and woman, experiencing multiple conflicts in a wide range of situations. Brunet's character lives her social and existential condition in terms very similar to those described by Beauvoir. María can never quite resolve her splitting, living what she calls "a half life" and feeling alienated. The freedom that entering the public world gives is here related to feelings of abandonment and disconnection rather than empowerment. Being alone, which being single and economically independent entails for María, unveils a world in which social bonds have been severed. Moreover, social interaction and others constitute a hostile reality that threatens to imprison the self. María withdraws and separates herself from an environment experienced as unfriendly and intimidating. She is aware of being the object that others look at and judge. Loneliness in this context represents a debilitating and negative condition for the self that reveals the need for the Other as inescapable.

> A veces la soledad pesa.Es como un molde que se va ciñendo al propio cuerpo hasta oprimirlo. Hay algo que duele adentro. . . . Son sensaciones que duran menos que un segundo, pero que dejan la horrible frialdad del vértigo en el pecho y en el corazón el aletear de un pájaro caído. Entonces se busca a alguien alrededor, alguien para alargarle la mano, temerosa de no lograr el movimiento y hallar en la otra palma una certeza de calor vital, una especie de cuenco en que acurrucarse. (118)

> [Sometimes loneliness weighs. It is like a mold that tightens around your own body until it oppresses it. There is something that hurts inside. . . . There are sensations that last less than a second but leave a horrible coldness of the vertigo in the chest and the flapping of wings of a fallen bird in the heart. Then you look for someone, some-

one you can extend your hand to, scared of not accomplishing the movement and finding in the other palm the certainty of a vital warmth, a type of vessel to curl up in.]

María has been viewed as an existentially distraught individual whose actions and discontent become circular or unresolved. This is essentially the view taken by José Promis, who associates María with other existentially desperate characters in the Latin American novel. Promis also notes the circular structure that governs her search for a meaningful center.[27] In my reading, María embodies a new subjectivity whose multiplicity and difference oppose hegemonic social discourses and models. In contrast, the women in Colloco not only accept tradition and Catholic femininity, but also become guardians of tradition.

Resisting this phallic womanhood, the protagonist rejects the status quo and its devitalizing social rationality. María's withdrawal and displacement are twofold, encompassing both social and psychic dimensions. Finding no common ground or friends to support her, María retreats to the private realm without really finding refuge. Being alone is lived as a negative experience in which the lack of an Other (male or female) is interpreted as being unrecognized. "llena de ilusiones ante un ser que parecía 'ese,' el que esperaba, lista para intercambiar con él—hombre o mujer—toda mi ternura, mi abnegación, mi conocimiento, mi mínimo caudal de cultura" (117) ([I was] full of illusions in front of a being who seemed 'the one,' the one I was waiting for, ready to exchange with him or her all my tenderness, my abnegation, my knowledge, my little culture. In this passionate and unconventional search for the other, we may see that sexual orientation is not an issue for María and that she could actually find company and fulfillment with either a man or a woman.

In modern rationality, alienation is reconfirmed in the negation of the other subject, the Other's needs and feelings, in sum, what Jessica Benjamin calls intersubjectivity, that is, the recognition of the self that the Other is another subject who is different and alike. When intersubjectivity is foreclosed, the self continues to live in the world, "untransformed by the Other."[28] Forms of modern and rationalized relations in the public sphere are thus defined in terms of their production and effectiveness, negating recognition.[29] The public and private fields are widely separated and private life is devoid of social significance. The women of the town of Colloco identify with this negativity and through this rationality become a social function rather than an identity. The best example is Petaca, who, being a restaurant owner, gives her life energy to it, alienating herself in an economic and functional position. On the other end stands María's passion destabilizing the dominant cultural regime. Her vitality is not reproductive and generates a sexual panic that resorts to regulations in order to contain her. The townwomen try to reduce and control her through the discourse of madness, evil, sexuality, and legal bonds. In an inexorable and adamant social closure, repressive mechanisms are unleashed against María. Melecia, María's older co-worker in Colloco's post office, declares a war against her:

> Una mujer sola, sin familia, es siempre sospechosa. Sabe Dios qué pájara será ésta. . . . Y para colmo se llama María López. ¡Miren qué nombre y qué apellido.
> María López—. . . siguió hablando llena de ascos—es como llamarse María Nadie. Un nombre tan vulgar y un apellido que lo tiene cualquiera. Los nombres empiezan por hacer a las personas. . . .
> ¿Y le parece poco? Una loca suelta, vestida con pantalones y una chomba que le deja todo a la vista. Y con ese pelo color de choclo. (56)

> [A woman alone, without a family, is always suspicious. No one knows what sort of bird she might be. . . . And on top of that, her name is María López. Look what a name that is!
> María López, she went on disgustedly, it's like being named María Nobody. Such an ordinary first name, and a last name anyone could have. The name makes the person. . . .
> And what do you think? A wild, crazy woman, who wears pants, and a sweater that lets you see everything, and that hair the color of corn.]

María's public image is progressively colonized by Melecia's classist and sexist discourse. Her statements reproduce social hierarchies and status in Chile through the preponderance of prestigious family names that in the majority of cases relate to landownership. As an older woman, Melecia fiercely rejects everything new and different that María embodies, namely, freedom, eroticism, and nonconformity. In contrast, she is a devoted Catholic who values social and economic hierarchies and the privileges with which she identifies. Religious fervor and daily mass substitute for marriage and give meaning to her widowhood. Furthermore, dogmatism and a reactionary spirit shape her view of the changes taking place in the workplace. The post office has added the position of telegrapher that María has filled, alongside Melecia and her sister, the postmistresses. Their past ability to open and read personal correspondence and know everyone's private affairs provided them, especially Melecia, with a sense of power and superior knowledge. Their status as de facto censors of others' lives is altered by María's presence in the office.

Work becomes a defining aspect of her subjectivity in that it determines María's public life and her journey through Chile. Yet female work and independence are intertwined with the rationality that articulates modernity in binary cultural and gender oppositions. María's dilemma and inner turmoil disclose the effects of social rationality on authorship and agency in the passage to modernity, as Benjamin notes.[30]

In the Chilean context, this transit incorporates the predominance of traditional patterns of domination within more formal and legal forms of rationality. María's existence discloses that the incorporation into the workforce that this new rationality offers to women expropriates their value through serialization and anonymity. Her productive work illustrates the gendered quality of labor and the specific forms alienation takes. Despite women's entrance into the workforce, gender dichotomy prevails, acquiring new meanings and forms. In Brunet's narrative, gender polarity limits and devalues femininity, leaving María without a sense of confirmation. Instead, she becomes the epitome of the harassed female within a modernity that has kept traditional forms of power in which women have become asexual figures impersonating masculine public values and traits. In this context, a woman like María is watched and suspected by other women, not only for her autonomy but also for her erotic power.

Gender relations, and relationships in general, represent conflicts that undermine individual freedom in the novel. María's view of the other has been shaped by negative experiences and by her ability to detect what she calls the underside, "la contrafaz," or the contradictory layers that constitute subjectivity. María's idealized search for "pure beings" who give themselves completely clashes with the contradictions people display (109). Her parents, for example, stand as the incarnation of lies, manipulation, and coercion. As most others in María's personal relations, they are "amasijos," negative and shapeless identities, that strongly clash with hers. Her parents are precedents to Colloco's inhabitants, belonging to the same symbolic constellation in which cultural and social values are class defined. Rural as well as urban morals are part of the same cultural matrix in which Catholic morality and social and gender stratification are pivotal.

Brunet's last novel, *Amasijo (Hybrid)* (1962) revisits the notion of hybridity from the very title by underscoring the way subjectiv-

ity and sexual identity are constituted. Here the male protagonist, Julián, cannot separate from his mother's omnipotent and
castrating power, even after her death. The mother's overwhelming and ultimately destructive attachment is central to the narrative and to the protagonist's identity crisis. Her desire to turn
him into a girl and play with him as she would play with a doll
develops a masculinity forever fused with the mother that can
only tragically escape through suicide. In this way, *Amasijo* concludes Brunet's revision of phallic mothers who are unable to separate from their sons and in the process make them victims of
their "maternal passion," as Melina poignantly shows (45). Petaca's overprotective attachment to her son, Conejo, is a foretelling
of Melina's symbiotic relation with Julián in *Amasijo.*

In *María Nadie,* on the other hand, authoritarianism is sustained by the women of Colloco, who, as mothers, wives, and wid-
ows, embrace patriarchy and its ethos in a new *amasijo.* In their
hybrid hegemonic role, women enforce tradition and impersonate
masculine power through their ability to ostracize, silence, and
simultaneously be the head of the household. The town operates
through these powerful females who perpetuate cultural and social structures. Brunet's insight into the way power and gender
intertwine is clearly revealed here. From her arrival, María is dis-
trusted. The disparity between her life in the city and Colloco's
rural and traditional culture highlights the uneven and discontin-
uous forms modernity takes in Latin American urban and rural
spaces.

In Colloco, respected women are devoted mothers and model
housewives. They keep the household perfectly running and its
budget steady. They are fundamentally mothers who make self-
sacrifice their defining value. Through them, Brunet reiterates
the cultural and gendered operations that dispossess women of
their sexuality. Simultaneosly, the erotization of the economic
role that the incorporation into the labor force results in works
as a compensation for their desexualization by religious ideology.
In this sense, we see Catholic ideology join with economic modernization in desexualizing women through different venues and
rationales that ultimately subordinate them.

Petaca (Don Lindor's wife) not only is responsible for the home
but also supports the family economically. While Petaca cooks,
works, and manages the restaurant and the home, her husband
lacks the motivation to work. Petaca's drive to move upward in
Colloco is fulfilled by becoming a restaurant owner. She embodies
the hard worker whose effort is geared toward making a better

life. However, her business success contrasts with her emotional and physical health. Her frustration and dissatisfaction surface through the endless fights with Lindor. Motherhood and an obsessive concern with her son, Conejo, become substitutes for an emotional and erotic lack in her marriage.

Petaca's best friend, Ernestina, a devoted mother too, also sublimates disappointment with motherhood. Her husband, Reinaldo, escapes boredom and monotony through adultery. His inability to see his wife as an erotic subject underscores the forms of domination within marriage. As I have said, the fear of her sexual and sacred power paralyzes Reinaldo with the threat of castration. His platonic infatuation with María, on the other hand, reiterates previous actions toward women. Seduction and an unavailable female are conflated in Reinaldo's desire with the endless search for the perfect lover.

In this local context, Melecia's centrality is linked to her status as a widow, and more importantly, to her knowledge of secrets. The sublimation of sexual desire, in her case to attain social respect, transforms her into the old female figure of the *beata,* in which religiosity and hypocrisy meet. Religion appears to offer women a place where desexualization is not only valid but a source of status and identity. From the very beginning, Melecia dislikes María and expresses it in the negative epithets and adjectives she uses against her. She calls her *ladina,* "bad bird," "crazy," and "hypocrite," words that point to Melecia's rejection of strangers, particularly women whose social background is unknown. Unsatisfied with these negative descriptors, Melecia decides to change María's last name from *López* to *Nadie,* displaying the widow's ability to devalue and deprive of social identity. The form of *ninguneo*[31] that the name *Nadie* implies places María in the margins of the community. She is not only seen as a stranger but as a nobody. The discomfort and fear felt by Melecia and others like her are neutralized by diminishing María and making her the target of stigmatizing categories. In this way, Melecia instigates a process of devaluation in which social origins, physical features, and appearances are key. Without a husband or a family, María is socially effaced by Melecia's relentless persecution of a woman she hardly knows.

María's dwelling in the capital marks her sociability and performance. She dresses unconventionally (she wears pants and no shoes), she walks by herself, and she relates to others openly and informally. In sum, her social behavior lacks the restrictions that rule values and actions in a rural town, where strict boundaries separate acceptable from unacceptable behavior. The character's rejection of patriarchal mandates and cultural expectations puts her increasingly in conflict with the social context. This also explains María's rather oblique perspective and her understanding of social performance as simulation. Her views demand authenticity in a world governed by the cult of appearances and self-aggrandizement. Furthermore, María fights alienation and pursues the satisfaction of her desire. For this reason, she represents the modern split after realizing that the world lives in a state of alienation. As a result, she dismantles two literary and cultural utopias: the one embodied in the city (Civitas Dei) and the one incarnated in the country (Locus Amoenus). Through her disappointing journey, María realizes that there are no utopias left but rather a landscape undergoing irreversible changes in which the image of the train sets a new pace. In the novel, the countryside appears contaminated by the city and is part of the same process in which economic modernization has been equated with progress and civilization.

As a female protagonist in Latin American fiction, María is a modern subject. Her awareness that marriage is a legal contract that legitimizes the purchase of a woman is awakened at an early age by observation of her parents. María is brought up in the mercantilist and alienated marriage contract her parents have, that is, a bourgeois heterosexual model in which self-interest and social mobility predominate. In her view, their marriage operates for mutual profit sanctioned by the social law. The long and detailed description of the parents' relationship and their identities emphasizes how they work in tandem for social and economic advancement. María's father is described as a weak and wretched bureaucrat controlled by his wife. The mother, on the other hand, is portrayed as a social climber and a sexual object. According to her daughter, she used her looks in order to get what she wanted from men and to help her husband's career (105). The mother's sexual objectification is harshly criticized by María. The disidentification with and repudiation of her mother are related to her willing transformation into merchandise, becoming completely alienated in the process. Colloco serves to confirm this same heterosexual conjugal model, though it is altered by a gender substitution in which women take the place of authority, becoming masculinized and asexual in the process. As a consequence, María is caught between these two perspectives of gender and modernity in the sexual arrangement, rejecting both for their denial of passion.

María's experiences constitute a new narrative discourse that progressively undermines the literary conventions about the novel as well as cultural models of gender. Her autobiographical narration is formalized in a monologue that reveals her life story to a pregnant female cat. Right after the scandal in the theater led by Melecia and Petaca in which María is the target, she revisits the events and tells them to a stray cat.

Y ya ves tú, gatita, lo que ha acontecido. Unas pasiones enloquecidas me han rodeado. Desde el primer minuto me han envuelto en sospechas, en malos pensamientos, me han cercado los hombres creyéndome presa fácil, me han supuesto las mujeres intenciones aviesas, hasta los niños me han abandonado. . . .
    —¿Qué te parece a tí? ¿No te parece absurdo que yo, María López— María Nadie en el idioma gentil de misiá Melecia pero que no sabe con cuánta verdad lo dice—, está aquí en la noche pueblerina hablando contigo . . . ? ¿No te parece que soy un poco loca?
Al amanecer pasa un tren rumbo al norte. Me iré, gatita ¿oyes? Me iré a esa hora en que una *mala pájara* debe regresar a su nido. Me iré. María Nadie también tendrá ante sí una puerta abierta. Seré de nuevo María López. Una puerta abierta ante mí. Puede que hacia una vida radiante. Puede que hacia inenarrables sufrimientos. Pero será la vida. . . . (136–38)

[And you see, little kitten, what has happened. Insane passions have whirled me. From the very first they have wrapped me with suspicion, in evil thoughts; and the men have besieged me, thinking me an easy catch; the women have assumed that I had lewd intentions; even the children have turned their backs on me. . . .
    What do you think? Doesn't it seem absurd to you that I, María López—María Nobody, in the gentile language of Mistress Melecia, who doesn't realize how true her words are—that I am here, in the night, in this village, talking to you . . . ? Don't you think that I'm a little crazy?
    At dawn the train comes through going north. I'll go away, little kitten, do you hear me? I'll depart at the hour when a bad bird ought to return to her nest. I'll go away. María Nobody will have an open door before her. I'll be María López. A door opens before me, leading perhaps to a brilliant new life, perhaps to untold suffering. But it will be life,]

In this section, María's marginality is evidenced in the solitude of her monologue. After being unjustly accused, the character is once again alone and alienated from a society in which her new values find no place. The shift here to a testimony highlights

María's gender experience and the lack of cultural referents within a fundamentally traditional society. María's failure is related to the impossibility of cultural transmissibility. Her voice has no resonance or interpellator within the context of an eminently rural culture characterized by economic, technical, and cultural deficit. The sociologist José Joaquín Brunner has pointed out that until 1950, the national education level of the majority of Latin American countries was below 1 percent. High culture had a very slim public in a social context composed by emergent middle sectors and a varied and heterogeneous culture of a popular, urban, and rural majority that was not literate.[32]

María's case in this landscape represents an exception in that she is educated and holds modern gender values that are alien to the majority. Brunner emphasizes that modern Latin American culture is not so much the result of ideologies but rather of universal schooling, electronic communication media, and the conformation of a mass culture with an industrial base.[33] Taking this sociological approach, we may say that Colloco has a traditional culture undergoing a process of modernization. María, on the other hand, represents a novel ideological break fighting for recognition within this cultural map that counters its potential with the hegemony of rural life and its institutions. Consequently, her tone and attitude are symptoms of her increasing alienation from a cultural system she opposes, as Ojeda comments.[34]

Moreover, this confession makes evident the sexual contract and its role for the public insertion of women in Chile. María reviews everything that has happened to her and her reflection points to marriage as the only legal alternative available. As a result of this imperative, she is proscribed, since what legalizes women in the public sphere in a traditional culture is marriage and not work. María's physical features, furthermore, suggest her resemblance to female icons in the Hollywood film industry. Marilyn Monroe comes to mind through María's blondeness and the sexual attraction she provokes. We must also consider that telegraphers, operators, and secretaries were among the first working women to be showcased in Hollywood classics. For instance, in *Hometown Story* (1947), the sexy blonde secretary played by Monroe in the supporting role of Iris Martin displays not only American modernity but also new public and gendered positions for women. In his book *Tradición y modernidad en el cine de América Latina (Tradition and Modernity in the Cinema of Latin America)* (2003), the film historian Paulo Paranagua argues that the film industry dramatically changed values and behavior in Latin America on a large scale. Hollywood films introduced certain genres, among them the melodrama, that were nationalized and served as narratives for the main film industries in the continent, namely, those of Mexico and Argentina. Cinematic images join the *folletín,* the *novela rosa,* the tango, the bolero, the fotonovela and the radionovela among the most important popular genres.[35]

Brunet's awareness of the impact of the media and American films in Chilean culture can be traced as far back as her novel *Bienvenido* (*Welcome*) (1929). In this *novela rosa,* the character Enriqueta fashions her identity with the repertoire provided by film stars such as Bebe Daniels, Constance Talmadge, and Mary Pickford, showing how American films and their icons became new models for female identity in Chile. Berta López has also pointed out Brunet's early incorporation of popular culture, which in my view seem to be rather the representation of the media imaginary and its function in the construction of female identity. In this way, Brunet's use of film images anticipates the much later trend followed in Latin America by such writers as Manuel Puig, Osvaldo Soriano, and Angeles Mastreta.[36] The impact of the radionovela is also present in "Piedra callada" in the oligarchic wife's daily rituals. She cannot miss a day of listening to this melodramatic narrative. It captivates her attention and interest much more than the real drama of her staff.

In *María Nadie,* María embodies the new urban woman who is not bound by traditional social norms. The fact that she is a virgin conflicts with this modern image, as well as her later pregnancy. Rather than believing that her pregnancy was unplanned, Gabriel assumes that it had been intentional in order to catch him. The difference between the two characters in relation to maternity and paternity highlights the ways gender determines parenthood in a traditional culture. Motherhood for an unmarried woman in Gabriel's hegemonic perspective is not only morally reproachable but also unviable for a working female. For him, paid labor appears implicitly linked to a male worker who has no domestic tasks or children to care for. In this dominant view, the double shift that marks the lives of working women is completely absent as a social or cultural referent, because of class and gender biases.

Moreover, in this cultural horizon, single motherhood as the result of choice rather than fate is unthinkable. As a consequence, motherhood is defined by the paradigms of a traditional and patriarchal culture in which marriage sanctions the sexual pact and its progeny. Within this patriarchal context, María tragically realizes that Gabriel finds her unfit to be a mother, particularly the mother of his children. His statements also show that the control of female fecundity is the place of domination par excellence of one sex over the other, as the French historian Yvonne Knibiehler has argued. [37]

Brunet's novel anticipates the contradictions of a gendered modernity and its double discourse for women: one that celebrates the individual and its autonomy, and another that glorifies self-sacrifice and self-effacement for mothers. Her novel reveals the moralist and conservative reactions to the social change and dislocation of the traditional feminine ideal that the incorporation of women in the workforce and their access to education produce in the first half of the twentieth century in Chile, as Diana Veneros Ruiz Tagle shows.[38]

Feminist Sharon Hays has also noted the cultural contradictions present in Western modernities, particularly in the United States, arguing that there is a tension for working mothers who are faced with opposing ideologies in a market economy. According to Hays, the historical construction of mothering arose with the ideological separation of private and public spheres in which the values of family and intimate life appeared, explicitly rejecting political and economic life. Motherhood in contemporary society persists as the place where an irreducible ambiguity is played out in a society based on the competitive search for self interest in a system of contractual relationships. The ideology of intensive motherhood, as Hays calls it, demands selflessness and ongoing care from the mother for the innocent child, conflicting with the values of individualism prevalent in the market.[39] This ambivalence is shared by most working mothers, who are split between the prescribed cultural choice of the mother's adequately intensive sacrifice for her children and the status, money, and satisfaction that paid labor provide. This model of motherhood emerged before World War II and has maintained its predominance, as Hays shows, despite the increasing number of women in the workforce.[40]

In developing countries, the tensions undergone by working women were greater if we take into account that by 1950 more than half of the population of Latin America was rural and a small percentage lived in the city. For the majority of the population, culture was based on local and oral communication, linked to the cycles of daily life, to the church and to the transmission of stories and beliefs shared by the community, as Brunner points out.[41]

María's miscarriage then reiterates the inability to become the mother demanded by tradition, while it also opens up the possibilities offered to a female by being single and childless. The tensions and contradictions that the ideology of motherhood enfolds in a process of modernization, however, are already present in this novel through María's life. María's final affirmation of choice and mobility is implicit in her reappropriation of the expression "bad bird" that Melecia coined and the image of the train. Instead of becoming domesticated by a traditional ideology, María chooses to leave the familiar and oppressive world of Colloco and begin anew.

The end of the novel leaves the future open and without definite answers. Brunet presents the search for female autonomy and female identity as a paradoxical and ambiguous modern project. María is defined by novel gender values and ideas that find no common grounds with a fundamentally rural community. Hence, working and educated women like María face the contradictions that allow the circulation of symbolic ideals of freedom and independence for women but deny their practice. Despite constraints and alienation, María's desire to move on and start in another place points to a hopeful perspective. The train going north underscores that she will not "be left by the train," as the popular saying had it for unmarried women in the past. On the contrary, she will catch the train being single, despite and against what traditional values and commonly held beliefs say. In the final redefinition of bad bird, we find a new take on the female journey toward modernity. In it, a single woman is not bound by marriage and masculine authority but may actually travel unsupervised to other cultural and urban settings.

3

María Luisa Bombal, or the Feminine Writer

MARÍA LUISA BOMBAL (1910–80) WAS BORN IN VIÑA DEL MAR AND spent her early years in this coastal Chilean city. When she was eight years old, her family moved to Paris, where they lived as other wealthy Latin Americans did during the early twenties. As the account of the Chilean writer María Flora Yañez (1902–82), from one of the most prominent liberal families of Santiago, vividly shows in her autobiography *Historia de mi vida* (*Story of My Life*) (1980) Bombal's family joined other South American elites in Paris during the crazy twenties.[1] While living in France, Bombal began studies in French literature at the Sorbonne and also took theater classes at L'Atelier, founded in 1921 by the prominent actor, director, and producer Charles Dullin. As a result, she became versed in European theater, the avant-garde, and French literary tradition. Coincidently, in 1921 the French poet, actor, and theorist Antonin Artaud (1896–1948) acted at Dullin's atelier. In the early 1930s he wrote his two manifestos (1931 and 1932) on the theater of cruelty, where he posited a new approach to theater as a means to disturb and vitalize Western civilization. Theater for Artaud was sacred and constituted a communion between actors and spectators. Danger and terror were used as primary methods to unveil metaphysical truths for the spectators through the loss of reason.[2] Some of these surrealist features and the notion of art as a ritual in which language and mystery join to open up a world of primitive forces that reason and logic cannot reach resonate throughout Bombal's literature.

In 1932, María Luisa Bombal returned to Chile for the first time, remaining there for two years. It was a time of unprecedented political and social turmoil in the country. Six governments rose and fell before the presidency of Arturo Alessandri Palma (1921–25 and 1928–32), who became the first middle-class head of the Chilean state. Surprisingly, Bombal's fiction develops without any direct reference to the social and political changes that were taking place. Instead, her narrative is shaped by an aesthetic that claims art for art's sake and the autonomy of the artist's creativity. Her literary production is brief, yet it includes two novels, several short stories, *crónicas,* and filmscripts.

María Luisa Bombal embodies the ideals and models of modern urban women of the upper classes in Latin America in the late thirties and forties. The degree of freedom she displayed and the disregard for convention may be attributed to her class privilege and social position. Bombal writes of the construction of class identity and what it offers the members of the landed oligarchy. In this depiction, however, the patriarchal restrictions imposed on women represent the kernel of her exploration of female identity and femininity.

While she lived in Santiago, Bombal befriended Chilean artists and writers, among them Marta Brunet, who would be instrumental in supporting Bombal's novels as well as involving her in theater and performance in several plays. This friendship would also enable the circulation, among the group of intellectuals and writers who surrounded Brunet, of Bombal's first novel in Santiago, *La última niebla (The Final Mist)* (1935), published in Buenos Aires. It should be noted that Bombal's works in the 1930s were not published in Chile; the three works mentioned here were all published first in Buenos Aires. *La última niebla* was first published in Chile in 1944 by Nascimento. This explains why until the 1940s only a very small group of Chileans were familiar with her work. During Bombal's stay in Argentina, she published much of her fiction, which was celebrated by the Argentinian literary and intellectual elite, among them Jorge Luis Borges, Norah Lange, Bioy Casares, and Victoria Ocampo. Ocampo, editor of the internationally acclaimed literary journal *Sur,* would help bring to public light *La amortajada (The Shrouded Woman)* (1938) and the short stories, "Las islas nuevas ("The New Islands") and "El árbol" ("The Tree") in 1939. Other *crónicas* and film reviews written by Bombal also appeared in *Sur,* providing her with a well-established and highly prestigious platform for her writings. The fact that paradoxically the first editions of most of Bombal's highly acclaimed works were published in Buenos Aires rather than in Santiago had a great impact on her reception in Chile.

Bombal's fiction is articulated through two frameworks that shape its distinct ideological contradictions and aesthetic features. Class identity, the first of these frames, constitutes a key cultural device in her narrative discourse and in the hegemonic gender ideology legitimized through the marriage contract. The project of modernity, on the other hand, presents a new set of cultural expectations that urban women and women's rights incarnate. Bombal's characters are placed at the crossroads of these two ideologies, with most of them unable to choose between the old traditional model of femininity that wifedom presents and the new one, represented by the independent working woman that modernity offers.

Femininity and sensibility are among the features that male critics of Bombal have highlighted when discussing her personality as well as her literature. The critic Ignacio Valente described her as "the princess of Chilean women writers,"[3] revealing the degree to which Bombal was equated in Chile with the feminine par excellence. Images of femininity and unfulfilled romance were associated with the writer throughout her life.[4] Among Chilean critics, the prestigious *Alone* (Hernán Díaz Arrieta) had a great impact on the way Bombal's fiction and personality were interrelated. He was the first to note her contribution to Chilean letters and the dramatic shift of her work from the realist literary tradition. His critical eye immediately acknowledged the rupture that Bombal's fiction introduced to the descriptive and regionalist literary schools. Poetic imagery and subjectivity were Bombal's signature; however, they were also samples of a delicate and feminine sensibility. With this ideological frame and to the detriment of her literary work, Bombal's writing and biography became conflated, heightening the public interest in her personal life. Furthermore, Bombal's numerous interviews served to reinforce these notions through her social identity and conservative views on gender difference, as we will see in the coming pages. Nonetheless, her novels define and reveal many of the symbolic devices that organize public and intimate space.

The writer's creative and innovative literary contributions have tended to get lost in the anecdotes that surrounded her life and her later effacement from public life. The paucity of her production and the fact that she spent a long time in the United States (1942–69) translating or rewriting her own texts and exploring other genres also contributed to her public image as a mysterious and somewhat bizarre woman. Her image as a bohemian and a dangerous femme fatale was also accompanied by the princesslike qualities. Furthermore, Bombal's failed marriage to the Argentinian homosexual artist Jorge Larco, as well as the scandal caused by her earlier attempt to murder her former lover, Eulogio Sánchez Errázuriz, placed her on the list of female authors who shocked the Chilean public.[5] In a certain sense, Bombal was a predecessor to the writer María Carolina Geel (1911–96), who actually killed her lover in 1955 and served time in jail for the crime while writing her autobiographical account of it in the novel, *Cárcel de mujeres* (*Women's Jail*) (1956). The authors experienced similar public notoriety for the crimes of passion they committed in broad daylight in the middle of a Santiago street (Bombal) and at a famous restaurant (Geel).

Bombal received numerous awards, among them, in 1941 the Premio Municipal de Novela (Municipal Award for the Novel) for *La amortajada*. In 1974 she was awarded the prestigious Ricardo Latchman Award. In 1976 she received the Premio Academia Chilena de la Lengua (the Chilean Academy of Language Award) and, in 1978, the Joaquín Eduards Bello Award. Despite the number of times her name was proposed for the Chilean National Prize in Literature, it was never awarded to Bombal. Her long, self-imposed exile only served to mythify the writer's life. With her marriage to a French nobleman, she exchanged her dreams of bohemian life for stability in Connecticut for a number of years, until his death and her definitive return to Chile in 1973. The last years of Bombal's life were characterized by neglect and poverty. During her final days, she lived in a nursing home, with neither public recognition nor the support of relatives or friends. She later died in a common room in a public hospital, as the writer Diamela Eltit recalls with astonishment.[6]

NEGATIVITY IN *LA ÚLTIMA NIEBLA*

In her book *Foundational Fictions: The National Romances of Latin America* (1991), Doris Sommer shows how the institution of marriage is intimately linked to the discourse of the nation in the nineteenth century. The Chilean novel *Martín Rivas* (1862), by Alberto Blest Gana (1830–1920), is the epitome of interclass alliance and the configuration of new national ideals through the sexual contract between the characters Martín and Leonor. The latter's acceptance of Martín's marriage proposal ends the novel with a happy marriage that shows the mobility of the middle class (Martín's) and the formation of new social identities within a liberal paradigm. Rather than focusing on marriage as part of the national discourse, Bombal's narrative in the 1930s opts for gendered subjectivities and the ways the sexual contract shapes them. She replaces foundational arrangements with the daily sense of failure felt by the oligarchs' wives in the confinement of the countryside. This universe displays the experiences of "perfect" women who live with wealthy, powerful men and who seem to have it all. They have the most valued attributes for women: they are cultured yet traditional in their acquiescence to the status quo. Most of them either play the piano, write diaries, read, or carry on seductive conversations showing the unique traits of the socially cultured. These protagonists tend to have the attributes of the elite "mujer de salón," the female socialite who has naturalized class distinctions, performing them with mastery.

However, María Luisa Bombal's fiction depicts the effects of gender inequity, sexual repression, and passivity in the lives narrated by wealthy and unsatisfied women characters. Bombal is one of the first Latin American authors whose literary focus is an interior world told exclusively from a female point of view. Her tales share the themes of love and personal experience that have been attributed to a literature produced mostly by women authors who have favored a subjective viewpoint.[7] Bombal's texts show how gender identities are intertwined and constructed through class differentiation and social hierarchies. The characters, though sheltered from material need and work, are subordinated and secluded in the patriarchal household of the hacienda. They are trapped in marriages that are meaningless sexual contracts in which they are reduced to exchangeable commodities. In this way, the narrative shows the failure of gender models in the countryside where the modern city woman, her productivity and gain, are absent. In contrast, in Bombal's world women do not produce: they vegetate, wasting themselves away in a temporality that has been left outside the promises of modernity. Instead they live in the negativity of modernity, a state of timelessness without traces of history. Here we can see what Jorge Larraín calls the decline of the oligarchic modernity, and the impact of its overarching feature of exclusion of difference.[8]

As a result, the reader is presented with two perspectives on women and modernity within this narrative discourse: the liberal and enlightened view that is critical of women's subordination and rural oppressive mores that slight individual rights, and the oligarchic, semifeudal position in which women are to be secluded and obedient to their fathers and husbands. Female characters are faced with these two perspectives and their configurations, confronted with gender offers that pretend to civilize them through their social integration by means of marriage or work—a choice that is absent from the characters as a result of class ideology.

The narrative textualizes the inner drama of a female consciousness in all its emotional and psychic turmoil when faced with the reality of objectification. This makes Bombal's writing essentially hybrid by bringing together the *folletín,* the melodrama, the diary, and testimony of females who reveal their victimization and self-sacrifice within marriage as a sexual contract in which women are the subordinate. Their sense of powerlessness is revealed through their dreams and obsessions, in which the body and sexuality are central. Within an aesthetic akin to surrealism, female passions and the unconscious coexist in conflict with a rational and factual order that is lived not only as hostile and self-destructive but also as masculine. In this way, the world of modernity remains threatening and subject to forces beyond female comprehension. Women's withdrawal and altered states show the dislocation of a subjectivity that is determined by a sense of melting away. What is new here is that disenchantment constructs an essentially disembodied self. In this psychic scenario, sexual difference is experienced as an absolute that produces ongoing fragmentation and decentering of identity. The possibility of an autonomous self is unattainable for characters whose sense of self is defined by inadequacy and fragmentation. Furthermore, the marriage contract appears bound by class demands that alienate women and condemn them to a purely biological existence.

In this cultural context, the dynamics of intimate relationships is restricted by thoughtless and repetitive patterns in which social appearance and status dominate. Gender and social hierarchy allocate greater power to males, who make decisions, control people and objects, and live for the public sphere. Isolation and withdrawal, on the other hand, determine the split psyches and altered states suffered by wives, who are condemned to the imprisonment of a domestic time and space.

The narrative conflict lies in the protagonist's split between the body and consciousness. The world depicted also echoes this division in the opposition between rationality and imagination that coexists to the point of blending in critical or extreme moments of female existence. A linear and phallologocentric perspective is subverted by a metaphorical language that represents subjectivity as a lived and imagined experience. The unconscious, dreams, and eroticism inexorably conflict with a regimented social reality in a narration that shifts from biology to consciousness and vice versa.

La última niebla (1935)[9] displays a new aesthetic style in which gender, class, and modernity are structures of discipline and repression for women. According to Freud, the aim of repression is to consolidate a civilized and cultured society. In his book *Culture and Its Discontents* (1929), he goes to great lengths to show how Western civilization is founded on the repression of individual drives, in particular those that are perceived to be threatening to the maintenance of patriarchal ties and rights, namely, incest, in his interpretation. In Bombal's novel, we also find a coincidence with Antonin Artaud's theater of cruelty and modern subjectivity in that social identities and behavior are radically disturbed by experiences that shake the foundations of rationality and morality. Roles and identities in Bombal's theater of genders are predetermined by a biological discourse in conjunction with *marianismo* to the reproduction and maintenance of an oligarchic and masculine modernity. Only passion as a life force provides meaning for these women, and in its absence the sadomasochist theater remains the last bastion of modernity in which to become equal subjects (of domination or subjection).

Thus, Bombal depicts the sinister side of a social class whose gender ideology is constitutive to the formation of identities. Her female characters must leave reality through insanity, daydreaming, hallucination, or a postmortem state in order to be able to speak from a nonrole or no place in which they have stopped being what they were.

The novel, *La última niebla,* presents a phantasmagoric narration told by an evasive and uncertain woman who remains nameless, insisting on her exclusively bodily existence. The old order of the landowning class appears closed and deadly in the hacienda, where subjects operate through scripted lives and rituals shaped by patriarchal and masculine values and privileges. In this social scenario, the female psyche is progressively dissociated from the landowning world it inhabits. This explains why the novel ends almost exactly as it begins, with only a greater sense of defeat for the anonymous narrator. Dismal marital circumstances motivate her inner journey of self-discovery and a search for passion in a desolate existence. The absence of love in an endogamous union between two cousins who have married for the sake of marrying is evident early on. The fact that they are blood relatives suggests the ruling class's tendency to marry within the family circle in order to secure its power and *latifundia* ownership. Through the emphasis on the domestic realm, Bombal, as does Brunet, shows the contradictions and stratifications prevalent in the public sphere, where an endogamous social structure secures the hegemonic power of a few Chilean families dating back to the previous centuries. Despite the changing political climate and populist alliances of the 1930s, a closely knit upper class still binds its economic interests in arranged marriages that preserve the property of the land. Bombal exposes this practice together with its foreseeable shortcomings and failures in marriages between relatives as well as in those where the parents choose the husband from among their friends (as *La amortajada* [1938] and *"El árbol"* [1939] show).

In a way we already know the end of the story in *La última niebla* when the narrator describes the excessive rain the day she arrives at the hacienda as a newlywed. Here the narrative presents images of the destructive power of nature, the heavy rain and winds, to foreshadow the protagonist's fate. In the opening scene of the novel, the rain threatens to dissolve the world, both natural and human. The narrator reveals her anxiety at seeing the water pouring down onto the soil, the fields, and the house. Shingles on the roof are soaked and every room in the house is leaking. The signs of decadence and datedness are evident from the start, underscoring the lack of future projection with the first sight of the oligarchic household. The house here is a hostile space rather than a refuge, evidently linked with a patriarchal family tradition that is life threatening for the narrator, as María Inés Lagos has pointed out.[10]

The narrative presents a reversed story and an upside down world in which the bride instead of happiness sees her biological destiny: to age and die. This abandoned and crumbling house is the place that culture has assigned to the wife. *La última niebla* focuses on the protagonist's interior turmoil and maladjustment to the social expectations of being a wife. Here the house and femininity are expressions of fissures and the flaws of an old and worn-out tradition. Thus the woman's jouissance becomes a pure symptom that reflects the traces and marks of mystical ecstasies, allowing her to deny the passage of time.

The narrator's sense of displacement and inadequacy shapes her self as a devalued other whose life is empty and insignificant. The absence of a proper name also underscores this sense of lack. Susan Fraiman describes this gender identity process as a failed apprenticeship that is really about "unbecoming."[11] Otherness is here inextricably linked to the negativity of gender: to being out of place and feeling inferior in a hierarchy where man is the locus of authority and meaning. The woman, in Bombal's novel, is apparently older and has married without love in order to escape spinsterhood. Marrying Daniel provides her with the status of being a wife, a role that gives her an identity in a world where unmarried females are irrelevant, as her husband cruelly reminds her. He makes clear his role as her savior, having rescued her from the grim fate of the spinster, a social failure and a marginal female. His hostile gaze is followed by cruel remarks:

—¿Sabes que has tenido una gran suerte en casarte conmigo?
—Sí, lo sé -replico, cayéndome de sueño.
—¿Te hubiera gustado ser una solterona arrugada, que teje para los pobres de la hacienda?
Me encojo de hombros.
—Ese es el porvenir que aguarda a tus hermanas. (57)[12]

["Do you know how lucky you are to have married me?"
"Yes, I know"—I reply, as I am drifting off to sleep.
"Would you have rather been a wrinkled old maid, knitting things for the poor folks on the hacienda?"
I shrug my shoulders.
"That is the kind of future your sisters can look forward to."]

Negativity defines female life and identity in this context. Daniel's words show not only his position as a male, but also the model that regulates gender relationships. As do most men in Bombal's works, he represents a rigid and hierarchical order. His attitude in Bombal's narrative universe is typically masculine[13] and cultural in the patriarchal perspective that presents females with the proposal to be part of the vital modern project. Underneath his arrogance, however, the protagonist senses a fear of being alone. His anxious gaze reveals to the new wife his need for companionship just a few months after becoming a widower (56).

The protagonist, on the other hand, has escaped a bleak future by marrying for convenience's sake a man whom she has known her entire life and who is also a blood relative. She reveals having married "for the sake of being married," feeling no particular attachment (57). The preceding exchange reveals the protagonist's limited social chances and her lack of value as a woman. Daniel, from her perspective, seems to be unaware of why he has chosen to marry or the impact of his former wife's death on his decision. He will remain obsessed and constrained by the memories of his late wife and never live in the present.[14] Moreover, in the wife's account, Daniel's necrophilic drives and tendency toward control are acutely expressed in his demand that she simulate his dead wife's appearance and behavior as the perfect wife. The husband's gaze is not only the dominant gaze in which woman is the projection of a phantasmatic masculine desire. In her case, she experiences a total sense of lack since she does not fulfill the feminine signifiers. The narrator tells her story through a split subjectivity in which there is a suffering body that is discursively dissociated from fantasy.

The way the male gaze has constructed the world is here suspended through the predominance of a female point of view. Knowing in a patriarchal social context means holding power over the female other to desexualize and objectify her. In a presumptuous way, Daniel tells his wife that nothing escapes him about her body and that he knows every inch of it by heart:

> —Te miro—me contesta—.Te miro y pienso que te conozco demasiado. . . .
> —Hasta los ocho años, nos bañamos a un tiempo en la misma bañera. Luego, verano tras verano, ocultos de bruces en la maleza, Felipe y yo hemos acechado y visto zambullirse en el río a todas las muchachas de la familia. No necesito siquiera desnudarte. De ti conozco hasta la cicatriz de tu operación de apendicitis. (56)

> [—I look at you—he answers—. I look at you and think, I know you all too well. . . .
> —Up to age eight we took our baths together, in the same tub. Then there were all those summers when Felipe and I would crouch down in the weeds and hide, waiting to watch the girls in the family come down and dive into the river. I don't even have to take off your clothes. I know you right down to the scar from your appendix operation.]

Daniel is apparently not attracted to a woman's body that he has watched and assessed over a long period. His emotional detachment is integral to the process of desexualization of his wife's body. The absence of eroticization is even deeper in this case since it is embedded in the substitution of the former/dead wife. In this way, the narrator realizes that the place culture had promised for the constitution of identity in marriage does not exist. What becomes apparent instead is that the sexual contract is a perverse fraud. Irigaray's notion of feminine intelligibility may be applicable in this instance, since woman does not speak within a phallologocentric discourse that defines and circumscribes the real to its laws and logic. The organization of phallologocentrism, as Irigaray argues, restricts what is perceptible and intelligible, maintaining the submission and exploitation of the "feminine."[15] By denying to the female subject the possibility of speaking from its own experience, this phallologocentric binary system of representation essentializes women and denies them their historicity. In her essay "The Power of Discourse and the Subordination of the Feminine," Irigaray suggests that the feminine has historically been assigned as mimicry, as a subordination that maintains sexual difference. This mimesis is what defines her position and her veiling in language. However, Irigaray also suggests that the transgressive possibility of women's play with mimesis reveals that they "remain somewhere else," a place she associates with pleasure rather than with logos. In Bombal this resistance takes the form of autoeroticism as well as self reflexivity through the use of deictics constructing a narrative world that turns onto itself.

Furthermore, Irigaray asserts that a feminine style of writing may be linked to the image of self-touching that is based on the desire for proximity and "disruptive excess" rather than a desire for property, suggesting a "mode of exchange irreducible to any centering or centrism."[16] In this reading, Irigaray sees a way out of essentialism as well as of the repetitive cultural pattern of female mimicry, finding a common ground with Julia Kristeva's semiotic *chora*.[17] Excess, the presymbolic, the body cannot be entirely contained or reduced to a linguistic system of representation.

The nameless woman is only matter that has been equated with a biological body in the patriarchal discourse that defines her. In this way, she incarnates the signifiers provided by culture, unsuccessfully trying to reproduce what is expected of her. She does encounter, however, a theater of cruelty in which Daniel fantasizes and demands her imitation of the perfect (dead) wife. She is thus placed within a theater of genders that she equates with the cruelty of preassigned roles and predetermined identities. The mechanisms of control are displayed in a mise-en-scène in which woman mimics the model of womanhood and wifedom.

Gilles Deleuze, on the other hand, reminds us that coldness is the essential feature of the structure of perversion in sadomasochism. It is evident in the apathy of the sadist as well as in the ideal of the masochist and in the absence of affect in their respective fantasies, which narrate them only as roles and what Jessica Benjamin terms self-objects. Coldness is thus the precondition of pleasure, an instantaneous resexualization of the object of passion where what matters is repetition rather than the experience of pleasure.[18] The lack of recognition is played out in the representation of the master-slave theater where the other is transformed into an object in order for the self to be confirmed. In the case of Bombal's novel, the nameless wife takes the place of the dead wife, but the husband desires the dead not the "copy." The implicit sexual model at work here arises from enlightened values in which Daniel identifies himself with a higher moral ideal that constructs him as a rational and apathetic male. This morality is grounded on his rebuke of the living wife as well as his sexual rejection of her.

In this way, the Catholic oligarchic marriage reveals a theater of cruelty in which the female is not only subordinated to the moral superiority and rationality of the male citizen but to the sanctity of the institution and obedience to the husband according to the church. The conflation of Catholic and civil elements in this sexual model and contract erases female rights while postulating sacrifice and obliteration as the wife's obligation and most exalted virtues. This is how gender arrangement works in the public sphere, where, despite the greater number of women, the ideals and expectations remain those of obedience and self-sacrifice.

The reiteration of Daniel's scrutinizing gaze and his comments succinctly establish the ground rules and the wife's position in a household governed by coldness in the system of gender roles. Daniel's disclosure of a long, voyeuristic practice reveals their close relation, on the one hand, and an insurmountable distance on the other. In this perverse male gaze the formula is coldness (in desexualization) and comfort (in resexualization).[19]

Paradoxically, the wife's solipsism elaborates her subjectivity in a kind of resistance to all her mimetic actions. Thus, despite her silence in front of her husband, we know what she is thinking: that Daniel's body is big and clumsy, and also too well known (56). Apparently, there is nothing to challenge either spouse to discover the other or what they are as a couple. This sadomasochist form of desire is reinforced in Latin America by its patriarchal oligarchic system where *machismo*[20] and its heterosexuality assign woman a sacrificial position. Her victimization in this theater of cruelty is close to melodrama in that roles are not only assigned and acted out but construed as unchangeable. Melodrama becomes the emotional and aesthetic structure that best represents female resistance to a gender social law whereby the woman becomes a martyr. Bombal's *La amortajada* is the best example of this sensibility, as a woman in a shroud struggles with her passions even after death. Women in both novels are among the sacrificed bodies in a system in which they become subjects only through suffering and pain: hence the emphasis on pain through a failed search for love in *La última niebla,* an impossible and fatal love whose basic form is a sadomasochistic attraction.

The absence of love in the couple is made clear again when Daniel weeps, apparently for his late wife, and the protagonist ignores his pain. She pretends not to notice and settles for an easy way out of this awkward situation. This series of exchanges establishes a "psychological distance" from the beginning.[21] Traditional decorum shapes her interaction with her husband, whose emotional withdrawal increases vis-à-vis her "existential petrification."[22] Intersubjectivity is replaced by accommodation that shifts between the woman's passivity and submission, according to the masculine heterosexual discourse.

The wake of a young dead woman that follows soon after the protagonist's arrival in Daniel's hacienda takes a highly surrealistic form, providing no reference to the deceased or the relationship with the narrator. The fragmentary quality of the entire scene resembles a dream, or, more precisely, a nightmare. The atmosphere of death that prevails at the wake presents people and objects without clear form and meaning. In the foreground is the dead woman, whose face and body are striking, and, ultimately, terrifying for the narrator. Death is embodied in the silent and immobile female body she is looking at. She is seeing herself in the dead female body she cannot embody. The body's static position and facial features signal the finality of death, as if the young woman had never been alive (58). The closed eyelids, without vital signs or makeup, underscore the absence of sight. The absence of cosmetics also shows that the theater of identities and roles may only cease with death. Furthermore, the attention given to makeup points to the narrator's realization that death is an experience that cannot be hidden or simulated. The expressionless face shows the lack of feelings as well as her definitive immobility in the coffin. This cinematic episode with a motionless and dead woman at the center will be revisited by Bombal in *La amortajada* as the most significant event that allows the protagonist, Ana María, to evoke the past from an all-encompassing point of view.

The nameless wife's consciousness of what the signifier death means for her makes her escape with horror at what her own materialization of it signals. Married, she will have to represent the dead woman as the perversion demanded by the marriage contract. The narrator's rejection and fear of the corpse's lifelessness and the death rites are expressed in her experience of silence, which becomes a hostile presence that invades the room and her consciousness (58). Silence turns into a destructive force threatening the protagonist with physical and mental destruction. The "silent" and mournful figures dressed in black and the "horrible" artificial wreaths increase her fear and her urge to escape the death scene. The lifeless atmosphere, however, follows her outside, where a fine mist has erased the landscape and increased the stillness of nature. Even the house she has just left suggests a tomb isolated amid cypresses—trees commonly found in cemeteries and the landowning landscapes of the central and southern regions in Chile.

The transformation of nature into a gothic and tenebrous landscape reminds us of the gothic romance. Patricia Rubio has commented that Bombal's novel written in English, *House of Mist* (1947), is a type of palimpsest of folk legends and fairy tales that are joined with the gothic novel and the melodrama.[23] In *La última niebla,* the gothic atmosphere is recreated through the dead body and the decay it conveys for the protagonist. Thus, the fog that surrounds the woods when she runs out works as a reminder of the inexorable passage of time, a truth the character will fight against until the end of the novel. Here the fog alters the landscape and reality with its power to blur and change the familiar, making the world strange and threatening. In this ominous setting the woman is forced to face the fact that roles imply a symbolic death for her, foreshadowing the question that will haunt the shrouded woman: how many deaths can a woman undergo?

While going through the woods, she stamps to hear her footsteps, but the wet and decomposing leaves absorb the sound. Death is literally at her feet during her walk through the woods. At this point, the character begins to doubt the reality of her surroundings and touches the trees to confirm their existence. The memory of the dead woman and the stillness of the fog are experienced as life threatening. Her reaction to this feeling of terror is to assert her existence as embodiment:

Y porque me ataca por vez primera, reacciono violentamente contra el asalto de la niebla.

—¡Yo existo, yo existo—digo en voz alta—y soy bella y feliz! Sí, ¡feliz!, la felicidad no es más que tener un cuerpo joven y esbelto y ágil. (58)

[And because it is attacking me for the first time, I react violently against the assault of the mist.

"I exist, I exist,"—I say in a loud voice—"I am beautiful and happy! Yes, happy! Happiness is nothing more than having a young and slender and graceful body."]

With this vehement assertion we are introduced to the protagonist's basic beliefs. She is far from analyzing her feelings about death and womanhood and instead verifies her existence in terms of her body. Happiness is defined as being alive and having a young and beautiful body. Despite the seemingly stereotypical values that inform her words, a deeper conflict surfaces in her fear of stillness and silence, perceived as omens of self-destruction.

The first scene of autoeroticism occurs right after she first encounters the sexual triangle among her sister-in-law, Regina; her young lover; and Felipe, the betrayed husband. The protagonist is intensely affected by the adulterous couple's erotic attachment as well as by Regina's disregard for convention and morality. She goes out to the woods and presses herself against a tree, disclosing her hidden sexual desire out in nature (61). She undresses and enters a pond, contemplating her sensual body for the first time as she is embraced by the aquatic plants and "kissed" and cooled by the breeze (62). This moment represents, as Saúl Sosnowski has argued, her immersion in a formless and diffuse world. The fact that it takes place in the water highlights the return of the unconscious and renewal through "the water of life"[24] in a kind of rebirth ritual. On the opposite end stands the still and tomblike house, which embodies social regulation and sanctioned morality. Here the narrative discourse reveals the predominance of the nineteenth-century metaphors, civilization and barbarism, as symbolic determinants of the protagonist's plight. In the cultural paradigm, she is defined as being biologically determined for marriage and motherhood; however, she cannot fulfill any of these gender demands despite her attempts, remaining on the margins of civilization.

After this episode, there is another encounter with Regina's lover that presents the core of the protagonist's desire and the way in which it is shaped. The men have returned from hunting and with "mutilated bodies" and "a profusion of death wings." Regina's lover carries a bleeding bird that he places on the protagonist's knees while it is still warm (63). This symbolic "offering" combines violence and sexual attraction in the image of a dying dove. It also highlights the links among masculinity, seduction, and death. As Georges Bataille discusses in his book *Erotism: Death and Sensuality* (1962), cruelty and eroticism are conscious attempts to trespass the field of accepted behavior; the separation from animality is thus imposed through the taboo.[25] Regina's suicide and the narrator's own failed attempt to kill herself reiterate later on that these are fatal erotic attractions precisely because they transgress marriage vows and female obedience. Desire and pain fuse in the hunting scene to show that heterosexual attraction is founded on violence and the ultimate suffering and sacrifice of the female. Hunting is another form of the sexual theater in this context, an unveiled expression of gender positions and their implications for women. The imagery of hunting in several of Bombal's stories reveals its link to classical and medieval French literature, where this activity is characterized as a courtly sport that may be quite violent. In a similar way to the males in the hacienda, the "courtly hunters slog through bushes and marshes in order to pursue their prey" or another lady.[26] In the novel the signifiers *presa* meaning "prey," and *presa* meaning "prisoner," trigger the entrapment that discourse reserves for women.

For the narrator, imagination becomes a refuge that allows her to become the wife she would like to be according to social expectations. At another level, the imaginary realm that she creates for herself with her desire and sexual aims enfolds autoeroticism. The body and writing thus become the same through the inscription of the letter in her body rather than in hegemonic discursive models. The break with social expectations is also achieved through the figure of the lover that provides a venue for an eroticism directed to an other, yet since it is imagined, her goal is conflated with her self. Consequently, the female body is homoeroticized in conjunction with the landscape through the transformation of the body into a source of pleasure. The transgression of breaking with social expectations that this claiming of the body implies may be seen as a source of meaning for heterosexual female identity in the real absence of a male other as well as of pregnancy. Here eroticism becomes the only vital and meaningful experience of the female self, whose power imbues even nature. Consequently, every natural element is an extension or reflection of the self in multiple ways: the water in its various states, the earth, the trees, the sky, the wind all are inextricably linked to this disembodied subjectivity in which the sexual drive is not directed to men or to hegemonic culture but to the self.

The protagonist's feelings of otherness are expressed in letters that reveal her search for passion and meaning. The epistolary correspondence includes a fictional male and a female character who engage in various love scenes following the *folletín* and its sentimental scripts. Lucía Guerra has called attention to the different narrative discourses that Bombal incorporates in her novel; among them, she identifies the romantic heroine and the female characters of the *folletín* and the sentimental drama who are passive, subordinate, and determined by biology.[27] Writing in *La última niebla* becomes a way to halt the passage of time and seal off a hostile world.[28] Here the protagonist's letters reproduce heterosexual models where she fulfills the romantic narrative that the invention of a lover provides. She pretends that reality disappears, and by doing this she creates a false memory of her own existence.

She invents countless secret encounters, conversations, fights, and scenes of jealousy where she and her lover are the protagonists. In this imagined and written romance, the narrator recreates a self who is loved, contemplated, and desired by a man. The latter is depicted as the ideal lover, the embodiment of an overwhelming sensuality that subdues her. In contrast, her uneventful existence is restricted to the space of the hacienda and the husband's control. By shutting the spouse off from her inner world, the narrator is able to slip into an imagined passion that gives meaning to her life for ten years. In a similar vein, Ana María in *La amortajada* compensates for her husband's indifference and affairs by allowing Fernando to listen to her secrets. In this case, the oral word takes precedence over the written. The narrator in *La última niebla* instead remains outwardly silent as she writes down her erotic plot in order to resist domination and a mediocre marriage, as Soledad Bianchi argues.[29] Despite their mimicries, both characters fall under the gender system and its imitative codes while time devours them.

The lover's warm and attentive gaze sharply contrasts with Daniel's suspicion and mistrust. The eyes convey desire or power, depending on who is looking at the protagonist. In the (imagined) case of the lover, his gaze equates to an intense passion in opposition to the husband's cold control. This contrast reiterates the cold versus warm opposition as life-enhancing or life-threatening experiences. Confined to a stagnant rural reality, the landowner's wife reveals the failure of marriage as a life project. The narration is shaped by her discovery and final awareness of the desolate meaninglessness of conventional cohabitation. Dwarfed by social constraints and the evident erasure of her identity within marriage, the protagonist of *La última niebla* escapes reality through evasion. The narrative discloses the fantasies of a lonely and silent woman who is besieged by persistent hallucinations, dreams, and nightmares that blur the distinction between fiction and reality. Furthermore, even her romantic fantasy results from unconscious cultural commands of what a woman ought to be.

Water, in the form of fog, shapes the narrator's mind and the way she experiences reality. Bombal states in the prologue to *House of Mist* that her women characters live in "casas de niebla" (houses of mist), disconnected and unaware of social and economic reality. The presence of the fog and its defamiliarizing effect diffuses the space, making interior places strange, a quality that Rubio relates back to the gothic romance.[30] From its first appearance in the woods after the wedding night, the fog never leaves the heroine. The fog steadily envelops her feelings and thoughts with a phantasmagoric dreaminess. Imagery associated with the mist covering the countryside and the two city episodes serves to split reality in the protagonist's psyche.[31] It also allows her to cross from the realm of the real to the unreal in search of passion.[32] The imagined lover becomes the power source that halts the fog and its threatening power to dissolve everything. Through this fantasy and her ability to imagine a complete story with her beloved, the narrator succeeds for a time in asserting her vitality against the destructiveness of time. Nevertheless, the fog evidences that everything is doomed to disappear, herself as well as the oligarchic order.

The narrator's inability to rebel and break away from old patterns leaves her with daydreaming and writing as her only ways of expressing and affirming (her)self. The lover becomes the emblem of imagination and suggests a kind of "artistic freedom" that responds to the woman's most intimate feelings. On another level, Bombal connects this fantasy to the act of writing, which is perceived as a personal search for a kind of transcendence. Interior monologue allows the narrator to wander from the present to the past, reliving daydreams as well as old memories with no specific reference to historical time.[33] It is as if time were suspended in the realm of passion, where only the lover and the woman exist. The woman's passion for the body and her autoeroticism resignify her identity, allowing her moments of pleasure. Experiencing the body in the pond returns a new and sensual image of the body as a site for sexual gratification. Bombal shows the need to link sexuality to gender since gender roles are what define sexuality. This explains why the narrator claims autoeroticism as a valid sexuality, redefining female sexuality in the process.

The uncertainty, however, surrounding thoughts and actions adds a contemporary quality to a text that makes this self-doubting point of view the source of the narration, as Cedomil Goic discusses.[34] Everything is perceived through and reduced to the motives and concerns of the protagonist, who writes and imagines from a silent and virtually invisible subject position. She is able to deal with her own dissatisfaction and disappointment by resorting to an erotic fantasy. Significantly, in this imagined experience the protagonist discovers the power of sexuality and its connection to identity. By looking at herself in the mirror and in the water, the woman's consciousness opens to a new and different sense of herself through the body. In the natural world (as in the narrator's perceptions), forms and shapes alter while becoming highly sensual. All of nature seems to speak to her as if she had only to listen and decipher a hidden code and its secrets. Subjectivity becomes tightly connected to Eros as a force that gives life and meaning in a stifling and destructive social order.

The character's own desire surfaces after seeing another woman's erotic object. The other is Regina, her sister-in-law, who with her lover form a symbolic triad with the narrator. Ricardo Gutiérrez Mouat proposes that Regina is the real presence that enables the protagonist to produce a discourse where she may invent herself. Consequently, her imitation of Regina gives birth to a form of copied desire whose object is valuable because it is desired by another woman.[35] I agree with this interpretation, but I would add that Regina is the signifier woman, its best embodiment, while the narrator is the phantasmatic and fallen copy produced by the male gaze. In *La última niebla,* the narrator wants the passion, intensity, and defiance that Regina displays and that she associates with having a lover. Regina is an inverted image of the protagonist's passivity and fear of breaking the rules. Her sensual power awakens the narrator's desire and her search for an erotic narrative. As she does, the narrator will attempt suicide after her passion has faded, as Cedomil Goic notes.[36]

Regina's character asserts unconventional behavior and defiance of society's laws as the only possible ways of living with passion. Her presence, her hair, and her body attract the protagonist and trigger her desire. She compares herself with Regina and sees in her a model of the femininity she would like to incarnate. Their first encounter and the scene after, when the narrator looks at herself in the mirror, underscore the body and its significance in female identity. Experiencing the body and claiming it as a place of pleasure through autoeroticism become the first gestures of female sexual transgression in the text as well as in Latin American narrative.

Regina's hair entangled in her lover's shirt is revisited in the mirror scene, where the narrator focuses on her own hair. She remembers her past appearance and comments about the former brilliance, redness, and wildness of the hair, which resembled "un casco guerrero" (a warrior's helmet) (60). This Athenian image of female power contrasts with the character's tied braid following Daniel's wishes for her to resemble his dead "perfect wife." In this way the signifier wife is tied to death and to perfection in a model provided by the husband. In a paradoxical way, the protagonist is never able to take the place of the dead wife nor fill the void left by her. Despite the fact that individual traits are erased in order to imitate the dead woman and play her role, the new wife always feels like a simulator or a substitute. However, she seems to be aware of the effort she puts into forgetting who she is to impersonate another woman. Her autonomy and individuality are given up to become the double or copy of the late wife, linking Daniel and marriage with death of the self. Thus, when the narrator notices the changes in her hair, this event metaphorizes her loss of identity and sense of powerlessness. The hair motif underscores the woman's fear of losing herself. The contrast with her past, projected in the image of the hair as helmet, emphasizes her loss of strength and will by being a wife. Her graceless and pulled-back braid points to her obedience and fate in marriage, which requires not only her social isolation but also her erasure. Yolanda's wing- and seagulllike appearance in "Las islas nuevas" (1939) ("The New Islands") is also linked to a sense of strange female identity; however, she is evidently more undomesticated than the nameless narrator precisely because of her rejection of marriage. The hair motif resurfaces in the story "Las trenzas" (1940) ("Braids") and becomes central to female knowledge and women's power in various fairy tales and legends, living as a symbol of a past memory and age. In "La historia de María Griselda" (1946) ("The Story of María Griselda"), María Griselda resembles a beautiful and graceful gazelle whose real nature remains beyond and outside the human realm. In this way, Bombal aestheticizes those qualities or physical features that enable her female characters to live in a natural and primitive state within yet separate from a patriarchal and modern culture. These qualities are part of what condemns them to live as estranged and disembodied ghosts in a world that is ruled by a cultural logic in which women are defined by biology.

Gender relations are incarnated in Bombal by the figures of the hunter and the prey. Several male characters in these works hunt and kill birds for sport. They are also characterized as hostile, inclined to ravaging and pursuing endless and futile activities. The short story "Las islas nuevas" reiterates these motifs, transforming Yolanda into a birdlike figure who hides her wing and herself from her pursuers. In *La amortajada*, María Griselda resembles a gazelle, a magical and tragic quality that is revisited and expanded in "La historia de María Griselda." Both protagonists are misunderstood and victimized by the men who endlessly pursue them without possessing them. Patriarchal power is presented through the hunting image that marks all areas of the hacienda culture and its gender relations, making sex in particular a most attractive and dangerous practice for women. Sexual attraction and desire are the cause of their enslavement in a repetitive and cumulative series of dramatic scenes in which women are most of the time the sacrificial victims.

Sexual imaginary is here represented in the narrator's desire, which is ambivalently structured through fear, attraction, and pain. The urge to lose one's identity and to be taken by the other's force develops a female masochism that is illustrated in *La última niebla* in the famous sex scene. Subjection here is inextricably bound to a desire to please and submit to masculine power. The imagined romance shows eroticism and intercourse within a hierarchical and dichotomous framework where gender roles and sexuality are overly codified and fixed. In the one-night event with an overpowering and almost supernatural male, pleasure is conflated with submission. In the sexual act, the lover becomes a seething wave that reiterates passion as an overwhelming and primordial force where identity and consciousness drop off. As Alicia Borinsky has shown, the perfect lover is the one who makes the protagonist forget who she is. Her longing is to be carried away by a man whose energy endows her with a special passivity.[37] However, this passivity is present only at the level of the story since discursively, the narrator constructs the signifier for a man. Thus, in the story, the stranger becomes the perfect lover, who is represented by a wave. Interestingly, we find a similar description of the initiation into sexual passion in Brunet's story "Ruth Werner," from the collection *Reloj del sol (Sun Clock)* (1930). Ruth Werner, as the nameless narrator, lacks love and passion in her marriage and is also initiated in a rite of passage in a trip to the city, as Helene C. Weldt-Basson points out. In both cases, the stranger provides a new identity for the wives as well as a sense of self-fulfillment and self-understanding.[38]

The lover the nameless protagonist invents is the equivalent to Daniel's dead wife, a figure that separates and disables him from actually seeing his new wife. The invention of the lover shows the falseness of both ideals (Daniel's perfect wife and the protagonist's perfect lover) in that in reality, what really exists are sexuality and her masturbation:

> Casi sin tocarme, me desata los cabellos y empieza a quitarme los vestidos. Me someto a su deseo callada y con el corazón palpitante. Una secreta aprensión me estremece cuando mis ropas refrenan la impaciencia de sus dedos. Ardo en deseos de que me descubra cuanto antes su mirada. . . . siento correr la sangre dentro de sus venas y siento trepidar la fuerza que se agazapa. . . . Su cuerpo me cubre como una grande ola hirviente, me acaricia, me quema, me penetra, me envuelve, me arrastra desfallecida. (68–69)

> [He barely touches me as he loosens my hair and begins to remove my clothes. I submit to his desire in silence, my heart pounding. I tremble with secret anticipation when my clothing resists his impatient fingers. I burn with a desire for his gaze to uncover me before another moment passes. . . . I feel the flowing of the blood in his veins, and I sense the pulsing of a force that lies in wait . . . His body covers me like a great seething wave, it caresses, it burns, penetrates and envelops me, it drags me along, I feel faint.]

Sexual attraction and intercourse are described from a visual perspective, where most of the activity is performed by the imaginary male. The narrator's desire in her sexual fantasy is revealed as autoerotic and self-centered. Everything we read is a product of her imagination and her ideal erotic scene. A precedent to this scene may be found in the pond where the woman discovers the sexual possibilities of her own body through autoeroticism. This self-directed desire is expressed in the need to be contemplated and possessed in a sexual fantasy whose ultimate goal is pleasure of the self. However, the sexual ritual is codified within patriarchal and heterosexual gender positions that assign a sacrificial role to the female even in the imaginary realm.

In this episode, the narrator's subjectivity is shaped by submission, erasure, and passivity. Masculine desire and performance, on the contrary, are marked by an active protagonism. The lover undresses her, unties her hair, and penetrates the woman in a near-death experience. In these erotic images, pleasure and death coexist to articulate one of the protagonist's most important events in her life. María Luisa Bastos comments that this mysterious union actually takes place between the narrator and her husband if we are to follow the narrative (presumably from the husband's perspective).[39] Rather than focusing on what is true in the factual world, I would argue that what is significant is that despite the humiliation that intercourse implies with the husband, the woman finds her own eroticism and actually has pleasure. This is particularly important if we keep in mind the precedent in the pond scene and its consequences for the protagonist.

Later, the woman's desire to be sexually possessed intertwines with her daydreaming as she waits for something to alter a monotonous and isolated existence. In this setting, masochistic pain surfaces when the woman unsuccessfully attempts to find the ideal man in the real world. As Deleuze has pointed out, masochism depends entirely on waiting and repeating the experience to the point of becoming a mise-en-scène of it with scripts and rituals to follow.[40]

In the narrator's psyche, marriage is like a prison in which she wastes away her life. In her husband's house she weakens and progressively loses her mental balance. Since she invents everything that happens to her with the lover, the matrix created is not supported by anybody else. Within her cultural horizon the lover does not exist, making progressively obvious that it is a construction of the woman's imagination. Her days indoors shift between languishing states of self-absorption and feverish angst to flee an inactive and confined life. Thus, the wife languishes as a result of self-effacement and inanition in order to fulfill her traditional role. Signs of self-immolation may be seen here, as she gives away her vital strength to a consuming identity. As the novel progresses, the woman's health worsens, leaving her in a kind of invalidism that requires others to look after her, particularly her husband, Daniel.

In this way, *La última niebla* shows us the inexorable way to female victimization through the effects of anxiety, delusion, and depression. Isolated and cut off from a community, the narrator's body becomes virtually immobile in the house. The body's interdiction thus echoes the narrator's censored identity and desire. Her physical symptoms reveal the cost of living in a psychic split. Faced with the impossibility of unity between consciousness and the world, the body turns against itself. In this instance, Bombal's language shows the body/mind division. This is the negative of the narrator's experience in the pond and in the love scene, where she dissolves into the world around her, becoming a single and total body.[41] Body and soul become one when desire and consciousness are aligned, something that for Bombal's female characters seems impossible outside imagination or altered states.

Psychic life is here bound up with bodily pain. The inability to breathe, weakness, and acute aches are part of the narrator's married life.

> Mi dolor de estos días, ese dolor lancinante como una quemadura, se ha convertido en una dulce tristeza que me trae a los labios una sonrisa cansada. Cuando me levanto, debo apoyarme en mi marido. No sé por qué me siento tan débil y no sé por qué no puedo dejar de sonreír. (65)

> [My pain of those days, that sharp pain, like a burn, has turned into a sweet sadness that brings a tired smile to my lips. When I stand up, I must hold onto my husband. I don't know why I feel so weak and I don't know why I can't stop smiling.]

The body and the psyche deteriorate in the closed and hierarchical world of the hacienda. Emotional/physical pain is experienced as ambiguous and diffused, shifting among sweetness, sadness, and incomprehension. The physical need for the husband, however, is stressed; the narrator is almost disabled and can hardly walk without assistance. Her dependency on Daniel is virtually total at this point. Within the cultural and social context of the novel, marriage is a prolongation of the father-daughter relationship in which the latter submits to paternal authority. The husband is the mentor and power figure in the patriarchal marriage and family. Daniel embodies a type of paternalistic authority that denies the protagonist's individuality from the very start.[42] He replaces the father in his duties and privileges over a woman who can barely exist without aid.

Physical and psychic frailty become feminine features, as the narrator increasingly falls into her husband's care and firm grip. She comes close to becoming a sacrificial female, exemplifying perfection as she yields her identity and health in a futile attempt to fulfill societal ideals of the perfect wife.

During a period of almost ten years, as her letters and thoughts show, the protagonist is confined to the countryside. Her physical deterioration corresponds to an ever-increasing emotional disconnection and estrangement. Her extreme withdrawal and silence develop into a state of acute depression followed by periodic hallucinations. As her consciousness increasingly focuses on her inner life, the wife daydreams, fantasizes, or remembers, in order to escape reality. Her humiliating performance as a wife, especially in sex, contrasts with her lyrical and primordial experience of pleasure with the lover.[43] In both instances, however, we find the same masochistic position in which pleasure and pain coexist, ultimately to constitute a confined female subject who can only mimic the model provided by Regina.

The novel ends as it began, returning to the same solitude but with a more acute sense of its inescapability. Rábago has noted this movement out of and back into loneliness in both spouses, pointing out that both sought to escape this condition through marriage and that, ironically, their union left them lonelier in the end.[44]

As reality begins to seep in and undermine the narrator's erotic fantasy, she is increasingly faced with the need to produce evidence. Her doubts about the realness of the romance mark the beginning of her final return to the rational order. These are the first signs of her awakening into an empty and lifeless reality. The urge to confirm her affair reaches its culmination when she prefers to get sick or feel physical pain rather than face life:

> ¡Si pudiera enfermarme de verdad! Con todas mis fuerzas anhelo que una fiebre o algún dolor muy fuerte vengan a interponerse algunos días entre mis dudas y yo.
> Y me dije: si me olvidara, si olvidara todo; mi aventura, mi amor, mi tormento. Si me resignara a vivir como antes de mi viaje a la ciudad, tal vez recobraría la paz. (84)

> [If only I could fall very ill! Some days I wish with all my heart that some serious ache or fever would come between me and my doubts.
> And I said to myself: if I'd just forget, if I'd just forget everything; my affair, my lover, my suffering. If I resigned myself to living as I did before that trip to the city, perhaps I would be at peace again.]

Oblivion through resignation appears as an alternative to an ever-increasing uncertainty. The protagonist tries to forget by engaging in small pleasures and trivial daily activities. Her desire undermines her doubts, however, when she feels the lover's mystical presence all around her (85). Imagination transforms every aspect of this silent self who cannot live without a romantic present and past. In the realm of imagination and writing, she finds a temporary solution to an overarching lack of meaning through the invention of this male signifier.

Her lost hat and Andrés, the only witness, fail to provide the evidence and ultimate proof of the lover's existence. After a decade, the protagonist's struggle against uncertainty gives way to doubts and the inability to recall and relive her love story. Her suicide attempt underscores the death motif as well as the passage of time. Ironically, Daniel saves her from being run over by a car. She also realizes the futility of an imagined passion in contrast to Regina's cultural performance. The parallel between the two is made more significant by the fact that nothing in the narrator's life has actually happened. The inner journey ends with a sense of failure that determines the narrator's outlook on life. Daniel, on the other hand, remains unconcerned with her thoughts and intentions. In this way the cycle of coldness comes to a close, as every action, thought, and desire is automatized.

Without hope, condemned to a repetitive and prescribed existence, the unnamed dreamer is finally invaded and symbolically killed by the destructive force of the fog, now definitely omnipresent and ominous. She is left at the "crossroads of the old and the new," as Phyllis Rodríguez Peralta lucidly points out, caught in confusion as to who she is.[45]

Passion gives way to hopelessness and the reinstatement of mimicry. In the end, the awareness of a false and wasted life fills the narrator. Her words are pronounced like an empty script to be performed mechanically:

> Lo sigo para llevar a cabo una infinidad de pequeños menesteres; para cumplir con una infinidad de frivolidades amenas; para llorar por costumbre y sonreír por deber. Lo sigo para vivir correctamente, algún día.
>
> Alrededor de nosotros, la niebla presta a las cosas un carácter de inmovilidad definitiva. (95)

> [I follow him in order to carry out an infinitude of tiny tasks; to accomplish an infinitude of silly little things; to cry habitually and smile when required. I follow him to live correctly, someday.
>
> All around us, the fog gives things a certain motionless character.]

This final passage reveals the woman's traditional position: to survive by repeating and upholding old and familiar practices. However, she also realizes that time has run out and that she only has meaningless tasks and obligations to follow according to her role as wife. The numbed inner monologue discloses the irrelevance of her actions and a stagnant existence. She is married to a man who feels like a stranger in that he ignores her pain and desire. In the end, the narrator is disarmed, without resources in a world that objectifies her.

This ending enacts for the last time the woman's inner conflict in terms of a desolate sense of failure and defeat. She finally accepts her disempowerment and a life of estrangement, unable to find alternatives to alter or change the situation. Despite knowing that staying in this marriage will eventually destroy her, she chooses to perpetuate the established patriarchal structures. She conforms to the hegemonic model of femininity and the dominant values it sustains. In this way cultural codes and sexist gender practices remain unmodified once the transgressor has been put back into her place. As the woman's consciousness fogs over, her final insight foreshadows a future of simulation and emotional death.

4

Sadomasochist Theater in *La Amortajada*

MARÍA LUISA BOMBAL'S RENUNCIATION OF THE FANTASIES OF THE sociosymbolic contract is best exemplified in the novel *La amortajada (The Shrouded Woman)* (1938), where negativity defines female existence. Here the feminine is shown to be a radical negativity in a literary discourse in which speech and reflection can only take place from the position given by death. Ana María, the protagonist, is a type of conscious corpse, suspended in time yet aware of her past existence as much as of the condition imposed by death. From this shrouded female body arises the voice of the woman who tells her story outside the patriarchal order and modern rationality. In this fashion, consciousness unfolds in the retrospective journey taken by Ana María's transformation, from a landowner's daughter to a landowner's wife to a corpse, throughout various love contracts.

The immobility with which *La última niebla* ended is also shared by Ana María, who has lived as if dead and is wrapped in a shroud in the narrative present.[1] In this netherworld, Bombal attempts her most dramatic presentation of a feminine subjectivity wrought by gender structures. The enigma for the reader is to distinguish who the narrator is and which events are real in a story in which negative passions govern. Perspective and focus are multiple in a novel that is defined by passionate and affective attachments.[2] The abundance of images, of juxtaposed time frames and otherworldly realities, makes *La amortajada* the epitome of the literary depiction of female unfulfilled desire and contained passion.[3] Through a fantastic turn, in the narrative present the senses of the "shrouded woman" are alive, as she can feel and see everything and everyone around her on the day of her wake. Ana María even feels pale and beautiful, as if time has not left the marks of age on her body. She also experiences the youth that the nameless protagonist of *La última niebla* desired as an assertion of being alive.

Feminine subjectivity is expressed as a kind of constitutive lack in Bombal's work that reveals the ideal as the (masculine) standard against which the sexuated subject is measured. From a Lacanian psychoanalytic stance, this lack appears to determine the formation of the subject through the abandonment of the real and the entrance to the symbolic realm. In the specific case of women, Collete Soler explains that everything can be said from the point of view of "being for the Other," but her "own being" remains foreclosed from discourse. Furthermore, the ability to "make [the Other] desire," which is characteristic of females in the symbolization of the sexual market as we know it, is enacted in the form of masquerade, adjusting to the Other's demands.[4] Thus, women in heterosexual relationships engage in a game in which they embody the Other's desire, seeming the phallus and the ideal images that are constructed by male fantasies. Bombal's female characters poignantly display the conflicts that the process of sexuation entails for women in patriarchal cultures.

The world of the hacienda and its traditions appear as places of domination where the oligarchy consumes itself in a gender polarization that vitiates self and life. In this rural context, symbolic models are established within a binary system of opposites in which the primacy of the male is asserted through the possession of land and women. The historian José Bengoa has addressed the evident interrelationship between the idea of the state in Chile and masculinity and their connection to power as force and domination.[5] From a sociological perspective, Pierre Bourdieu has lucidly discussed that the predominance of the male and masculine symbolizations in patriarchal cultures parallels the devaluation of the female and feminine images and values in a system of hierarchical oppositions.[6]

Bombal fuses fantasy and social criticism in this work, anticipating in the late 1930s much of what would later be called magic realism and would achieve worldwide recognition in the "Boom."[7] Her writing not only breaks with the previous literary tradition of regionalism, but, more importantly, undermines the paradigm of fixed and objective meanings of reality. The use of uncertainty, ambiguity, and numerous perspectives underscores the fracturing of modernity as the only foundational Latin American cultural and sociopolitical project. By inscribing unconscious and subconscious operations, Bombal decenters hegemonic cultural and literary discourses.[8] In a shroud, Ana María voices a failed life based on a contractual identity. Her rage and memory reveal the remains of a femininity sacrificed to modern reason (to capital) that is represented in the economic unit that comprises the hacienda and the marriage vows.

Through a disembodied conscience, Ana María tells the "muerte de los vivos" (the death of the living), as her life story and its end reveal. Her denunciation and complaint inscribe the female gender condition as an experience of alterity lived in hostile and negative terms that may only be resolved in the idealized image of the lady. In this way, the protagonist inverts the marriage contract (and herself as subordinate) and escapes her definition as subject of the law (civil and religious) through what I will call courtly love. This arrangement provides Ana María with a dominant position in relation to the male subordinate (her friend and courtier, Fernando), whom she despises yet keeps under her control. This love rhetoric and practice based on the impossibility of sexual consummation and possession with Fernando work to supplement the spousal model with Antonio. The process of making love the central axis of her life turns Ana María to one of the first cultural exaltations and idealizations of Western romantic love as it is expressed in courtly love. In this medieval and courtly tradition, we find a whole code of rules that organize the ritual of love between a lady and her courtier. For Denis de Rougemont in his book *Love in the Western World* (1983), this is one of the first perversions of religion since passionate love and sexual desire are given spiritual transcendence. More significantly, de Rougemont claims that language is equivocal since it "betrays what it wishes to say without saying it."[9] Thus the social function of the myth of courtly love is veiled while providing a manifestation for what no longer may be said. This contradiction proper to passionate love in its courtly form constitutes then, according to Jonathan Dollimore following de Rougemont, the dynamic of death/desire that shapes modernity and its flaws.[10] In the development of Western love, not only does passionate love become a substitute for religion as de Rougemont argues, but subjectivity suffers the effects of perversions brought about by modern contractual relations and identities.

The inversion of the traditional coming-of-age narrative is evident in the protagonist's passage from childhood to adulthood and the role of the father/daughter relationship. María Inés Lagos shows in her book *En tono mayor: Relatos de formación de la protagonista femenina en Hispanoamérica* (1994) that in several Latin American novels written by women authors the coming-of-age story unfolds a process of female stunting. Like Bombal's characters these protagonists are conscious of the gender norms and the price paid for rejecting them. Similarly, instead of having their dreams realized, for women of the elite the entrance into adulthood proves to be governed by their family and religious education. Both social institutions limit women's independence, disabling them from making personal decisions and living up to their expectations.[11]

From childhood onward, Ana María naturalizes a contractual relation between genders through negation of the self and differentiated and hierarchical gender roles. Masculinity is embodied in a distant and cold father who is incapable of emotional involvement, teaching Ana María the contract that she will sign as a wife and later invert in her relation with her confidant and admirer, Fernando. Through the father's distance, Ana María comes face to face with the coldness of the patriarchal oligarch, the man of power who is characterized by affective withdrawal.

Distance and emotional detachment show the protagonist of *La amortajada* the way to have control over the other as self-affirmation. Thus, becoming an adult woman is equated with learning how to contain emotions and feelings in order to protect the self against disappointment and rejection. As a consequence, Ana María experiences the world as conflicting opposites in which gender becomes an absolute and antagonistic determinant of reality. Men, such as her father, are characterized as being cold and inaccessible in their intimacy. The relationship with a cold father marks and shapes Ana María's relationships with other males and the way bonds are nurtured and perverted.

From a psychoanalytic feminist perspective, Jessica Benjamin has underlined how the fantasy of the homoerotic bond of the girl to the father is condemned to becoming female masochism, subject to envy and submission while always being a deferred object for both. Female masochism for Benjamin is related to the female desire of being like the all-powerful father and being recognized by him as similar.[12] In the case of Ana María, the lady she acts out allows her to take the inaccessible place of the father, and with that, a portion of power over others, making herself unreachable to masculine power. The fact that Bombal's female characters do not have mothers and that they have detached relationships with authoritarian fathers makes the fear of destruction of the self an ongoing issue in their lives. A possible explanation for the absence of the mother in Bombal's narratives is the complex cultural shift that took place in Western culture during medieval times. With the emergence of the courtly love rhetoric and practice the church felt the need to halt the mystification of love because it substituted God for the lady.

As de Rougemont points out, the worship of the Virgin is incorporated as a master religious narrative of the church from then onward. This may also explain the mutual influence in terms of language and the fact that the "vocabulary of courtship" resembles that of devotion.[13] As a result the social foundation of society, family through the marriage contract, legalized a perverted and unique fact that is the death of woman, understood as sexual mate, and the birth of the wife, understood as a sacred lady-mother. Perhaps the anxiety of male castration was felt by the church authorities with the decline of the cult of God and in the secular realm by husbands who reproduce the same model through marriage. This new cultural arrangement pervades the discourse of Catholic modernity in Latin America, where the paradox may be seen time and again.

Robert Tobin explains that the submissive perversion toward the other is proper to masochism and that it places submission in front of the dominant discourse. This exposure of the hegemonic narrative and what it hides makes masochism reveal that submission is not natural but rather is both an effect of symbolization and a discursive construction.[14]

Female self-effacement is reiterated and radicalized in Ana María's shrouded state since her consciousness exists somewhere between life and death, inside a coffin. Visual and sensory images predominate over introspection, underscoring the use of vision and hearing as vehicles of consciousness.[15] Consequently, the world of the senses and perception expands beyond human constraints and those imposed by wifehood. Ana María has had to die biologically to be able to reflect and have authority in the process of self-awareness. Walter Benjamin discusses the relationship between death and storytelling and shows how the former "is the sanction of everything that the storyteller can tell."[16] Narration in medieval times was for Benjamin "born from the pathos of an ultimate exchange between the dying and the living" where the dying man evoked his memories.[17] As does Benjamin's storyteller, Ana María narrates her past life and the trauma of the violence she experienced, which she can only put into discourse when she dies biologically. She spent almost thirty years in silence, finally to be able to tell her story from her deathbed. And as a storyteller, she juxtaposes death and birth as experiences determined by the process of silencing and telling the story.[18] Following Benjamin's take on history, Ana María's story is characterized by discontinuity and resembles the history of the oppressed. Moreover, her trauma remains a private matter, as in most of Bombal's characters, that cannot be exchanged or symbolized collectively, paralleling the traumatic experience of soldiers of the First World War, as described by Benjamin. When they returned, public discourse was dominated by commercialization and information dissemination, changing forever the role of language.[19] Thus silence as a manifestation of trauma is key in understanding the change that takes place in Ana María's account and, therefore, in her subjectivity.

In Bombal's novel, the afterlife provides her protagonist with the opportunity to examine her life for the first time. From a cosmic perspective, Ana María views her present, past, and future life through selective cinematic frames in which resentment, frustration, and suffering predominate. Through a mystical journey after her physical death, Ana María's consciousness reconstructs and reexperiences her life as a montage of interrelated images and motifs.[20]

First- and third-person narrative voices conflate to tell Ana María's story from the omnipresent viewpoint conferred by the end of life. Walter Benjamin argues that the thought of death declines during modernity, together with a diminished communicability of experience after the atrocities of the two world wars. Bombal's narrative discourse seems to question the course of modernity by linking storytelling and death in her protagonist's dramatic biographical retrospective. Ana María progressively comes to understand the meaning of life, which death discloses. As readers, we share the experience of her death and the character's fate.[21] In this hybrid novel, storytelling, denunciation, the fantastic, and mysticism unite to reveal the sterility of Ana María's passionate and dramatic existence. Furthermore, a melodramatic mode defines the conflict in *La amortajada* that depicts the protagonist's inner plight and the ways she relates to others, particularly men. Peter Brooks has suggested that the melodramatic mode is related to an "inner drama of consciousness" and the way it shapes life choices.[22] Expression and intensity of feelings, coupled with an "impulse toward dramatization" and "acting out," characterize the melodrama, according to Brooks. Its semantic field is linked to excess and the force of desire.[23] Ana María, as do most female characters in Bombal's work, suffers because of the absence of love and an erotic object around which she can center her life. The compromises she makes and the love contracts she accepts unleash and heighten her emotions, as well as show her theatrical resources.

When asked about the social content of her novels, Bombal asserted her interest in "sentimental drama" and her passion for the personal, the internal, the heart, art, and nature."[24] Her novels reveal heightened passions and how they define subjectivities in which gender equates to a biological destiny. Because of these traits, *La amortajada* may be read as a sequel to *La última niebla,* where the passionate subject is still unable to understand and ultimately accept her gendered condition. Her battle against an intolerable reality continues, without immediate respite or the promised rest of the Christian afterlife. Ana María's defiance of the established gender laws represents an individual outcry against the patriarchal relationships that oppress her. The impact of sexist cultural values and institutions such as the *Patria Potestad* plays a decisive role in the construction of gender identity and the development of female identity in Latin American culture, particularly in the case of Chile.[25] Social values and civil status, in Ana María's case, press her into accepting her role as a bourgeois wife despite her husband's affairs. Nevertheless, her untimely death may be interpreted as her rejection of a diminished identity and position. Naomi Lindstrom has said that the protagonist's decreasing power to perceive and articulate her experience as an adult dramatically contrasts with her rebellion and insights as an adolescent. Her resistance is systematically curbed and ultimately tamed by a sentimental rhetoric and the rigid conventions of the oligarchy. Being a wife in this context represents acquiescence to a limited identity and subordinate position. Thus Ana María learns to live within the established order of marriage, despite persistently feeling out of control, as her memories reiterate.[26]

Through diverse forms of identification and rejection, Ana María is constituted into a subject constantly resisting gender domination from the landowner (her father and her husband). Exclusion and the impossibility of recognition constitute gender difference as emptiness and death that the figure of the shrouded woman expresses in a radical fashion. The day of her funeral, Ana María is contemplated as a dead woman, recognized and seen by others as a still and inert body, a kind of wax figure who resembles a virgin. At her funeral, Fernando reiterates her condition of "estatua de cera" (a wax statue) of a female body that is "lívido y remoto, cuya carne parece hecha de otro material que la de ellos" (139) (livid and remote, whose flesh seems made of a substance different than theirs) (215).[27] In the narrative, a woman without love is a dead woman, just as the presence of death remained with the narrator of *La última niebla,* as María Luisa Bastos points out.[28]

The social order is questioned from the outset with an afterlife perspective that focuses on Ana María's intimate relations with men. Ricardo, Antonio, and Fernando form the triangular structure that reveals different and problematic aspects of the protagonist's experience. Ana María adapts her passion to "a mediocre love," learning to restrain herself with her husband and her children, as Soledad Bianchi notes.[29] To her dismay, Ana María senses that everyone holds in and stifles feelings. As she grows older, passions constitute the axis around which her relationships to others turn. They deeply mold her own development and movement, which are reduced to what her husband, confidant, and children dictate.[30]

The sense of personal inadequacy and the negative attachments that the protagonist develops set the stage for her inner conflict and resentment. According to the melodramatic discourse that informs the novel, women like Ana María are emotionally victimized in the web of gender relations. Her entire life has been defined and centered on a man. With the shroud she still feels her emotional world, reliving the agony of being rejected and abandoned again and again by the men with whom she was in love. The romantic heroine found in the *folletín,* or sentimental melodrama, is the predecessor of Bombal's females and their search for love, as Lucía Guerra argues.[31] Their emotionalism works as a form of complicity with the reader, who is able to identify with their drama.[32] It also highlights erotic passion as the only significant reality, blurring the dichotomies of social and cultural systems. For Bombal's women characters, love is the purest and truest form of self-recognition. Most significant is the need to be loved in a "total" and "eternal" way.

The need for an absolute here is at home with a conservative view of society and its institutions. Agata Gligo notes these contradictions in Bombal and relates them to being both old-fashioned and modern, caught between two periods without being aware of it.[33] Similarly, the characters aspire to find in marriage evidence of the stability and permanence they seek. The absence of love, therefore, leads fatefully to suicide or death in an order where power is expressed as domination.[34] Marriage in this context is a reproductive and constraining institution that supports heterosexuality and a cultural ideal that binds nation with gender and sexual imperatives.

In Bombal's writing, female characters withdraw as a reaction to the external world, where they feel powerless. Although the social dimension is kept in the background of the novels, it is interwoven with the protagonists' emotional world through the impact of marriage. Thus the position of women becomes the focus of Bombal's works and their most remarkable element precisely because marriage is "the central issue of their [women's] lives." But instead of directly criticizing the social structure, as Ian Adams argues, Bombal focuses on how it is experienced by women, and how their feelings, reactions, and dreams are intricately related to their lack of power. This leaves them emotionally helpless without a satisfactory resolution to their situation, as opposed to men, who have choices and become "an external alienating force" for women. An oppressive conventionality and a limited social world shape female disempowerment.[35]

In *La última niebla* and *La amortajada,* the protagonists have been defined by sentimental memory and what Brownmiller calls "the secrets of the heart."[36] The heart is one of the greatest symbols of feminine vulnerability and sentimentality. Gender demands that a woman devote her life to maternal, romantic, religious, or other forms of love and care for others. The loss of love or its absence is what guides these characters, leading them to a final sense of truth. Passion is lived as an absolute power that dramatically changes being and sustains life. In this respect, the writer seems to attribute to passionate love the same qualities that Breton gave to "l'amour fou" (foolish love)[37] and "le point supreme," (ecstacy) an energy that transforms the lover in radical ways by affirming the self. For the narrator of *La última niebla,* passion occurs in a timeless dimension, outside human chronology. Love blurs the distinctions between the sacred and the profane, and it makes sense only in terms of its existence. The anonymous protagonist lives submerged in her sentimental existence, where she experiences the outer world in an uninvolved way.[38] Remembered and imagined time encompass most of *La amortajada* as well as a narrative present that is only a day and a half, the span of time between Ana María's wake and her funeral.[39]

Bombal's textual retreat to a closed and private subjectivity is related to her critique of a desacralized world that has lost meaning and cohesiveness. Her protagonists resist an aggressive outer world that appears to be governed by self-propelled and destructive forces. In their interiority, women find refuge from an overwhelming sense of pain and desire that is defined as eminently feminine. This allows them to evade reality and fulfill the longing for the perfect man through numerous imaginative and theatrical strategies.

In many ways, Bombal shows an essentialist understanding of gender differences when she attributes love and self-sacrifice to women and cold intellect to men. In an interview with Marjorie Agosín in 1977 she said:

> no creo que los derechos sociales reconocidos oficialmente en la actualidad a la mujer puedan hacer cambiar lo íntimo de su naturaleza. Creo que somos y seguiremos siendo la mujer eterna. La idealista, sacrificada, ávida ante todo de dar y recibir amor.

> [I do not believe that the social rights now being granted to women officially can change their basic nature. I believe we are, and will continue to be, the eternal woman: idealistic, sensitive, self-sacrificing woman, eager above all to love and be loved.][40]

This dichotomous gender paradigm is also evident in the characters' experience of love. The ability to feel or not feel love is at the core of opposing gender identities, thoughts, and values within an essentialist framework that attributes innate gender qualities to the sexes. The fact that conventions are lived as natural demonstrates Ana María's limited situation and awareness. In discussing Bombal Adriana Valdés has called attention to the fact that her characters do not think through what they feel. Connecting feelings and reflection with other alternatives available does not take place.[41] Ana María lacks the means to reflect on reality, her sense of emptiness, and her fear of change.[42] This explains that she has to die to be able to think about her existence and analyze it with perspective.

Notions of femininity and masculinity derive from the dominant values of the period that conceptualized woman as "pure heart," the giver of love and peace to the public man.[43] There is, however, a critique of the institutions that shape private life and female identity. The private realm and the experiences of these "problematic heroines," as Guerra calls them,[44] are marked by negativity and oppression. According to Bombal's literary discourse, the male other undermines not only the autonomy but also the constitution of the female self. Even though Ana María dwells among and needs others, she is constantly disrupted and frustrated by them. Conflict thus governs this disjointed female subject, who anticipates the existence of a permanently decentered self whose life is in flux and whose identity becomes lost in the process.

Ana María's complaint about the difference between men and women echoes Bombal's previous statement quoted earlier and the destructiveness of patriarchal sexual arrangements from a gender perspective. Ana María experiences gender identity as opposed and inferior to masculinity when she asks:

> ¿Por qué, por qué la naturaleza de la mujer ha de ser tal que tenga que ser siempre un hombre el eje de su vida?
> Los hombres, ellos, logran poner pasión en otras cosas. Pero el destino de las mujeres es remover una pena de amor en una casa ordenada, ante una tapicería inconclusa. (142)

> [Why, why is the nature of woman such that she must always revolve around a man?
> Men are able to put their hearts in other things. But the destiny of women is to turn over and over some love sorrow while sitting in a neatly ordered house, facing an unfinished tapestry.][45]

Ana María echoes Bombal's claims for gender differences as biologically rather than culturally and socially constructed. Having a proper female destiny means an inescapable loss of identity in exchange for the social and economic security of marriage. Thus death—both literal and symbolic—becomes the only alternative to escape frustration and disappointment. Ricardo Gutiérrez Mouat has suggested that Ana María's passion resembles a Christ-like passion in which she suffers and dies for love.[46] Ana María claims a sacrificial erotic passion, thereby symbolically redeeming women for their passive suffering. It is no surprise then that she should make her husband "lord and master"of her death in a metonymic displacement and comment on her own life as a wife. In death she finds the answers to her questions and doubts, achieving understanding and self-acceptance through the disintegration of her body and identity. Death in the end becomes a resurrection of sorts as Ana María fuses into a kind of intercourse with the earth, as Gutiérrez Mouat suggests.[47]

The dominant themes in the novel are pain and death, enacted in Ana María's body, and melodramatic sensibility. Her sickly condition, as for the main character of La última niebla, works to justify her past seclusion within the home and her abstention from worldly pursuits. For both women the figure of a man represents the ultimate reason for a search that is essentially erotic.

Love, upon which foundational marriages were contracted in the nineteenth century, as Doris Sommer has explained, is here substituted with a contract in which female identity oscillates between masochism and sadism.[48] In the specific case of Chilean culture, the Virgin Mother also represents an ideal, as Sonia Montecino argues in her, *Madres y huachos: Alegorías del mestizaje chileno* (*Mothers and Huachos: Allegories of the Chilean Mestizaje* [1991]), the virginal mater is the cultural ideal embodying the mother of all Chileans and the people. This Magna Mater is a power unto itself rather than an advocate between humans and God; she incarnates maternal power over the creatures she has engendered.[49] In this way, the cultural myth shapes maternal ideology and female identity, providing women not only with an expectation but also with a validated social place and experience.

Males in this paradigm are defined by arrogance and sexual aggression. As most of Bombal's stories show, men's attraction to women is perverted by domination and possession. Ana María's confidant and silent admirer, Fernando, demonstrates his submission to an arrangement wherein resentment and humiliation are central. Their relationship seems to suggest that heterosexual relationships, with or without intimacy, end in perversion. More significant is that sexual attraction and desire inevitably trigger negative feelings and responses that range from emotional numbness to outright aggression toward women.

The highly theatrical sense of masochism is seen in its tendency to a mise-en-scène in which desire perverts the rules of a conventional romantic love. Masochism uses submission and weakness to sustain while subverting the structures of daily power, as Tobin states.[50] Ambivalence and opposition of feelings are essential in the emotional repertoire of this identity. Within this tendency we can understand Ana María's behavior in front of her husband and her admirer. Distance and aggression are constitutive of the relationship with the husband. With Antonio, Ana María shifts between resentment and withdrawal, as well as heated arguments and tears. With Fernando, she reactualizes the emotional distance of her father while she reveals Antonio's infidelities. Antonio, Fernando, and the father seem to share the same arrogance toward and distance from women, following closely patriarchal ideology and its cult of virility through its Latin American version of *machismo*. Lorna Williams notes that Ana María becomes aware of the disparity between her expectations and marriage the very day of her wedding.[51] Threats to individuality and self-development are central to Bombal's characters and their sense of a gendered identity that is progressively stifled within the institution of marriage and patriarchal models of femininity and masculinity.

For Ana María, inviolability is constitutive of masculinity, a feature she appropriates and that witnessing her husband's aging questions for the first time: "Como un resorte que se quiebra, como una energía que ha perdido su objeto cae en ella el impulso implacable de morder" (158) (Like a spring that snaps, as a force that had kept her implacable and venomous") (229).

Her marriage to Antonio as a result of her father's negotiation proves to the daughter the rigor of the sexual contract and the lack of recognition of the female subject, who becomes a role. In her essay "Commodities amongst Themselves," Luce Irigaray points out that women, like signs, currency, and commodities, are exchanges among males in patriarchal societies. She further adds that the sociocultural order itself requires a homosexual organizing principle and that heterosexuality is basically the "assignment of economic roles." Men in this regime are the producer subjects and agents of exchange, whereas females as well as the earth are commodities.[52] Bombal shows the value of females as commodities particularly through arranged marriages, as in the cases of Ana María and Brígida in "El árbol." Both women are married off to men chosen by their fathers without ever being asked their own feelings. In this way, the business transaction takes place according to male prerogatives establishing a social and economic order in which females have no place as subjects.

Once married, Ana María performs her role and duties as a wife and mother according to the law. The two failed attempts to free herself from the marriage testify to the impossibility of constituting herself outside the cultural mandate and show the alternative of courtly love as the only way out. The relationship with Fernando while the protagonist is married represents the inversion of the marriage arrangement through a parallel relationship. Her renunciation of the body's pleasure and the rejection of masculine power are pivotal to the exertion of a female power identified with the hegemonic model. Fearing being abandoned and betrayed, Ana María identifies herself with the figure of the unreachable lady who is respected and admired for her extreme sexual indifference and aloofness. Thus, self-denial becomes central to the constitution of the lady's power over the distant admiration of her devoted servant. Love here resembles warfare language, as de Rougemont claims in regards to courtly love, in that life is analogous to passion for death and shares many of its qualities and strategies. The lover is expected to *besiege the lady, deliver amorous assaults, press her, take her by surprise,* and *overcome her modesty.*[53]

The love triangle in the protagonist's sentimental life that the bond with Fernando introduces to her married life shows the relevance of courtly love within heterosexuality and the ways it becomes a sadomasochistic arrangement. The origin of this idealized rhetoric on love defines erotic experience between desire and containment, making love sensual and self-disciplining as well as humiliating and exalting. In this love convention the male becomes the lady's idolizer always available and trying to win and please her. Interestingly, the language of piety is transferred into the conventions of courtly love, making the lady an ennobling spiritual force that in many ways resembles the Virgin Mary.

Ana María becomes the lady who stipulates the rules through her rejection of and indifference toward her admirer, embodying the inaccessible object of sublimation in the purest sense. In his *The Metastases of Enjoyment: Six Essays about Woman and Causality* (1994), Slavoj Žižek points out that the obstacle of courtly love centers around the impediment of physical contact that makes the lady unreachable and shows that this love will never be consummated. In *La amortajada,* the woman scripts male actions, providing norms and prohibitions for his position as a vassal to the idealized figure she performs.

The mise-en-scène of this feminine inaccessibility of courtly love is provided within the masochistic transaction that is required so that desire is deferred. Enjoyment and renunciation are essential elements in this amorous theater of the genders in which sexual identities are thought to be binary and absolute. The mutual dependency of the subject and the other that cannot be controlled is resolved here through subordination, making the other recognize without being himself recognized. The inability of the subject to accept dependency in relation to the other is transformed into domination. The desire for autonomy and recognition is thus resolved in the fantasy of erotic (sadomasochistic) domination through the master/mistress-and-slave paradigm. In the novel, this is expressed in the figures of the lady and the lover. Ana María's relationship to Fernando shows the fantasy of domination in which she controls the other according to her enjoyment, in the Lacanian sense, keeping physical distance as the insurmountable obstacle. Passion here conceals a longing for death in which suffering and obstruction elevate the object of love to a higher and idealized form. Furthermore, in the "feudalization of love" that courtly love reveals according to C. S. Lewis, we find a hierarchy in which there are a superior lady who grants rewards as well as a morality in which renunciation and deliberate obstacles are essential.[54]

The dichotomy enforced by *machismo* and class distinction confines emotions not only to the private domain but also to femininity. Men in the oligarchy appear devoid of emotional depth and driven by futile external goals. As critics have noted, they are figures that remain indistinct and nebulous in the majority of Bombal's texts.[55] Their purpose seems to be to frame the narrative and the elusive nature of the feminine.

Surprisingly, despite the impact of patriarchal and Catholic ideology, motherhood is not central in Ana María's life. Her three children surface only in relationship to some aspect of herself rather than for their own sake. The experience of maternity rather remains tangential to Ana María's self-identity, which is shaped primarily in relation to heterosexual bonds and the power they allow or disallow.

Within their social context, Bombal's characters are educated into being marriageable to men who provide them with an identity and support for life. The protagonists' inner conflict in *La última niebla* and *La amortajada* is to a large extent the result of discrepancies between desire and social demands. As in other Latin American novels written by women writers, the development of a heroine's childhood, adolescence, and married life is the focus of the story.[56] Bombal's works in general belong to a kind of narrative that depicts the conflicts of growing up female in a society where women are subordinated. Alongside Ana María stand the nameless narrator, Brígida from "El árbol," Yolanda from "Las islas nuevas" (1939) ("The New Islands"), and María Griselda from "La historia de María Griselda" (1946) ("The Story of Maria Griselda"), all of whom share the problematic and distressing process of becoming women through marriageability. Marriage represents the most significant rite of passage and works as a kind of masquerade in which the father passes the daughter to the husband, arranging it as an economic transaction. In this order, women's social success or failure is determined to a large degree by their ability to be wives, the only identity that provides them with legitimacy. María Inés Lagos, in her discussion of Latin American women's fiction, highlights that the masculine process of learning independence and autonomy portrayed in the

Bildungsroman is absent in the novel of development written by women authors. The major difference between women's fiction of development and men's is that learning in the latter is depicted as gradual. In contrast, in women's fiction female characters grow through sudden awakenings at different intervals. This may explain why Bombal's protagonists realize fundamental truths about themselves and others in unexpected ways that resemble epiphanies. Understanding and self-understanding in particular are a sudden phenomena that tend to take place as a transformative illumination of consciousness.[57]

Most relevant is the fact that females are excluded from taking an active role in public and national affairs. *La última niebla,* as we have seen, focuses on how the narrator comes to terms with a failed marriage and an invented romance. In a similar way, Ana María and Brígida confront the reality of marriage and a meaningless life. Brígida, however, stands as the only character in Bombal's literary repertory who completely turns around the discourse that has excluded and numbed her by leaving her husband and beginning anew. Paradoxically, according to social and gender expectations the silliest and laziest of all the women characters in the author's narrative, Brígida, becomes the only one capable of breaking the marriage contract and actively questioning the patriarchal model of female identity within it.

RICARDO

Rainfall announces the return of old love memories with Ricardo's arrival at Ana Maria's wake. He evokes the happiness of summers in the countryside, of childhood and adolescence. Ana María's long braids are loose while taking horseback rides with him, emphasizing her freedom and sensuality. The image of hair here metaphorizes the discovery of female sexuality (107). Falling in love soon gives way, however, to feelings of torture. Ana María oscillates between intense desire and the pain of not being loved enough. The attraction to a sexual object that does not reciprocate engenders the first signs of passion for men who are indifferent or do not respond. The character's subjectivity is thus determined by a masochistic perversion where pain is interconnected to desire in a cultural system that admires female suffering. Freud and others have noted the relationship between women's masochism and their suffering in a patriarchal culture. More recently, from a psychoanalytic perspective, Otto Kernberg

argues that masochism "is centered on motivated self-destruc-
tiveness and a conscious or unconscious pleasure in suffering."[58]

Masochistic rituals evidence relations of power and their arbi-
trariness through a theatricality that is played out in the "appearance of subordination." In this light, women's masochism
shows itself as the imitation of male-male power struggles, the
bonding that constitutes the basic structure of domination and
patriarchal society.[59] Women's masochistic theatricality may be
subversive, however, in that it suggests that power in interpersonal, private, and sexual relationships is arbitrary and can be
manipulated, as Tobin asserts.[60] The slave/master dynamics inherent in masochism disclose pleasure through submission as
well as the fictional and polyvalent nature of perversion.[61] Hence,
the "pretended pretense of powerlessness reflects what it undermines," namely, that power is what is being displayed in a highly
aestheticized scene.[62] Francine Masiello's discussion of melodrama "as a way to insist on the perversity of gender relations
and the crisis of individual subjectivities" is especially pertinent
in this context.[63] Ana María spends her life chasing the wrong
men, becoming infuriated by their abandonment or rebuff, experiencing endless disappointment and self-doubt. Ricardo's unexpected desertion turns him into her enslaving torturer. She
becomes his victim, whose only desire is to die when he leaves, as
her suicide attempt further reveals. Again she is enraged at the
realization of how she gave herself to him, how much she loved
him, and the fact that she became pregnant. She also recalls her
abortion[64] and her obsessive need to understand why he had left
her. His behavior remains an enigma she cannot resolve or accept.

Ana María's transgression in her first love relationship is twofold. First, she has sex without being married, disobeying the sexual taboo imposed on single women by Catholic ideology and the
cultural myth of virginity. Second, she has a miscarriage that
seems to be induced, representing an even greater social and
moral transgression. Textualizing this experience represents a
literary challenge, on the one hand, and a questioning of sexual
morality and reproductive rights, on the other.[65] Unfortunately,
these transgressions remain invisible to Ana María in a memory
marked by a sense of rejection and humiliation (107–8). At the
end, she asks herself why one has to die to understand a man's
love, confirming Ricardo's feelings for her and the fact that he
had not forgotten her.

FERNANDO

As Fernando makes his entrance, Ana María hears his voice. He blames her for having hurt and avoided him for years. Amid complaints and resentment, he declares his unrequited love for the shrouded woman. From his viewpoint, we find that he has been the recipient of Ana María's disappointment and rage. In Ana María's most perverse relationship, Fernando is the source of both repulsion and attraction. She could not tolerate his intimacy and the fact that he felt her equal (127). They victimized one another in a relation where pain was equated with pleasure. Fernando subjected himself to her repeated abuse and aloofness, knowing that she would ultimately come around to reveal her secrets.

In this sadomasochistic attraction, sexual pleasure is deferred and transferred to the realm of language. Ana María opens herself to Fernando and voices endless marital complaints. As we enter his perspective, the masochistic arrangement establishes him as the listener (servant) whose presence grants recognition to the lady (mistress). This scenario shows that power and meaning are not stable nor always in the hands of the culturally dominant subject. The theatrical nature of this pact, where power is control, is best illustrated by the reversal of pain and pleasure, as Victor Taylor argues.[66] He also comments on the contractual nature of masochism and underscores suspension and deferral of objective reality in favor of subjectivity and its internal meaning.[67]

Ana María's pleasure arises from containing Fernando and keeping herself unreachable. The subtext of courtly love may be seen here in the lady's idealized image and the chivalrous lover who admires from the distance granted. The parodying of religion implicit in the courtly etiquette shows that love is understood as a higher sentiment, forever pursued and never attained, to which even life should be sacrificed, as Lewis argues.[68] As he speaks to himself, recalling their virtual affair, Fernando recognizes his own selfishness, envy, and inability to support Ana María emotionally (129). In his case, wounded pride made him unable to express the love he felt for her in positive ways. Despite his dissatisfaction, Ana María nevertheless kept up the relationship for years, using it as a buffer for her marriage. Her rejection of change and the fact that relationships are subject to it allowed her never to break away from Fernando. This virtual adultery and its implications, however, never enter Ana María's awareness, as she is blinded by her need to have a confidant and an unconditional admirer. Their relationship is governed by a system of rules from which care and reciprocity are absent. Naomi Lindstrom has shown that in this attachment Ana María resembles the classical adulteress, who tries to make up for the lack of communication in marriage by breaking the loyalty pact that convention demands.[69] The perversion of love results in resentment and degradation as the memories of both characters unfold. Ana María hated Fernando's desire for her yet felt pleased by his undemanding tribute (137). Her death, on the other hand, relieves him of the anxiety that her "llamado de una mujer ociosa" (call of an idle woman) produced in him (139). With these harsh words about the woman he presumably loved for so long, Fernando's negative attachment ends.

ANTONIO

The most significant fact in Ana María's life is that Antonio is chosen by her father as her husband right after Ricardo has left her. The daughter's feelings about marrying are never solicited. However, Ana María, though still in love with Ricardo, marries Antonio in accordance with her father's command. Her obedience to patriarchal law underscores her disempowered position in a sexual arrangement established between the father and the husband-to-be.

Ana María is transformed into an erotic object whose gender position facilitates the masochistic play of passivity and self-inflicted punishment. Female sexuality and identity appear to be conditioned by the power relation that spawns them. Judith Butler's theory of subjection and subjectification helps us here in understanding the process of identity formation and its intricate link to power. For Butler, the strategies and performances that subjectivity implies are spawned by power in a process that oscillates between resistance and subordination.[70] Our position as subjects of discourse is negotiated in these opposing venues within power structures that determine us while providing discursive identity positions in an ongoing and open movement.

As wife, Ana María experiences sexual pleasure for the first time in a dissociated way, as her romantic feelings are split. The struggle between her feelings and sexuality is polarized to the point that Ana María leaves Antonio to go back to the parental house. She escapes her husband in order to deny her own transformation into a sexual subject, holding on to her past as daughter. Romantic memories and fantasies conflict and arrest Ana María's becoming a wife while being sexual. Antonio's erotic desire is met with her passivity, in which pleasure and shame join (143). She is unable to recognize her own body, which is experienced as alien and in disguise under her new dresses, which metaphorize her identity as a wife (146). The clothing metaphor reveals the process of self-transformation that marriage entails and the protagonist's rejection of the concrete ways in which it affects her by experiencing her body sexually.

Her marriage to Antonio changes Ana María to the point that she feels dead. This fearful and life-threatening experience is poignantly expressed in the pond episode, when she says in terror:—"El fin del mundo. Así ha de ser. Lo he visto." (144) ("The end of the world. It must be like that. I have seen it") (219); metaphorically she is referring to her experience as a newlywed and to sexual pleasure. Susana Munnich argues that this is a very frightening experience for the narrator, who experiences this particular change as the void and horror of becoming invisible.[71] Antonio's words, implying that her image can be put back together, make no sense to Ana María, who remains terrified by the fragmentation and absence of her self-image while looking at herself in the water. Here, as in *La última niebla,* water is inextricably linked with female identity and sexuality. In Ana María's case, however, rather than providing a sensual and autoerotic experience, water returns the pieces of a shattered self. Ana María can only see her image as broken fragments, an experience that becoming a wife has revealed to her. The lack of intersubjective connection in the marriage, from the protagonist's view, may be understood as "the breakdown of the tension between affirmation of the self and recognition of the other, from a psychoanalytic perspective."[72] Instead of sharing and mutuality with Antonio, she experiences oppression and separateness. As in this instance, identification with the other in Bombal's texts happens as a dual unity where the self is represented as a need and the other as the answer. In the characters' experience there is no being with the other as a continual and evolving awareness of difference and a sense of intimacy.[73]

The protagonists in *La última niebla* and *La amortajada* experience marriage through their husbands as threats to psychic survival. How they live in their bodies is also linked to this hostile other, who, rather than affirming them as subjects, turns them into passive objects (for sexual pleasure and social status). Antonio's progressive detachment defines his power over the unsatisfied wife, who becomes a "tolerable" but inescapable presence in his life (152). Watching him kick her slipper, unaware that she sees him, reveals for Ana María his true feelings. From here on, she withdraws, limiting and measuring her relationship with him. The range of emotions she displays in order to regain Antonio's affection range from tenderness to muteness to harassment. However, all this energy is met with her husband's avoidance or feigned ignorance. Once she left him the first time, his behavior changed as well as their positions in the relationship. He stopped being the passionate husband of the beginning and instead withheld his feelings, remaining detached and later unfaithful.

Married life engenders disappointment and jealousy in a cycle of perversions. Antonio's emotional negligence feeds Ana María's resentment to the point of rejecting and denying her own pleasure and sexual intimacy with him. The narrator of *La última niebla* shows a similar rejection of erotic interaction with her husband in which sexual intercourse with him makes her feel humiliated. Both women devalue intercourse, in spite of the pleasure they experience, as a revenge of sorts against husbands who are perceived as uncaring and unloving.

In *La amortajada,* jealousy is what breeds insecurity and doubt and an obsession with interpretation for Ana María. Antonio becomes the source of multiple and equivocal signs that Ana María attempts to decipher. In this instance, knowledge is the result of a violence that mobilizes the unconscious and what is involuntary, as Gilles Deleuze shows in his study of jealousy.[74] Ana María feels betrayed and denigrated as she learns of her husband's multiple infidelities. Her failed attempt to put an end to their marriage reveals the extent to which social convention determines female dependency and subjectivity. The intense hostility that shapes the relationship between the spouses is finally accepted as integral to the marital contract that secures Ana María's economic and social status as the landowner's wife. The lawyer's cynical advice emphasizes the constraints due to gender and class position imposed on the wife. As a lady, Ana María cannot behave in a way that is beneath her and should disregard her husband's affairs in order to show her moral superiority (155). This demands that she occupy the semidivine place of the Virgin Mother and become untouchable also for him. In this way, she accommodates herself by resorting to periods of extreme aloofness and others of brief passionate encounters with Antonio. These alternating poles, however, leave her feeling enraged and out of control.

Years into her marriage, however, Ana María recognizes her simulations and melodramatic theatricality. Her sudden realization reveals to her the effort she has put into acting out and self-inflicted pain: " 'Sufro, sufro de tí . . ,' empezaba a suspirar un día cuando, de golpe, apretó los labios y calló avergonzada, ¿a qué seguir disimulándose a sí misma que, desde hacía tiempo, se forzaba para llorar?" (156) ("I suffer, I suffer because of you . . .' she began to sigh one day, when suddenly tightening her lips she remained silent, ashamed. Why should she continue to hide from herself the fact that for a long time, she had had to force herself to cry?") (227). Her love for Antonio had turned into a mute yet fierce hatred that only increased over time.

By distancing herself from this highly sentimental rhetoric, Ana María becomes aware of her own melodramatic performance as a victimized wife. She realizes then that she resents Antonio's power to remain unchanged despite her outbursts of anger and frustration. Thus she claims feeling "cierta irritación y un sordo rencor, secaban y pervertían su sufrimiento" (157) ("a certain antagonism, a mute rancor was withering and perverted her suffering") (227). Esther Nelson has also highlighted Ana María's narcissism and excessive intuition as part of the melodramatic tenor of the novel. She has called attention to the repetitive use of the word *never,* the abundance of rhetorical questions and Antonio's unwonted tenderness.[75]

Ana María is filled with anger and resentment toward Ricardo, Antonio, and Fernando. Through her relationships with these men she loses a sense of herself and of the passage of time. Moreover, it could be said that despite herself, she wastes her time yet is unable to accept it. In the shroud, she is finally able to contemplate her life and the cycles of rage and fear that bound her. Ana María's enslavement to passions (love, hate, fear, and resentment, among others) is not only an individual flaw but a social evil in the melodramatic structure of the novel. Since men are the guardians of law and order, they are also the ones who are ultimately responsible for women's well-being. Ana María's existence stands as a metaphor for the inexorable sacrifice of female bodies to the project of modernity. This rationality, through the institution of marriage, demands that women reproduce the heterosexual and patriarchal system by symbolically dying, or becoming zombielike or disembodied ghosts who give up their vitality.

The stagnant condition of the landed oligarchy, as disclosed in gender relationships, reflects its imminent political and social decline. Exclusion and subordination, which are inherent to the hacienda culture, are patently illustrated in the marriage contract and family structure. Marta Brunet develops this aspect in a more comprehensive way than Bombal, as we have seen, by depicting a system of domination that cuts across class and gender lines. In her novels the countryside is founded on a social order where a few owners enforce their privileges over all others. Bombal's narrative, on the other hand, focuses exclusively on the landowner's wife and how the world of the hacienda and its culture feeds on her vital energy.

Furthermore, Ana María's descent into the entrails of the earth shows her the bodies of women and girls whose untimely deaths confirm the existence of a world where female self-destruction prevails. After death, however, these women, as Ana María does, seem to find liberation from past constraints. In this archetypical realm, the main character finally returns to the origins, to a place and time in which woman, earth, and water belong to the same natural order, as Lucía Guerra suggests.[76] Bombal displays a conception of life and death in which the self realizes its ultimate truth in its connectedness with the cosmos and its dissolution into wholeness along the lines of Buddhism and Eastern philosophies.[77]

This cosmic motif remains in most of Bombal's later stories, reiterating woman's connection to primal and natural forces. The melodramatic conflict stems from the character's awareness of the evident separation from the natural realm and the assignment of a biological destiny and a role in the social order. Furthermore, modernity's attempt to master nature is extended to women, who become commodified as do all other properties belonging to oligarchic and powerful men.

The internalization of rage turns Ana María into a shrouded woman who adopts the identity of a lady as the only dominant female position within a contractual love model. When she proposes to Fernando the pact of courtly love, she is able to invert her subordinate gender role and state the new terms of her dominance. However, this alternative does not give her a vital identity but instead falsely identifies her with a new form of legal investiture. Oligarchic modernity shows clear signs of its termination, revealing the need to replace it with a new cultural and social alternative. In Bombal's narratives, however, the alternative can only be found in archetypes[78] and fantastic worlds beyond rationality.

The transformation into the lady is thus completed in the acceptance of the shroud, a condition that allows Ana María to constitute herself as untouchable and immaculate (like the Virgin). Through the rites of death, the lady is evoked and consecrated as a shrouded woman through the last possible identity in rigor mortis. In this way, she regains her lost youth and beauty, qualities that distinguished Ana María's exchange value in the world of capital that also allowed her to marry.

Bombal's critique shows here the equation between the shroud and the lady who becomes a corpse that exercises absolute power over others. This inverted virgin/martyr image provides a double testimony of subjectivity in the novel. It shows that the only possible love is provided by courtly love, a highly ritualized form in which a woman controls a man through keeping an absolute sexual difference and distance. It also constitutes a female identity that can only assert itself in a new contractual arrangement and its perverted effects.

The narrative makes evident a desacralized order where religious and humanist values have been replaced by coldness and perversion. As a consequence, the transformative effects of love and imagination have a marginal and even destructive outcome, as several female characters illustrate. Bombal's view dismisses the discourse of modernity and its belief in progress as it is understood in the first half of the twentieth century. Instead, her utopia is founded in an archetypal female paradigm evidently absent in the cultural and political Latin American projects of her times. The attention and focus on the unconscious and feminine desire specifically reveal what modernity and its rational logic slight and ultimately condemn as unproductive. In contrast, Bombal's fiction highlights these other rationalities and their marginalization from a social and cultural system governed by capitalist logic and its untrammeled negation of passion and affective attachments.

Bombal's women characters are positioned at the intersection of imagination and reality, of remembered and lived experience, unable to choose with awareness and to act independently. The social order, and gender cultural mandates in particular, are lived as ominous, constraining women and ultimately consuming their lives. Ana María dramatizes this in extreme form by displaying herself shrouded, a totally confined and repressed body. In order to reach freedom, she needs to die biologically and become a disembodied voice in a timeless realm—the only position that allows her enunciation.

At the end of the novel, the limitations of the body, language, and thought imposed on the character are transcended by a kind of greater knowledge in which everything is interconnected. This rendition of the afterlife deviates from orthodox Catholicism and incorporates many of the elements present in Taoism, Buddhism, and other Asian spiritual traditions.[79] Bombal seems to find an answer to women's dilemma in non-Western traditions, particularly in systems that move beyond representational thought.

The original state of oneness and what Freud calls "oceanic feeling" is experienced by Ana María at the end of her journey through the final merging with the natural order. The boundaries of the self break down with the "pleasure of oneness," eclipsing separation and difference. Oneness, as Jessica Benjamin explains, cannot coexist with the sense of separateness that relations with the other make paradoxically evident throughout life.[80]

The passionate subject is thus transformed into a disembodied consciousness that transcends her previously dualistic mode of thinking and experiencing the world. Ana María's absorption into a universal energy produces completion as the body disintegrates and consciousness expands. Resentment and despair are replaced by a life force that links every creature and thing in the cosmos. Ana María's ego finally dissolves into a boundless and organic process that seems to extend beyond human rationality and history. Enacting an inversion of the Virgin's ascent to heaven, Ana María descends to the earth, resurrecting in a new life without separateness. The spiritual overtones of this journey toward self-knowledge overcome the sadomasochistic perversions. Body and ego boundaries finally break down, together with what had been a source of pain for the protagonist. At the end of the novel, the cosmic perspective takes over, erasing social and personal views. Nothing remains of Ana María, who becomes one with the whole universe, another element in a timeless cycle. From this discursive position, the character's self-sacrifice gives way to the disappearance of the self. As a consequence, the disappearance of sexual difference and ambiguity proper of human existence can only take place through the final dissolution of being. Since the body is the locus of life and experience and can restrict or affirm our freedom, as Carl Olson points out, its boundary position represents our being at the crossroad between bondage and liberation.[81] However, in the afterlife, as Bombal's novel illustrates at the end, female identity as otherness ceases alongside the permanence of the self. Without the body to symbolize self and other, what we know as human life disappears, signaling instead impermanence as the true nature of being. In this way, Ana María's melodramatic life is transcended by the stillness and silence of a universal and cosmic order.

5
Diamela Eltit
The Body of the Letter

THE WRITING OF DIAMELA ELTIT (B. 1949) MAY BE CONSIDERED ONE OF
the most transgressive literary projects among Latin America
women writers today. This narrative displays awareness of the
construction of gender and the ways cultural systems operate in
subject formation. Her beginnings as a visual/performance artist
and member of the collective resistance art project Colectivo de
Acciones de Arte Collective of Art Actions (CADA) during the
early eighties of the Chilean dictatorship strongly shaped Eltit's
understanding of art and writing as forms of cultural belligerency
to dominant modes of representation and authoritarianism. In
1984 the fourth art action, considered the most significant by the
group, took place. The members of CADA went out every night to
write on the walls of popular urban neighborhoods the word
NO +. This graffito aimed at positioning art in the popular areas
of the city as a form of resistance to official culture and repression. Through the use of graffiti, the public could participate directly by adding phrases to the NO + (e.g., NO + Pinochet, NO
+ gobierno autoritario), as the critic Robert Neustadt discusses.
For some, the NO + project was a precedent to the democratization of Chile and the plebiscite that brought down the dictatorship through the NO campaign of the opposition.[1]

The artists and poets identified with the neo-avant garde were
part of the "escena de avanzada" to which Eltit and CADA members also belonged. The cultural critic Nelly Richard has stated
that they collected the fragments and residues in the margins of
an epic of resistance as well as reelaborating the fracture and dislocation provoked by the military coup. The group resisted the
illustration of ideology and took an ethical and critical position
that dethroned institutional forms of representation.[2]

In the book *Campos minados Literatura Post-golpe en Chile:
(Mined Fields: Post-Coup Literature in Chile)* (1990), Chilean

critic Eugenia Brito points out that during the dictatorship traditional literature and art were simplistic and reductionist while the "nueva escena" did not conform to these parameters. This new literature radically diverted from the literary mainstream in ways similar to the "escena de avanzada" in the visual arts. Both cultural expressions crossed discursive boundaries and "worked with fragments, *coupures,* sparks and discontinuities, and remained skeptical of all totalization," as Nelly Richards points out.[3] The city and the body became "social materials" to "intervene," producing alterations in subjectivity as well as making a "radical" critique of representation that differed from that of the traditional Left.[4]

Its members, Raúl Zurita, Gonzalo Muñoz, Soledad Fariña, Eugenia Brito, and Eltit, were avid readers of Latin American literature and art as well as their European and American counterparts. Moreover, the works of Lacan and Derrida were circulated and read in the Departamento de Estudios Humanísticos, where they were students of literature and philosophy. In 1983 when the novel *Lumpérica* (*L. Iluminata*) was published, Diamela Eltit was the only woman in the "new literary scene." Her participation in CADA allowed her to absorb the tendencies that Chilean artists such as Juan Carlos Leppe, Carlos Altamirano, Eugenio Dittborn, and others, had propagated through the use of the body as a signifier and the conceptualization of language as a space.[5]

Eltit presents a new paradigm, revolutionizing the Chilean socioliterary context in creating new representations and ways of reading. Her narrative provides alternative positions for a woman protagonist for which fiction is conceived from a nonrepresentational stand. Eltit's precedents may be found in the Latin American post-Boom literary movements, in contemporary visual arts, film, and video. Her studies of Peninsular literature and a degree in Spanish allowed her to approach language freely, as Góngora did, by bringing Latin into Spanish, observes Brito acutely.[6]

In the book *Margins and Institutions: Art in Chile since 1973* (1986), Nelly Richard emphasizes Eltit's break with a traditional and Eurocentric understanding of art and her refractory aesthetics. Eltit's perspective on Chilean culture as a colonized and peripheral social formation would surface in her earliest novel and reappear through her different narrative and nonfictional texts. The borders of the social and the symbolic intertwine to become privileged narrative spaces. Social margins and discursive fragments are the material of a relentless effort to textualize a subject on the verge of collapse in a world where certainties have vanished. In this literary scenario, the body becomes the site of experience, the place where ideological systems struggle to impose their regimentation. In Eltit's work the body is staged "as the indomitable other—or inverse—of language."[7] This understanding of experience as embodiment stresses the materiality as well as the specific location of the subject's body. Embodiment becomes "the site of possibility and necessity of difference," as Anne Cahill along with other postfeminists who theorize the body have claimed.[8]

Physical violence, pain, pleasure, and reproduction are among the repertoire of experiences that the body goes through in Eltit's narrative. Her text dismantles the binary oppositions upon which the epistemology of modernity is based and displays the contradictions and displacements that the project of modernity reveals in Latin America. Most important, however, is the role the body plays in her alternative model of reasoning. One of the original traits of her writing is the way it challenges and expands the expressiveness of linguistic codes to the point of exploding them. As a consequence, language stops representing by acquiring a life of its own in which sense is closer to experience. This literary project confronts and alters the phallogocentric discourse of modernity and the unidirectionality of the linguistic code inherited from the Western philosophic tradition of Aristotelian and Thomistic thought. Contrary to this legacy, Eltit experiments with the languages of art and literature by sculpting and volumizing the letter, thus transforming it into a body to work with for its productive materiality.

Refractoriness is Eltit's political signature in that it reflects an obstinate resistance to authoritarianism and hegemonic cultural codes. The conditions of production are inscribed in her texts in their peculiar and distinctive twists and extreme and excessive gestures. Eltit's antirepresentational mode, as Neustadt notes, displaces the allegory of the dictatorship by means of a transtextual performance that seizes control of the body via "corporeal, literary, and visual texts."[9]

Traditional readings of Eltit's texts have charged them with being cryptic and difficult, demanding great work from her readers. The critic Carolina Pizarro, on the other hand, points out that Eltit's creative itinerary may be linked to the avant garde, the neobaroque, as well as psychoanalytic and filmic terms. She adds, however, that entering her particular linguistic system is "difficult" and demands "effort."[10] In a way, this criticism echoes what a sector of the readership has expressed regarding Eltit's work. Both receptions, I would argue, share and present a gender bias. Readers' efforts and literary difficulty, as we know, tend to be considered strengths rather than weaknesses in a literary piece written by a male author in which literary density is celebrated.

Another reception of Eltit's literature within the "escena de avanzada" is presented by the Chilean critic Adriana Valdés in the book *Composición de lugar* (*Composition of a Place*) (1996). Here she underscores the peculiar mode of these "situated" texts, which were produced during the time of the dictatorship. Eltit's early novels, namely, *Lumpérica* and *Por la patria* (1986) (*For the Fatherland*) (1986), may be considered part of the cultural production that gave special attention to ambiguity in order to generate multiple readings that would sidetrack the repression of the Pinochet regime. In this light, the obscure nature of the signs was a necessity created by the conditions of censorship and repression in Chile.[11] Surprisingly, in this same period we find yet another reading of Eltit by Ignacio Valente, one of the most influential literary critics of the conservative newspaper *El Mercurio*. Valente recognizes Eltit's literary talents and the mysterious and suggestive power of her language despite his own shortcomings in understanding it. In his review of *El cuarto mundo* (1988) (in English, *The Fourth World,* 1995), for instance, he states that the "language convinces as a novel" and that this is a "logical fantasy" within the fantastic narration presented by the embryo in the first section. Valente, in spite of the fact that the second part of the novel seems "incomprehensible to the reader," insists on emphasizing its "experimental value" and the "enigmatic and powerful phenomenology of female existence, sexuality and the ineffable of human corporality" it presents.[12] His reading is part of the dual reception that Eltit's literary production has had in Chile. Contrary to this, in the American academic world Eltit's works have been thoroughly studied and commended for their originality and textual politics. Within this line of interpretation, the studies by Juan Carlos Lértora, María Inés Lagos, Francine Masiello, Robert Neustadt, Gisela Norat, Julio Ortega, Mary Louise Pratt, Djelal Kadir, Mary Beth Tierney-Tello, and Raymond Williams have contributed to Eltit's literary and academic circulation in the United States.[13]

The challenge that Eltit's texts posit to hegemonic forms of writing and the literary canon may also be extended to normalized ways of reading. She is keenly aware of the politics governing the readers' expectations, as the excerpt from the following interview shows:

> Las dificultades que un texto pueda ofrecer son el resultado de una ideología, de un sistema. Nada es muy cierto, el lenguaje es bien ambiguo. Incluso, el lenguaje más común. La misma habilidad que tiene un sujeto para descifrar cotidianamente la ambiguedad de ese lenguaje, la debería tener con la lectura. Cuando tú estás leyendo más allá de lo que te están diciendo, creo que ese mismo proceso lo puedes llevar a lo literario.[14]

[The difficulties that a text can offer are the result of an ideology, of a system. Nothing is very certain, language is very ambiguous. Even the most ordinary language. The same everyday ability that a subject has to decipher the ambiguity of that language, he/she should have in reading. When you are reading beyond what you are being told, I think that you can carry that same process over into literature.]

Consequently, reading is not an innocent activity but rather a social act that privileges specific discursive and cultural conventions. Literature, for Eltit, is a kind of rejection of the system's ideological inoculation. Thus, what is not understood is inadvertently linked to biases belonging to a form of politics.[15] Chilean critic Rodrigo Cánovas, following Cedomil Goic's periodization, in the book *La novela chilena: Nuevas generaciones. El abordaje de los huérfanos* (*Chilean Novel: The New Generations: The Boarding of Orphans*) (1997), places Eltit's literature within the creators of the "novela de la orfandad." This generation inaugurates a break with the precedent tradition in that it proposes a decentering of the notions of totality and harmony. According to Cánovas, in this new narrative an orphan voice calls for the vitiation of the categories that sustained a complete subject.[16]

Eltit's literature presents eccentric voices that problematize our understanding of representation and its relationship to gender and power. Her writing may be characterized as antioedipal in that it breaks down a linear and masculine textual economy by the overflow of signifying remnants. Eltit's focus on a localized perspective and her alliance with a marginal position resonate with Deleuze and Guattari's argument on minor literatures, as Chilean critic Juan Carlos Lértora has noted.[17] Experimentalism and an elaborate narrative discourse create a writing that is at odds with the literary canon and official culture. The predominance of body parts and fragments proposes the possibility of meaning that opposes any form of totalizing perspective. This not only is a postindustrial project that works with symbolic and cultural residues, but more importantly it makes of incompleteness the salient condition of experience. Consequently, fragmentation and mutilation of urban bodies and subjectivities are the modes of an aesthetic that takes issue with the utopia of neoliberalism in Chile.

The polyphonic and subversive qualities of the novel that explores language from a marginal cultural position are present in Eltit's literary work. Her literature displays an estranging quality of language, where worlds are unhomely and enveloped at once in enigma and violence.

INCEST AND *SUDACA* CULTURE IN *EL CUARTO MUNDO*

Diamela Eltit's *El cuarto mundo* (1988) (in English *The Fourth World*) may be read as a kind of dramatic repertoire of the flaws and limitations of familial bonds within the progressive disconnection of the citizenry from collective fields of signification. It is also noteworthy that the novel was published in the same year as the 1988 plebiscite that would produce the political defeat of Pinochet. Authoritarianism became embodied in the figure of the father present in the political discourse in Chile at the time.

Chilean critic Danilo Santos emphasizes that this novel shows signs of Eltit's abandonment of the avant-garde aesthetic of her previous literary production.[18] Brito also concurs with this view and sees in *El cuarto mundo* the first change in Eltit's literary development and search for new narrative scenes.[19]

The cultural and social context of this novel's publications dramatically shows the social cost of the project of modernity during the last years of the dictatorship. Brazilian critic Idelber Avelar has compellingly argued that a state of mourning characterizes the fictional works of the postdictatorial period in the Southern Cone. For him, the "untimeliness" of these writings is apparent "not so much as the epoch posterior to the defeat but rather the moment, in which defeat is unapologetically accepted as the irreducible determination upon literary writing."[20]

Eltit's sense of defeat of the literary, as a marginal lettered endeavor within a consumerist culture that is controlled by mass media and the market, takes a more acute and pressing exploration in *El cuarto mundo*. Santos, for his part, underscores this aspect of Eltit's neo-avant-garde project, which links those who have been deprived of their social and linguistic space, namely, the *lumpen,* women, and the autonomous writer, in a consumer-oriented environment.[21]

Another moment of modern authoritarianism may be seen in the cultural and social discourse during the time when this novel appeared. The figure of the military patriarch as the emblem of maleness and masculine identity becomes embodied in the father who should be obeyed and respected by all family members, but particularly by his submissive wife. The dictatorship as a political, social, and economic project promotes those identities that have been defined as desirable by modern rationality in the urban Chilean imaginary.[22] These models of gender identities are hierarchical, heterosexual, and Catholic, features that are embedded in the itinerary of the military nation and its family. Nelly Richard has pointed out that the doctrine of national security and its notions of order and integrity constituted a system of representation on which authoritarianism based its prohibitions and punishments. In this context, the signifier family had the mission of tightening masculine and feminine identifications to the system of representation and its dominant sexual ideology. Militarism and patriarchy joined to mystify the family as well as the most traditional gender identifications.[23]

As a novel published during the last years of the dictatorship, *El cuarto mundo* presents a view of an all-encompassing power that disciplines and watches over citizens and encloses them in the house. The family follows a hierarchical order and gender division where the father is dominant and the mother is a subordinate and suffering female. Two of their children who are twins become the transgressors of this family model and its statutes in which members have become watchdogs of one another. In this universe, the operations of power are intertwined with the formation of subjectivity, gender, and insanity throughout the complicities and betrayals that the family creates. In this sense, we find resonances with Brunet's family dynamics and its destructive interactions. The role of women, however, is in *El cuarto mundo* subordinate to that of men as a patriotic duty reinforced through the military dictatorship in which mothers are to inculcate the true values of the nation. The family in this discourse becomes *patria* rather than nation, reproducing the military state. Despite Eltit's avant garde, both gender and family structures are framed by a social problematic.

The title of the novel suggests a border that is acutely aware of itself and its distance from the center represented by the first world.[24] On another level, it also signals the existence of pockets of poverty and third world immigration in the first world and their formation of a fourth order. The Chilean psychoanalyst Francesca Lombardo provides another interpretation of the term *cuartomundistas* (fourth-world subjects), asserting that they are individuals who have become desocialized inside their homes.[25]

El cuarto mundo is divided into two parts that correspond to two gendered narrative voices and two very distinct narrations. As Brito shows, this duality undermines binary logic as the organizing principle of thought.[26] The novel begins with the male twin, who takes a distant and seemingly objective perspective to hide his weakness. His attempts at assurance and directness are articulated in a language that wants to be rational and certain even before birth. Intrauterine life and the womb are actually experienced by the male twin as threats to his survival, as a kind of prison. The confining space of the uterus, its chaotic fluids, and its irruptions, represent a source of terror for the male fetus. The way to control his own fear of death is reflected in his persistent intent to order and judge his mother and twin sister. The feminine that they embody represents the biggest threat to his sense of identity and power. He attempts to rationalize what he cannot control while literally being assaulted by his mother's dreams and nightmares, her physical spasms and bodily pains. The dependency on the maternal body motivates the male twin's desire to free himself and become autonomous.

His use of language and its sexual markers is another expression of his sexual identity and his affiliation with paternal power. The father is perceived as the only one able to contain and subordinate the mother's body from the very start. Critic Gisela Norat has noted the relevance of sexual difference in the twin narrators and the way it affects their identity and language.[27] Having a female and a male fetus allows a discursive counterpoint that reveals the link between sexuality and social regulation in contemporary society. The psychoanalyst Kathya Araujo argues that the forms of social regulation are intertwined with the forms that regulate sexuality and that support the predominance of the masculine. From this perspective, the ways sexuality is regulated may be considered the very structure of the modes of organization of societies.[28] Eltit, in this novel, explores passions, particularly "passions of the body," as Araujo would have it.

The space external to the family's house resembles an abandoned city, inhabited by people called Sudacas, who have no apparent links to the family. Chilean critic Raquel Olea explains that the term *Sudaca* is tied to a "subject in crisis" whose existence is off-limits and outside institutional relations.[29] It becomes a polyvalent and hybrid term that works to link a colonial past with the peripheral status of Latin American societies. The word *Sudaca* also brings to mind different forms of marginality, suggesting a critique of the Conquest and colonial power by way of its current use by Spaniards as a derogatory term to refer to South American immigrants. Eltit foregrounds the marginal characters who are represented by the term *Sudaca* in order to focus on postcolonial subjects who are socially and culturally excluded. She emphasizes, as Francine Masiello has shown, their aesthetic potential and the ways in which they create tales from the collage available to them in the city.[30] Thus, the term *Sudaca* with its scatological and derogatory associations is rearticulated as a hybrid (from the local perspective) yet historical experience within a global economic order.

The story line is reduced to a brother and twin sister who are born into an abusive family in a place that is governed by a nameless authoritarian and modern power. However, this initial illusion of storytelling is undermined in the end by the irreverent inclusion of the author's name in lowercase letters. This gesture inserts Eltit's choice of meanings and signification over the plot and her tendency to dismantle authority and authorship. She radically destabilizes the various power relations that link author and text by becoming the mother of the Sudaca novel, a hybrid and debased cultural/literary work.[31]

The voices of these two thinking fetuses emerge from a dark and fearsome womb. The incorporation of dreams and symbols emphasizes the dramatic permutation that links this avant-garde aesthetic to performance, particularly to the carnivalesque in the way Bakhtin and Kristeva have used the term. The fact that Eltit's novels tend to have scenes and speech performances further highlights the linkage between discourse and spectacle in her narrative. As Kristeva has shown, the scene of carnival is dream and game, stage and life, at the same time as drama becomes located in language itself.[32]

The first part of the novel develops the consciousness of the male twin, his power and gender position, in relation to language and the world around him. The narrator's sense of space and entitlement within his mother's womb is reinforced by his preexisting knowledge of reality before birth. He knows that his mother was sick and that her body was in pain the day he was conceived as a result of his father's repeated sexual assaults. This foundational rape scene reenacts colonial power exercised over the bodies of Latin American women throughout the different stages of colonization. The law is embodied in the father, who asserts his desire without limits or concerns for the other—embodied here in the mother as the powerless other par excellence.

The second section, belonging to the twin sister, displays a highly sexual and experimental writing where incest becomes the strategy "in the sister's bid for kinship and accession into culture."[33] The sexual motif, as Gisela Norat has shown, underlies the novel and reaches its climax in the second part, where the sister describes copulation with her brother.[34] The genital structure of the novel is especially evident in this section, where the female fights for her place in language and knowledge. Her writing unfolds her empowerment in a culture that expropriates and contains her creative and sexual energy. This text is a kind of "manifesto," as Norat asserts, an aesthetics that links procreation with creation in a new textual/sexual framework.[35]

The hierarchy governing epistemological oppositions appears unstable in a world where survival is at stake. The local perspective is here anchored and further problematized through a peripheral position that exposes the grip of hegemonic discourse over bodies by devaluing and restricting their differences. The fact that in Eltit most bodies are interdicted gives a political status to the carnivalesque by underscoring the exclusion undergone by low and popular sectors from official culture. The fact that they are frequently seized by hunger further underscores their material and symbolic need within a patriarchal and dictatorial modernity. The dismantling of social, political, and citizenship rights in Chile during the dictatorship through successive "modernizations" meant that most aspects of the welfare state became privatized, transferring the principles of the market to new spheres, as political scientist Susan Franceschet argues.[36]

The contemporary urban subject is displayed decentered, and crossed by multiple and heterogeneous forces that keep it in a state of flux. In Eltit's work, subjectivity appears wrought by a sense of inadequacy and lack, of not belonging to the constellation of hegemonic social identities. Females experience themselves as margins and borders to the system of cultural and symbolic categorization, as Nelly Richard asserts.[37] From the womb, the twins make their way into another form of confining space, that of the house. In this urban patriarchal modernity, private space reinforces feelings of splitting and isolation from the rest of the community. The house and its rooms become a de facto form of prison in which discipline regulates its inhabitants through rewards and punishments. This literary representation of the house resonates with the analogy made during the dictatorship between the fatherland and the home, or the fatherland and the family, in which women became the bearers of patriotic and moral values in the domestic sphere.

In the novel the family is haunted by insanity within a regime of hierarchical vigilance in which everyone is watched and spied on by the other. This link between power and vision runs throughout the novel, enfolding the ways the other's gaze shapes self-identity in multiple and intricate ways. Within this context, however, multiple rituals of domination are enacted that form each family member's identifications and subjectification according to gender. This hierarchical family structure functions in the private sphere as the military state did in the public sphere. Since all social referents and ties have been drastically severed, the family becomes the only institution that provides symbolic and affective connections. Within a highly threatening outside world, others figure only as potential enemies who might affect or hurt one's public image and status, or in the way of the Sudacas, the disenfranchised, who are the only human presence in the ghastly streets.

In the novel this public context does not emerge until the twins are adolescents and able to go out into the city. Both brother and sister stroll the streets of an urban setting crowded with marginal people, among them the young and sensual Sudacas. The restrictions in the household contrast with the provocative gestures the Sudacas display. They attract and interest the twins as they walk and observe what the city offers.

The public sphere, symbolized in the street, is fundamentally depicted as a marginal and masculine space. Consequently, the twins' mother does not work outside the home and instead volunteers in charities and tends the sick. She follows the military state's definition of women as mothers who are essentially apolitical. Natacha Molina asserts that government programs for women during Pinochet's administration displayed a perfect fit of the traditional role of women and the consolidation of authoritarianism.[38] The reorganization of the Centros de Madres (Mothers' Centers) and the creation of the Secretaría Nacional de la Mujer (National Women's Secretariat) by the military government had the purpose of spreading the values and ideals of women's roles according to this authoritarian model. As Ximena Bunster states, this ideological process turned "women volunteers" into "public

mothers" who participated in literacy campaigns, civic awareness, and education programs.[39] CEMA Chile, Foundation of
Mothers centers, implemented this ideal at a national level
through the volunteer work of women, mostly military wives and
upper- and middle-class professionals, with popular women
whose crafts were sold in CEMA stores. The mother in the novel
is enclosed in the house and only does volunteer work, echoing
the military definition of femininity.

Society is in a state of disintegration in the face of a repressive
power that reduces experience to private life.[40] *El cuarto mundo*
already displays symptoms of the progressive atomization of social experience through its sole focus on a familial world that is
disconnected from the rest of society. Experience and subjectivity
appear to be anchored rather in the position held by the twins,
first within the womb and later in the destructive home. Avelar
has noted the increasing presence of and focus on the private
realm in Eltit's narrative after the advent of democracy and the
prevalence of a market economy in Chile.[41] Toward the end of the
novel the exterior world is governed by the marketplace, where
citizens become frantic consumers. This image points to the dominance of global consumerism, which disembeds social relations
and leads to the scattering of cultural forms and identities.[42] The
market demonstrates its power to domesticate desire and parti-
tion urban space. Néstor García Canclini has argued that disintegrating cities reveal the globalization of the local through their
financial and communication networks while losing their sense of
space and cohesion.[43] Citizens' questions are answered more in
the private consumption of goods and the media than in the abstract rules of democracy or collective participation in public
spaces.[44]

The initial closeness of the twins in the womb develops into a
desire that permeates their relationship, leading to incest and, ultimately, to the conception of a Sudaca girl. This transgressive
union embodies a different understanding of temporality, relationships, and solidarity. They are an emblematic couple that
questions hegemonic forms of subjectivities, sexualities, and social relations. Recalling origins and blood ties, their bond calls to
mind past cultural legacies in Latin America that modernity has
disregarded or attempted to eradicate. The love and marriage between brother and sister were part of the pre-Hispanic tradition
of Inca mythology, as the foundational couple of Manco Cápac
and Mama Oclla symbolize. Within other non-Western cultures,
the matrilineal cosmogony of the Egyptian pharaohs finds in the

uterine love between Isis and Osiris another reference to incest between sister and brother, as well as a significantly different social position of women in comparison to that in Western patriarchal societies. The twins' union in *El cuarto mundo* drastically contrasts with their parent's marriage, which is based on a sexual and economic contract in which domination and violence predominate. As Eltit's analysis of Jorge Edwards's short story "El orden de las familias" ("The Order of Families") (1967) suggests, the twentieth century witnessed the progressive challenge to the dominance of the heterosexual and bourgeois family.[45]

The transgressive couple in *El cuarto mundo* affirm dialogue and plurality in a culture whose subjects and histories are heterogeneous. Thus Eltit's narrative discourse places the counterrationalities face to face with an authoritarian and technocratic modernization that is being imposed from above, as Vivian Schelling has highlighted for the Latin American case.[46]

The predominance of the childbirth metaphor in the text links the textual with the female body. Julia Kristeva's "Stabat Mater" reminds us that writing is inextricably connected to the painful process of childbirth for the woman writer. *El cuarto mundo* reiterates woman's body as the place where motherhood leaves its mark of anguish and pain. Eltit textualizes the experience of the mother as branded by cultural submission and violence. In the novel the mother and later the twin sister experience motherhood as a painful and deforming condition that radically transforms the body by making it the site of an overwhelming and primal power. The text here highlights the physiological and psychic toll of pregnancy, revealing women's vulnerability and dramatic physical transformations.[47] The representation of pregnancy and the expectant mother follows a grotesque rendition that confronts the virginal model proper of *marianismo*. In her book *The Female Grotesque* (1994), Mary Russo explains that modernity constitutes the female grotesque as an interior and tragic experience by uniting Freud's uncanny and Kayser's estrangement.[48] In *El cuarto mundo,* we find the collision of the popular representations with the dominant Catholic tradition as well as secular conceptualizations of the female body.

The ambivalence of maternity as yielding and suffering is foregrounded first through the male twin's account, and later through the sister's pregnancy. The female narrator says: "Mi cuerpo orgánico me dolía, mi alma orgánica también . . . , poseída por el maleficio de la fecundación" (119) (Consumed by the curse of fecundation, my systemic body was hurting) (79).[49]

Furthermore, the female twin dismantles the Catholic myths surrounding the figure of the expectant mother by sexualizing the body. Her sexual desire increases to the point of insatiability as her body gets heavier and bigger, radically breaking hegemonic images of the erotic and the sacredness of maternity:

> "A horcajadas, terriblemente gorda, estoy encima de María Chipia tratando de conseguir el placer. Va y viene. El placer va y viene. Cuando viene , viene un olvido total y el umbral lo ocupa todo. Me ocupa toda y María Chipia redobla sus movimientos porque sabe que estoy en el umbral del placer." (141)

> ["Terribly enlarged, I am straddling María Chipia, trying to obtain pleasure. It comes and goes. The pleasure comes and goes. When it comes, it comes with oblivion and the climax of pleasure fills the void. It totally permeates me and María Chipia intensifies his movements because he knows I am about to have an orgasm."] (99)

In this way, the novel becomes the countertext of the biblical story in which women are condemned to suffer when pregnant and to give birth with pain. Eltit's text contests this tradition of pain that defines and frames the experience of birthing for women as a curse that centuries of history have not erased and that is still present. Since the Bible is the only authoritative narrative on this subject, Eltit's grotesque and disfigured representation goes against the very foundation of Western culture. The female narrator in Eltit's account becomes a powerful priestess of sorts who is omnipotent as the lover and sister of her twin, María Chipia, as Pedro Granados argues. She is the leader and creator of a new myth that allows the integration of males in a fraternal community in which "emotional dialogue" is possible.[50]

The myths of motherhood and pregnancy as sublime experiences of womanhood are dismantled in the female narrator's defamiliarizing account. She reiterates the subjection of pain and swelling as well as her body's inexorable deformation:

> El malestar, el dolor. El malestar, el dolor constante, el sueño sobresaltado y de nuevo el dolor. La gordura me aplasta. Mi gordura está a punto de matarme. Altera mi corazón, infecta mis riñones, perturba mis oídos. La grasitud de mis párpados ha tapado mis lagrimales y la humedad estropea mi visión. Los tendones de mis piernas

parece que van a romperse por mi peso. El dolor generalizado no me
da tregua . . .

He incubado a otro enemigo y solo yo conozco la magnitud de su
odio. (147)

[The nausea. The pain. Constant nausea and pain, startling
dreams and pain all over again. I am crushed by the swelling. The
swelling is about to kill me. It alters my heartbeat, infects my kid-
neys, obstructs my hearing. My swollen eyelids have clogged my tear
ducts and the humidity has clouded my vision. The tendons in my legs
seem as if they are going to snap from my weight. The pain knows no
truce.

I have incubated another enemy and I'm the only one who knows
the magnitude of hatred.] (103)

Idealized and sentimental representations of maternity and the
mother/child bond are displaced by the physical toll and transformation of the body into a cavity that enlarges to disproportionate
size. Furthermore, the effects of having another being inhabit
and grow in oneself are presented through war imagery in which
the fetus becomes an enemy of sorts that will later betray the
mother. Norat has also noted the warlike representation of birthing in this novel that leaves scars and trauma for the mother.[51]
The female twin openly discloses the magnitude of the toll that
pregnancy and birth imply for a woman while also highlighting
female authority and creativity in these processes. In Eltit's novel
Los trabajadores de la muerte (*Death Workers*) (1998), the mother
also notes the unnerving demands of breastfeeding and the
unyielding needs of the two male babies (99). Similarly to the narrator in *El cuarto mundo,* both women underscore the grotesque-
ness and deformity of their breastfeeding breasts. As Marilyn
Yalon shows following Melanie Klein's findings, the breast becomes an oppressor to the child, who is not satisfied, biting and
devouring it.[52] In Eltit's writing the child's sucking the breast
turns into a destructive act from the perspective of the mother
who feels consumed by the other. The novel *Los vigilantes* (1994)
(in English, *Custody of the Eyes,* 2005) also displays similar feelings in the mother's harassment, not only by an authoritarian
culture and political system, but also by her own larva son whose
presence is both threatening and parasitic, as critic Magdalena
Maíz-Peña correctly asserts.[53] Moreover, in several of Eltit's texts
the mother avenges this extreme demand enforced by motherhood as the character of *Los trabajadores de la muerte* shows.
This popular Medea avenges her husband's betrayal and aban-

donment as well as the years of care of her two children. Eltit has discussed her interest in the Greek mother and the radical motherhood that Medea embodies, her own character "kills her sons in a more symbolic way."[54]

Embodiment, as postfeminist theory has claimed, is what defines subjectivity and gender experience. The ways the body is lived and felt subjectively are intertwined with the cultural images and values that dictate what being a woman means in a specific historical and social context.

Pregnancy in this writing is experienced as a psychotic physical transformation that follows a random and unimaginable course. Thus, in this novel the body becomes a site of signs located on the threshold of language and biology, reinstating previously obliterated female experiences. As in other texts by Eltit, the body displays its symptomatic language, or what Richard calls decodified excess.[55] Significantly, Eltit explores experience as gendered embodiment and the ways subjectivities and sexualities are shaped.

The myths governing the official discourse of the dictatorship are put in practice within the hostile and distrustful family that is bound by gender hierarchy and phallic values in El cuarto propio. Power cuts across the twins' relationship as well as the other family members, displaying the split and contradictions between experience and public discourses that the dictatorship polarized. Norbert Lechner and Susana Levy note that the disciplining of woman within the household in Chile, for instance, was one of the strategies of a patriarchal and authoritarian regime that not only excluded women from the political and public spheres, but also relied on their restriction to the private sphere. This realm was understood as a familial-patriotic nucleus and the only legitimate space for women.[56] As Lechner and Levy show, gender plays a major cultural role in how what is political is associated with the Paterfamilias and the domestic sphere becomes the realm of the feminine and the apolitical.

The novel El cuarto mundo, however, challenges patriarchal motherhood as a myth of a fractured fatherland. Authoritarian notions of gender and nation are deconstructed through experiences that destabilize social and symbolic orders. The womb, the body in pain, and sexual pleasure become sites where the symbolic wrestles with what cannot be translated into language. The body rather is textualized as the other of language for its power to disrupt, sexualize, and propel into crisis the dominant norms, as Richard points out.[57]

The female body in pain suggests a female subject who stands against death and the destruction of the social fabric, as the end of the novel reiterates. The female twin who has witnessed her mother's pregnancy and childbirth later becomes pregnant herself as an act of defiance against patriarchal prohibitions. Pregnancy remains the threshold between nature and culture, a heterogeneity that explodes by "extracting woman out of her oneness," giving her the possibility of reaching out to the other and the ethical, as Kristeva has shown.[58] This gesture toward the other is an ongoing motif in Eltit's work that allows for complicity and resistance. In the end, the female narrator stays with her sick brother/lover after the family has abandoned the house while the plague ravages the city.

The sister holds on to her maternity as a vital will against the cataclysmic effect of a modern dictatorial patriarchy and its consumerism. Citizens controlled by greed show up in an urban landscape that has become, in both a literal and a metaphorical sense, an open market. In the streets the Sudacas are exposed to currency with their own figures printed on the bills. The bills display their images while containing their desire through the numbing effect of consumption. The city is thus transmuted into a marketplace where everyone and everything is for sale.[59] The transformation into merchandise, into a seductive object that generates desire, is the irony, as Brito lucidly points out, that the text proposes as a way out. In this fashion, the future of the novel is the same as the future of these marginal figures, who have been socially defeated but who can still survive in a culture that punishes.[60]

María Chipia's name embodies those identities and desires that have been excluded from official culture. He is the result of his twin sister's creation, her double, the Other who makes alterity real. Retrospectively, he is diamela eltit's creation, as she also makes possible their incest, her pregnancy, as well as the final abandonment. Brito asserts that the most intriguing question is, Who is diamela eltit and who is the daughter who will go up for sale? The meta- discourse of the narrative stresses that this is a woman's fiction where a woman dreams of a man, whom she embodies only to leave him later. Her own bisexuality would thus be enacted through María Chipia's ambiguous and transgressive sexuality, first with the Sudaca stranger, then with herself.[61]

María Chipia's sexual experience with one of the Sudacas in the streets is a rite of passage for males into the public/social world. His sexual relation with his twin, on the other hand, reinstates heterosexuality for the sister's use. The parents' fight over the son's name results in victory for the mother, who calls him María Chipia, feminizing him and erasing the father, ultimately, giving him a witch's name, as Brito says.[62] The mother's recreation of the son resembles Brunet's mother in *Amasijo* (1962) *Hybrid*, who treats her son, Julián, as a girl. Interestingly, a year after the publication of *Amasijo,* the novel *El Río (The River)* (1963) by Alfredo Gómez Morel (1917–84) also shows names as markers of identity and resistance within the world of criminals. Each one has a name according to the type of crime he performs. Within this cultural context, names create a language that escapes and challenges the statutes of bourgeois ideology, constructing new forms of identities. Eltit's narrative project attempts something similar through the creation of a new language and situations that generate other subjectivities.

The poetics and politics of the name are also present in Chilean homosexual culture as shown by Pedro Lemebel's *crónica* "Los mil nombres de María Camaleón" "The One Thousand Names of María Camaleón" from the book *Loco Afán. Crónicas de sidario (Foolish Effort: AIDS Chronicles)* (1996). Here names multiply in order "to camouflage paternal names" within a language that affiliates with the feminine. Latin America has a filmic gallery of virgins, according to the urban *cronista* in the story, who have been homosexualized through the transvestites who copy them.[63] This is what María Chipia does when he dresses up and impersonates a virgin. He undermines the sacred signification of the image by making it a model to imitate, evidencing its constructed nature. Identity becomes a disputed territory to exalt or humiliate, to reward or punish. Revisiting the scene of the annunciation as Brunet did in *María Nadie,* Eltit further desacralizes and parodies the biblical story through gender inversion:

Mi hermano mellizo adoptó el nombre de María Chipia y se travistió en virgen. Como una virgen me anunció la escena del parto. Me la anunció. Me la anunció. La proclamó.
"¡Oh no!, ¡oh no!", dijimos a coro al percibir la catástrofe que se avecinaba. Evolucionábamos a un compromiso híbrido, antiguo, asfixiante que nos sumergió en una inclemente duda. (109)

[My twin brother adopted the name María Chipia and, like a transvestite, became a virgin, for a virgin could predict the birth. He predicted it. He predicted it for me. He proclaimed it.
"Oh, no!, Oh, no!" we said in unison upon perceiving the catastrophe that had beset us. An archaic, hybrid, asphyxiating compromise evolved, plunging us into apprehension.] (69)

The transgression of patriarchal law reveals a new perspective on the expulsion that Adam and Eve endured. In this way, the couple abandons the social and symbolic contract on which Western civilization has been founded and that modernity reinstates through the marriage contract. Furthermore, the male twin enacts the historical and political identity of the Latin American subject in terms of a psychic polarization constituted by the presence of subaltern and dominant elements. The critic Raquel Olea finds the precedents to the formation of this specific identity in Eltit's *Por la Patria* (*For the Fatherland*) (1986). This earlier novel presents the gestation of a multiple Latin American identity embodied in mestizo culture and irreconcilable social differences.[64]

Transvestism and the blurring of a clearly defined sexual identity mark María Chipia throughout the novel. Cross-dressing and wearing makeup further stress his eccentric subjectivity in which masculinity and desire are not hegemonic. The norms regimenting his identity as the firstborn and only male in the family are disorganized by the confusion that his name and sexuality produce. In this instance, the theatricality and parody of self implicit in transvestism (linguistic and sexual) serve to construct identity in a game of otherness. Speeches and bodies are confused and linked in a founding fraternity that takes on the *roto* (Sudaca) legacy as well as the mother's guilt, as Olea emphasizes. Patriarchy is here replaced by fraternity and dual relationships that are marginal and precarious. Fraternity, as Mary Green asserts, is the founding principle for the couple's love and the new utopia they embody.[65]

The circularity of the twins' confinement is evident in the mother's womb and later in the paternal house. From this position, watching and being watched construct subjectivity and reality in constraining conditions. Watching the mother being sexually forced by the father while she is sick determines the son's disaffection for the parents. María Chipia and his sister are conceived on April 7 and 8 in identical circumstances where the sick mother is raped by the father. The male narrator's memory and consciousness are forever split between a dominant male and a submissive and suffering female.

The fear of being lost and swallowed by the tumultuous fluids and forceful movements in the womb exacerbates the male's desire for separation. Sharing this space with his twin sister further heightens the feeling of encroachment and terror in his section of the novel. The sister's counterperspective, on the other hand, underscores her inventiveness and her search for affiliation with others, as Norat points out.[66] The intrauterine world in *El cuarto mundo* appears as an unpredictable and dangerous space, a kind of dark camera where the life of the thinking embryos is at stake. The description of blood emanating from the mother's body during birth underscores the intense and symbolic meaning of female blood and its potential to disrupt order and rationality. Blood—particularly menstrual blood—as well as other bodily fluids have the ability to shatter the limits of the body, instilling fear and awe. Menstrual blood, according to Kristeva, "stands for the danger issuing within identity (social or sexual); it threatens the relationship between the sexes within a social aggregate and, through internalization, the identity of each sex in the face of sexual difference."[67]

Blood and its link to women are salient motifs in several of Eltit's novels, reiterating its power to challenge and subvert the symbolic pact. It also reinstates the role of ritual through the female body as the depository of primal forces. *Vaca sagrada* (1991) (in English, *Sacred Cow*, 1995), *Los trabajadores de la muerte* (1998) *Death Workers*, and *Mano de obra* (2002) (*Labor Hand*), reiterate the relationship between women and blood. A sense of sacrificial sacredness surrounds the female body in *El cuarto mundo,* enacting the archaic bewilderment with a body that can bleed but withstand pain without necessarily dying.[68] In sharp contrast, modernity desacralizes nature and the female body. Consequently, rituals have been lost and the female body degraded and deprived of other meanings. In an interview, Eltit discusses blood and the different types of blood there are, highlighting two fundamental gender differences. She asserts that symbolically there is a heroic blood belonging to men and originating in the wounds endured in battle, and there is an impure blood related to female menstrual cycles. The latter, she continues, is related to a signifier and ritual where the female body becomes a ritual stage in which sacredness and degradation collide.[69] Consequently, woman's sexuality becomes either mystified or animalized in patriarchal symbolic discourses, as the title *Vaca sagrada* reveals.

The project of modernity sacralizes woman in her reproductive ability by mystifying maternity as the only form of social identity for women. On the other hand, the female body is degraded as a site of sin (religion), insanity and monstrosity (science), and crime (law). This rhetoric of the body is prevalent in Eltit's narrative and serves to deconstruct the ways in which the corporeal has been colonized by different paradigms. The body is understood both in its gendered and material meanings as well as in its social and political implications. The dynamics of attraction and fear that the female body mobilizes structures rituals and emotions that are connected to life and death. Female sexuality (in the mother's and the twin sister's cases) is presented in all its potential to alter and subvert patriarchal restraints. Despite the surveillance the mother is subject to, she engages in an affair that transgresses gender and social norms, stripping the husband of his power.

The interplay of normalization and precariousness shapes the mother's fate, however. The narrator comments on her adultery and the neighbors' rumors, showing the social control of female sexuality. The effects of gossip and its social functions as a form of control are particularly evident in the mother's position, as *Los vigilantes* reiterates. Gossip serves to enforce sexual morality and limits female freedom in a social order where the law is equated with masculinity and power.

In contrast to the mother's social condemnation, the father's numerous affairs are disregarded and considered to be part of his masculinity in *El cuarto mundo*. They remain unexamined by the narrator since they are seen as natural expressions of heterosexual male sexuality. On the contrary, the mother's affair destroys the family name as well as the honor of the husband. Masculine honor appears to be linked to a woman's sexual and public behavior, making her the carrier of reputation and status not only for the husband but for the entire family. The persistence of this Catholic Baroque topic highlights the conservative reproduction of sexual morality through man's honor and woman's guilt. The male twin's transgression of heterosexuality also reveals feelings of shame at being unable to take the father's place in the family. Guilt turns him into a social outcast who expiates his "crime" through sacrifice and repression, taking the place of the mother (36).

Despite sexual and moral control, the mother's body is deterritorialized. Desire becomes the mobilizing force that allows her to move out of the husband's dominating grip for a time. Her ostracism for having committed adultery and literally being watched in the sexual act by the husband highlight in a voyeuristic way how surveillance organizes and distributes gender privileges. When a woman sexualizes herself, patriarchal institutions and norms restrict and punish her. In *El cuarto mundo* this is apparent when the husband's pride and status are challenged by his wife's affair. His reaction and sense of possession alternate between pain and the need to destroy her (64–65).

In Eltit's narrative the female body is presented as sexual, maternal, or degraded in mythical narrations in which elements of the grotesque are evident. In this sense, the body serves Eltit as the site of the flaw and irregularity that breaks down the all-encompassing rationality of the project of modernity in its neoliberal utopia of progress.

Furthermore, Eltit's critique of globalization and the free market economy is patently encapsulated in her reelaboration of the Christian myth of abundance and scarcity toward the end of *El cuarto mundo*. The grotesque image of wild and possessed consumers who try to catch the bills and coins falling down from the sky recreates a kind of perverted manna in which money substitutes for bread. The rampant consumer-oriented society and the effects of world capitalism in peripheral modernities, as Jameson has commented, contaminate all of culture with economics.[70] In the novel, buyers and sellers mingle and confuse one another in the frenzy caused by this free money unbound from the effort of labor. Capitalism spreads its mythical discourse, offering miracles (money without working) while emptying out consciousness and politics. The myth of a triumphant and modernized Chile is here confronted with a society turned into a marketplace in which social action and subjectivity are equated to buying and selling. Eltit's essay "Se vende," (For Sale), in *Emergencias: Escritos sobre literatura, arte y política* (*Emergencies: Writings on Literature, Art and Politics*, [2000]), returns to this cultural and social paradigm in which the ideology of the market is hegemonic in a society where economic inequities and social marginalization predominate. The cultural penetration of the modernization model embodied by the "most powerful nation" in the novel reveals the hegemonic role of the United States in sustaining the neoliberal utopia: modernization is possible as long as there is an adaptation of habits and values to new technologies and modes of consumption. This new form of colonialism, as the Mexican writer Carlos Monsiváis argues, has given Latin American modernity an "American makeup" that has transformed the feeling of private ownership into the only bond among reality and sensations, consumption, obligations, and rights. The frenzy described in the scene of the market in *El cuarto mundo* parallels the Mexican process of denationalization and "plundering" that has taken place across Latin American in the last thirty years when the only conceivable ideology is consumerism. [71]

The commodification of bodies runs parallel to the pernicious influence of the market, which turns everything into exchangeable commodities. The prevalence of the free market economy in this rendition literally reaps everything from past values. Communal ties, social and civil rights, as well as political awareness have vanished from this new world order. The result, as the female twin declares, is an empty city in which no traces of history, memory, or human presence are left: "Sólo el nombre de la ciudad permanence, porque todo lo demás ya se ha vendido en el mercado" (159) ("Only the name of the city remains, because everything else has been sold in the open market") (113). In contrast to the twins' extreme poverty lies the city's mercantile and empty image. Society appears to be governed by a rampant consumption where "all of culture is available for purchase," as Francine Masiello has argued.[72]

The closing section of the novel returns to the twins' plight in a city that ignores them. The last sentences establish the last parodic twist by having the female narrator reveal her identity as *diamela eltit,* introducing the author's name as a fictional character: a writer and a mother. María Inés Lagos has stressed the symbolic nature of the birth at the end and the way the mother/author creates the novel from her experience of the margins of the city. Moreover, the mother conceives this work with the help of the other, the male twin who is also part of her and with whom she has shared the womb, family, and social life. In this way, the birth image recombines sexualities as well as noncanonical genres in the formation of the "Sudaca girl," a hybrid work of literature.[73]

The transgressive couple with their newborn constitutes a kind of degraded nativity condemned to poverty and stigmatization. A social system ruled by the law of the market, as the novel shows, not only erodes civil and social rights, but makes marginality invisible (contained in an "abandoned house"). The fate that awaits the newly born Sudaca girl, and of the novel itself, will be determined by market demands in a world in which God and reason have disappeared.

In this way, *El cuarto mundo* is located within and against the economic criteria that literature faces today. This challenge also confronts the readers as the publishing industry diversifies and new pressures are put on writers (particularly women writers) to fit into mainstream tastes and expectations in order to sell. Mercantilism thus extends to the literary and turns the book into a commodity.[74] Brito has astutely pointed out that the allegory of literary creation embedded in *El cuarto mundo* underscores, in a provocative and political way, the difference that being the "mother of a text" entails for the woman writer who has to confront the cultural web (literary and symbolic) that motherhood implies.[75] For the Sudaca girl and the novel the marginal position that gender as well as a minority literature have in the current social and cultural order is also reiterated in the challenge of confronting economic imperatives in order to survive. Robert Neustadt has noted the interrelationship between writing and prostitution at the end of *El cuarto mundo* with the imperative of selling, which the novel/daughter faces.[76] The literary work shares the marginal condition and commodification that the Sudacas face throughout the narrative. Furthermore, the novel radically defies traditional familial contracts (marriage and the patriarchal family) and the canonical literary representations that reproduce and maintain them. Eltit's literary aesthetics reveals, in contrast, a marginal world in which the powerless not only resist but confront hegemonic discourses and sexual morality, unabashed and unhindered by the material and symbolic violence they endure.

6

Motherhood on Trial in *Los vigilantes*

THE STATE OF SURVEILLANCE AND CAPTIVITY REACHES ITS CULMINA-
tion in Eltit's fifth novel, *Los vigilantes* (1994) (in English, *Custody of the Eyes*, 2005). This work was awarded the José Nuez
Prize for the novel in 1995 for its exploration of the different
"forms of distrust, control and manipulation" undergone by the
protagonist.[1] Following the confessional model proper to the mystical tradition and love discourse, the mother of *Los vigilantes*
gives herself to the task of reviewing her actions in order to write
her defense against numerous accusations and the harassment
planned by her husband.

The erasure of history that the dictatorship accomplishes is
embodied during the postdictatorship in a city turned into a ruin
of the lower classes and marginal groups: the poor and disabled,
the lumpen, and women, all considered surplus by the social system. They have become historical wastes of modernity and the
dictatorial regime that considers them a danger to progress. They
are cast as the new barbarians who threaten to take over an orderly, clean, and rational city.

In the novel, the city has been devastated as the result of a
major disaster that remains incomprehensible, unfolding an uncanny urban landscape. Critic Idelber Avelar describes this novel
as apocalyptic, particularly in reference to an end of the world
feeling that prevails.[2] The continuity of the modernization project, together with a patriarchal rationality, discloses the ways the
political consensus glosses over gender and class stratification.
We read the subjection of a desperate mother and the transformation of the city into a besieged place where the law legitimates
surveillance and political persecution. Woman is here the metaphor of the other, an excess that together with other marginal
groups circulates in the urban stratification of the modern dictatorial city. The female body, on the other hand, becomes a place
of resistance as well the depository of public and social abuses.[3]

186

The female character's feverish writing is the desperate answer to the accusations she receives from her absent husband and father of her abnormal child.[4] The novel is framed in two narrative voices, the son's opening and closure of the text and the mother's thirty-four letters. From the beginning, she is accused of being an incompetent mother and sexually promiscuous. Later she is declared insubordinate to the state for not complying with women's patriotic mission. Nelly Richard has shown how the dictatorship looked for cohesion in the ideological nucleus of the family through the indoctrinating identification of woman and nation as a symbol of continuation and guarantee of order. The mother became the official emblem and natural guardian of the sacred values of the nation. She represented patriotic life in contrast to the inner political war waged against the enemies of national security who were seen as the agents of death. In this mythology, motherhood was polarized in relation to the words *woman and fatherland,* which made some women adhere to the dictatorship and understand the conservation of life as the search for official security. At the other extreme, the reverse of the authoritarian/totalitarian power could be found in those rebel women who fractured the patriarchal model through civil disobedience. These females decontextualized the traditional link of motherhood and home and resymbolized maternity in the public sphere by going out into the streets, a space traditionally reserved for men.[5]

In a similar way, the narrator of *Los vigilantes* attempts to reinstate the lost links among the mother, life, and the word. The Italian philosopher Luisa Muraro has argued that culture separates us from nature and the mother by making us independent within the symbolic order of the father. Thus, symbolic independence, she states, is paid for with the loss or covering up of the original relation with the mother.[6] Writing in Eltit's novel is predicated upon this modern negation and loss that is politicized in the defeat of the marginalized, embodied here in the mother, her child, and the ghostly figures of a fragmented city.

Los vigilantes is an epistolary novel that attempts to connect the recent past with contemporary Chilean culture, where memory is still an ideologically charged territory. The mother's letters, however, claim memory as a sort of living legacy that is embodied in her affliction. Her writing also becomes the relentless self-defense of an imprisoned and condemned female. The myriad allusions that her letters convey may be read as the testimony of an injured psyche that has witnessed and survived a cataclysm that almost eludes representation. Kirby Farrell comments that the trope of trauma accounts for a world that seems threatening and out of control in the case of complex societies that have not come to terms with or worked through the aftermath of a catastrophic historical event.[7] Still today Chilean society grapples with the conflicts and conflicted memories that linger from its dictatorial past. Legal attempts clash with political and economic agendas, where forgetting and moving on are upheld as the only possible alternatives in a capitalist democracy.

In Eltit's narrative, the exclusion of Margarita, the mother, is reiterated in a desolate and frantic writing that reveals her struggle to survive amid hunger, cold, and political harassment. In this threatening world, she oscillates between delirium and ecstasy, logic and causality, explaining and defending herself through legal discourse. Her claim, however, is doomed from the start since man is the category for citizenship, excluding woman. Legal language shows how institutional and cultural ideologies about gendered identities are encoded in linguistic representations. Discursive formations shape the "kinds of identities that are produced," as Susan Ehrlich asserts.[8] As the circle closes around the woman, private and public domains begin to cancel each other out. In the process, her own defense leads to her criminal sentence. Her letters constitute a report of the grievances and distress brought about by her husband, his mother, and the neighbors. The narrator's life is determined by their rule, making her the victim of numerous intrigues and false accusations. Within Chilean literature, the mother's letters and the son's two texts may be linked to the writings of Carlos Droguett (1912–96) and José Donoso (1924–96). As Eltit does, both authors focus on sensibilities that are at odds with and uncontained by dominant cultural and literary discourses. The texts that come to mind are Droguett's *Patas de perro, Dog's Legs,* (1965) and Donoso's *El obsceno pájaro de la noche* (1970) (in English, *The Obscene Bird of Night,* 1973), in which monstrosity is a site of resistance. In Eltit's essay "Los bordes de la letra" "The Borders of the Letter", she points out the challenges and differences that Droguett's deformed character, Bobby, establishes in Chilean letters. The larva-child in *Los vigilantes* resembles in many ways Bobby and Donoso's El Mudito in his physical deformity and symbolic insurrection. He embodies a silenced and infantile idea of Chile that is unable to sustain itself without maternal care and attention.[9]

In *Los vigilantes* the uncanny atmosphere that prevails makes it impossible for the woman writer to integrate the outer world into her experience. She is unable to explain or translate the world that surrounds her as she is increasingly dominated by anxiety and fear. She writes faced with the incomprehension of a world governed by strict rules that must be obeyed and that resemble the early days of the military coup. Within a catastrophic sense of reality and the absence of historical meaning, threats multiply as the narrator dramatically tries to constitute herself into a subject while proving her innocence through the writing process.

The figures of a mother and a sick son represent subjectivities fated to be eradicated from modernity and its phallocentric structures. Rita Felski argues in her book *The Gender of Modernity* (1995) that for women modernity has created more oppressive and concealed forms of domination. Furthermore, she concludes that the modern "is predicated on the absence of the Other and the erasure of feminine agency and desire."[10] The novel *Los vigilantes* privileges two extreme and delirious voices whose alterity and affect hold them together. Eltit relates the voice of the son, which opens and closes the novel, to a kind of marginal epic in a minor key.[11] The first and last sections of *Los vigilantes* display the son's precarious existence as inextricably linked with and completely dependent on the mother. He embodies "the residue of affect" that the mother's writing cannot exhaust, as Avelar points out.[12] His sections expand the complexities and contradictions of this relationship and the shifting positions, feelings, and meanings that structure it. The mother-son relationship continues the reflection on motherhood started in *El cuarto mundo*. Here, however, the son takes over the work left unfinished by the mother, replacing her in the process. The mother, on the other hand, shows an oedipal maternity in her overidentification with the son against the father. Her alienation and complete dispossession at the end leave insanity as the only way out. The fictionalization of insanity in the novel coincides with Eltit's *El infarto del alma, The Stroke of the Soul,* (1994), a nonfiction text published the same year as *Los vigilantes*. In this visual and literary book, woman, madness, and writing join in Eltit's love rhetoric alongside the portraits of inmates, who are lovers, taken by the photographer Paz Errázuriz.[13] Insanity and love in this text display the absence of limits in an extreme form of passion in which there is no narcissistic identification with the other.[14] Blurring the limits of the ego and those of logical reasoning becomes a poetic journey of how two completely disenfranchised beings develop bonds of love. Furthermore, the close connection that traditionally has been established between woman and insanity in masculine rationality, as Richard suggests, has made the feminine incongruent with the systematic logic of meaning.[15] In this way, the interns participate in the same otherness attributed to those who take on a feminine rather masculine position in the realm of language and culture. Avelar has also noted that this novel faces not only the postdictatorial task of mourning but also its void. Margarita's letters are addressed to the absent other, who is the nucleus of her obsessive and written desire.[16]

In *Los vigilantes,* the son's opening section, BAAM I, foregrounds the impossibility of speech, on the one hand, and his love for his mother, on the other. His larval drooling wets everything that has contact with him, mostly his clay pots, the soil, and his mother's calf. His saliva reanimates the petrified world that surrounds him in which his presence establishes an inverse relationship to his mother's writing. She exists only when faced with the written page in a kind of shroud that seals her off from life. Her absorption and loneliness are interrupted by her son's saliva on her calf, making his body indistinguishable from hers. The son's discourse is anchored in the body (particularly his mouth and its fluids). Kristeva's discussion on the abject and bodily fluids highlights how cultural codes cancel out what society fears as dissolution of its moral borders and limits.[17] As the son here shows, he is not separated from the external world but rather lives without clearly defined lines separating himself, his mother, and the world. His loud laughter and drooling connect him to the exteriority he inhabits. He knows that his mother is annoyed by his laughter and uses it to get her attention and force her to stop writing. The world for him is a lived experience inextricably linked to his love attachment to the mother and his feeling of hunger. He is all need for the mother and the food (material and emotional) that she provides. From his child's perspective, the maternal body is perceived as a vital source that secretly keeps ("warm" and "sweet") milk that is only rarely given to him. Milk here acquires multiple meanings that relate to images of sacredness (the mother's milk as a source of life and sustenance) and to the persistence of a maternal politics that is present in the milk stain on Margarita. This motif resonates with the urban interventions of the art collective CADA and one of its performances during the dictatorship in which they distributed milk in the shantytowns of Santiago. Symbolically, the novel reintroduces Eltit's attention to milk as sustaining nourishment and the drama involving its lack or scarcity in Latin American popular sectors.

In *Los vigilantes,* bodily fluids (maternal milk, tears, and saliva) extend the limits and blur the borders between the internal and exterior worlds. They also relate to the abject by transgressing the limits of the body through its various openings (the mouth, the eyes). In the son's text other parts of the body are also linked to his fixation on the mother, particularly his mother's leg and calf as he crawls up and down through the trail left by his dribbling mouth. The abject is presented as disturbing "identity, system, order" and making evident the "the border of the condition of being alive," as Kristeva argues."[18] This mute and demanding child is still attached to the real as his babbling and onomatopoeic sounds reveal in the trail of fragments and signifiers that flood his psyche.

Judith Butler has shown that the relationship between survival and love attachments is inseparable. For the child, his relation to the parent can only result from a love that guarantees his social and psychic continuation. Love, Butler argues, is bound to life, and no subject can emerge without this dependency. The triumph of desire, on the other hand, reflects the threat of the subject's dissolution. Thus, subordination and desire/love are intertwined in the formation of the subject.[19] As the son in *Los vigilantes* shows, he intensely loves the woman he depends on for survival. His erotic life, on the other hand, centers around the activities of the mouth, which include drooling and inserting his fingers in his mouth and eyes. As Freud has pointed out, infantile autoeroticism is expressed in the repetition of the act of sucking from the mother's breast. When the child discovers this pleasure in himself, he sucks his finger rhythmically and maintains the mouth as his erogenous zone. This act makes him independent of a world he is still unable to control.[20] The larva-child of *Los vigilantes* displays his intensification of the lip area, where he searches for (maternal) sustenance together with the pleasure that he gets from making "holes," kissing, and "drooling" on his mother.

His two sections in the novel become the mother's containment, for he possesses a knowledge that is based on the body and is prelinguistic.[21] Through his outbursts of laughter and ongoing drooling, the son calls for his mother's attention and makes her focus on him, on his vital body, which when unattended turns "blue" or "freezes" to the point of near-death.

The woman's section is composed of thirty-four letters that highlight her position as a mother increasingly disenfranchised and isolated from collective ties. The epistolary structure of the novel emphasizes the crisis of a female subject who is confined and ostracized. Her first letter begins at dawn with a sense of urgency and restlessness. Like the other letters it is directed to a man, apparently her husband, who becomes the locus of power and meaning in her dramatic and desperate attempt to overcome hunger and captivity.

From her perspective there is no force capable of opposing the father of her child, his law, and his name.[22] He plays the role of inquisitor to whom the woman explains her every action and thought. His authority resembles what the Chilean sociologist Tomás Moulian has pointed out with regard to Pinochet's transformation from dictator to patriarch after seventeen years of rule. Moulian argues that his regime was supported by a triad (composed of the military, entrepreneurs, and neoliberal intellectuals) that gave birth to a bureaucratic machine that subordinated and coerced in vertical yet multiple ways.[23] In a similar way, Margarita describes her husband as the embodiment of a ubiquitous power in which his identity is multiplied through numerous institutional male figures: "No sé quien eres pues estás en todas partes, multiplicado en mandatos, en castigos, en amenazas que rinden honores a un mundo inhabitable. . . . Como si fueras un legislador corrupto, un policía, un sacerdote absorto, un educador fanático" (112) ("I don't know who you are because you are everywhere, multiplying your commands, in punishments, in threats that pay respect to an inhabitable world. . . . As though you were a corrupt legislator, a policeman, an obsessed priest, a fanatical teacher" (88).[24] The perversion of this social order may be seen in the gender relationship enacted by the couple. Metonymically the husband embodies the authoritarian state while the narrator becomes the voice of dissidence, considered barbaric by the hegemonic social discourse.

The narrator's writing shows the symbolic structures of a disjointed and alienating experience of modernity for a nonpatriarchal motherhood. Magdalena Maíz-Peña points out that the narrator's horror in the face of an omnipotent surveillance is shared by the reader, who also feels threatened by the uncertainty of an erratic writing that destabilizes a referential and canonical model.[25]

The postindustrial urban landscape shows a postdictatorial city without historical memory. Persistently, the narrator denounces the neighbors' plot and the culture at large in their complicit role to keep the city under the current political order.[26] Her complaint is also a testimony, a kind of open letter that grapples with the aftermath of state violence, the birth of a postindustrial and highly controlled society. The woman's imprisonment, her lack of rights, and her imminent condemnation recall the state of harassment and restrictions that the dictatorial regime imposed. The new political consensus and the advent of democracy, as this novel allegorically intimates, maintain gender inequity and women's lack of rights in contemporary Chile. Eltit presents a model that confronts Western modernity by disclosing the consequences of a dictatorial totalitarian power in the emotional and cognitive experience of the narrator. Within her mental space, the city is a metaphor of what remains in the collective and individual psychic imaginary after the dictatorship and its neoliberal economic order. The narrator becomes "the last survivor, the last carrier of the word," as Avelar points out, in an apocalypse of "collective defeat."[27]

The neighborhood surveillance begins in the fourth letter and continues for the rest of the novel. The female neighbor's ongoing snooping is linked to powerful citizens who want to eliminate difference and dissension in their utopic and uniform city. The narrator, furthermore, observes how increased control measures extend through the city in order to secure the neighbors' properties: "La vigilancia ahora se extiende y cerca la ciudad. Esta vigilancia que auspician los vecinos para implantar las leyes que aseguran pondrán freno a la decadencia que se advierte" (32) (The surveillance is extended now and encloses the city. This surveillance supports the neighbors' instituting laws, which, they assert, could curb the decadence they observe) (25). The neighbors' ever-watchful eyes help reinforce the city ordinances, highlighting the new power invested in each and every eye. In a divided city, mistrust and suspicion are central to a public sociability ruled by the fear of betrayal. The birth of a panoptic society may be seen in this ubiquitous public gaze, which contains and limits the subject's agency with the citizens' consent. Robert Neustadt has noted the centrality of this panoptic power in Eltit's novel and how it represents the ways relations operate "in Chile during the transition to democracy."[28] He also underlines how in contemporary Chile seeing and being seen provide a "safe" stage for consumerism.[29] The way the state operates in the citizens' daily lives is strikingly expressed when Margarita comments that people seem to live to watch one another. Parents watch their children, children watch their mothers, and neighbors watch strangers (74). She also notes the blurring of distinctions among official authorities, the neighbors, her husband, and her mother-in-law. They all seem alike, operating as parts of the same dominating matrix ruled by homogenization and discipline. Surveillance is managed and maintained by the citizens themselves, who guard the city from potentially threatening elements. The polity here imposes a single identity on all citizens, demanding that they conform or be excluded. In many ways, this novel foreshadows the implementation of a type of vigilante justice whereby each citizen is endowed with the duty to report suspicious subjects who put the nation at risk. Panoptical surveillance and the different technologies to which it resorts to exclude specific citizens in order to drive them from public spaces are also part of the modern machinery.[30]

The ominous feeling that dominates the narrator speaks to her sense of disempowerment and alienation. She is unable to recognize herself in the world around her, being overcome by a feeling of estrangement. In contrast to her son, she appears vitally weakened, reduced to a deadened existence inside the house, possessed by her compulsion to write and explain the inexplicable. Freud points out that the effect of the uncanny is produced when the distinction between imagination and reality disappears and what we consider imaginary appears in front of us as reality. There is then an overvaluation of psychic reality in relation to material reality.[31] Margarita's letters testify to the modes in which consciousness cannot recognize the city and cannot understand it, as well as the devastating effects of public surveillance, persecution, and confinement. Here the subject can only take the place of the persecuted, the watched over, and the scrutinized by a hostile other.

In the narrator's view, reality is reduced to laws that meaninglessly rule the city. The world outside presents itself as a flat theatrical set that holds no real affective or cultural significance. In the letters, we witness an increasing entrapment of a subjectivity whose social place is transgression and illegality in a system that administers every aspect of private and public life, particularly for women who rebel against patriarchal demands.

The ideals driving the social machine in the novel are uniformity and sameness of thought, action, and identity. In this neocapitalist society,[32] rumors and disrepute become parallel forms of control exercised by the subjects in tandem with public surveillance.[33] What is totalitarian about this kind of democracy, as Hardt and Negri have shown, is that society and the state/market are unified by an "organic foundation" that is not democratic.[34]

There are no boundaries between society and the state because power has ceased having borders since the collapse of the nation-state and its replacement by transnational economic governments. This also results in a change in the notion of sovereignty as national states progressively erode, reproducing in the local contexts the center-periphery dynamic of globalization, or what Hardt and Negri term empire. Paradoxically, this can be observed in democratic regimes and more poignantly in societies undergoing a process of redemocratization in which a neoliberal economy operates. As the case of Chile testifies, the transition to democracy left untouched the authoritarian and coercive mechanisms that the Pinochet dictatorship had put in place. From 1990 onward, the democratic governments of the Concertación were more concerned with finding a "consensus" that would leave the economic model and past authoritarian mechanisms of social control almost intact. The forms of surveillance introduced by the dictatorship and continued through the postdictatorial period became informal and parallel mechanisms carried on by the citizens themselves in which rumors, accusations, and denunciations played a major role. Globalization or neoliberalism in the Chilean version meant a drastic reduction of the state and its withdrawal from social and economic areas, letting the market rule. The previous welfare state and its protectionist social policies were replaced by a repressive social and political system during the dictatorship in order to implement a free-market economic model at a great social cost. Furthermore, the postdictatorial years, as the publication of *Los vigilantes* in 1994 signals, not only inherited but reproduced authoritarianism and policing, evidencing that they had become embedded in the social fabric and the neoliberal subjects. Eltit's *Mano de obra* (2002) explores further this dramatic impact on subjectivities and work rights in the fate of Chilean workers and the old working class under the dehumanizing economic conditions that globalization has developed in the local context, as the critic Fernando Blanco argues.[35]

The mother-in-law and the husband aim at making Margarita a loyal citizen by forcing her into seclusion and supervision (55). In this way, ordinary citizens enforce a police state by becoming the ideological guardians of an order that makes dissidence a punishable offense. Being a mother and daring to go out into the streets for food shape the narrator's political profile as an enemy of the fatherland. Her house becomes a prison in which fear, hunger, and desolation prevail.

Eltit revisits the crisis in the modern patriarchal family and exposes the fractures that cut off sustenance and attachments in this oedipal triangle. As the narrator's writing reveals, the husband's social and economic position is radically different from that of her son and her. He does not provide financial support and leaves them to starve and freeze in the middle of winter. Comments in her first letter illustrate the husband's sheltered material existence in contrast to the emotional and physical affliction the woman undergoes on a daily basis.[36] They also point to the discontinuities and emotional distance between the couple,[37] and the ultimate impossibility of a pact within patriarchal definitions of gender, gender relations, and motherhood. In *Los vigilantes,* gender politics determines the precarious condition of the narrator, the meaning of maternity, as well as her political practices. The son's gaze defines her as a mother and normalizes her. His need for food and warmth sends her into the city, provoking the father's anger. In this way, the text explores motherhood while placing the narrator in different historical positions with multiple demands. Being a mother is presented as one circumstance in the midst of many other demands that the narrator is confronted with as part of her historical experience.

Private space in this abrasive scenario turns into deprivation in a material and symbolic sense; it is the site of degradation. The hunger that mother and child endure and their captivity resonate with a dictatorial politics that encompasses public and private spheres. Furthermore, the mother's solidarity with the homeless transforms her into a collaborator, an insurbordinate to the state and the family, betraying what ought to be her patriotic and civic duties. The conflation of nation and family reaches a dramatic turn in the plight of this woman who becomes the traitor of the most sacred ideals of the civilized world. Her fate thus joins that of the lowliest social and moral elements of society who have been declared the outcasts of modernity and decency.

The mother's incursions after hours into banned public spaces echo the curfew regulations on the inhabitants of the city, evoking memories of the many years when this policy was in place for Chilean citizens. Thus Margarita breaks the law by going out into the streets, opting to follow her son's need to eat rather than the law of the state. Otherness within this urban and surveilled world is presented as a multilayered heterogeneity that official culture silences and makes invisible.[38] The fate shared by street dwellers and the mother discloses the ways hegemonic culture operates through its economic and legal structures to contain the socially undesirable and institutionalize their exclusion. In the text, they are transformed into the enemies of the social order and Western values upheld by "powerful citizens." Breaking the rules of unconditional loyalty to the system is perceived as criminal. The narrator writes that powerful citizens, furthermore, guard not only their neighborhoods with armed vigilantes but also the fate of the West:

> Yo sé que ellos persiguen una ciudad inmaculada que es inexistente. Si la consiguen, si la consiguieran me convertiría en una pieza más de esta ruda vigilancia. . . .
> No asistiré a sus oscuras reuniones ni daré mi consentimiento para establecer esas rondas de vigilancia armada que proponen. . . .
> Los vecinos proclaman que es indispensable custodiar el destino de Occidente. Díme ¿acaso no has pensado que Occidente podría estar en la dirección opuesta? (64–65)

> [I know they are in pursuit of an immaculate city which is nonexistent. If they achieve it, if it can be achieved, it will turn me into just another element in this crude surveillance. . . .
> I shall not attend their dark meetings nor shall I give my consent to the establishment of those armed surveillance patrols they propose. . . .
> The neighbors proclaim that it is indispensable to take custody of the fate of the West's destiny. Tell me, has it occurred to you that the West could be in the opposite direction?] (50)

Margarita challenges the patriarchal law that governs and that makes her the victim of the state and public discourse. Her progressive loss of status and authority, however, is led by a confabulation against her actions and thoughts in a hostile neighborhood and a threatening city.[39] Living alone with her son without food or heat becomes an ordeal of survival as well as a failed attempt to establish legitimacy through writing. Fatefully, the mother becomes inexorably transformed into a criminal by the propagated rumors and denunciations. The work of the husband and his mother is supported by the disciplinary unit that the neighbors constitute to defend modernity and progress. The cultural model demands Margarita be a mother in line with the patriarchal and national ideals in which family and nation are inextricably bound. In this ideology, the mother has an assigned role in the household that supports the husband's civic duty in the refoundation of the fatherland. In contrast, the narrator in *Los vigilantes* is part of a resisting maternal legacy that has questioned a political order founded on repression and death. Thus, she claims solidarity in a highly regimented and hierarchical order in which political resistance has been systematically crushed and the public sphere is governed by consumers rather than subjects of rights. Furthermore, in this mercantile world violence is rampant, beginning with the family and running all the way up to the state. It permeates all relationships and transforms them into relations of power in which authoritarianism rules social practices.

Furthermore, the husband's harassment is taken over by the mother-in-law, who sides with him in order to subdue Margarita's resistance. The mother-in-law shows her phallic identification in her complicity to discredit Margarita. She becomes her custodian, in the house as well as in the public domain. In fact, her denunciations provoke a process of stigmatization and criminalization against her daughter-in-law. In the narration, the patriarchal family is integral to a cultural system whose production and reproduction are bound by authoritarianism. Margarita's defeat is due to her failure as a mother, according to the values in place. In the social discourse, having an abnormal son makes her an incompetent mother who is unable to provide a strong and healthy citizen to the nation. Her biological role is thus called into question when she has a sick child. Margarita's competency as a mother is further undermined when the boy is expelled from school, making his father challenge her authority and educational methods. Her writing textualizes her "own story" (67) of the progressive erosion of civil and human rights under an all-encompassing power. Through the letters we see the dismantling of civil society and the foundation of the new patriarchal authoritarian state within a collapsed institutionality. The only possible imaginary in this scenario appears to be the patriarchal and its legacy from the dictatorship. The complaints that the narrator directs at the absent husband and his mother reveal their support of the new regime that encloses her. This is different from Brunet's world, where we still may see institutions working. In contrast, Margarita is completely alone, and there is no model to identify with because there is no system of cultural transmission operating. There are no parameters or reference points in place. The only law is the patriarchal Western law in front of which Margarita becomes a howling dog, stripped of language, as the end dramatically displays.

In Eltit's work the dominance of the West and its ideals is prevalent in the patriarchal gender ideology and a political postcolonial model where the economic dimension takes precedence over the political one to mediate with capital. Western economies—namely, Spain, Britain, and the United States—and their cultural paradigms have maintained and reproduced the colonial and postcolonial status of Latin America since its insertion into the world map through the Spanish conquest, as Elti's novel *Por la patria* reexamines. Even though this colonial status changes with time the legacy of Hispanic capitalism shapes the different development models that Latin American embarked on from the nineteenth century onward. Symbolically and socially this power deficiency has been acutely manifested in those subjects who have been marginalized at specific historical junctures.

Pinochet's dictatorship was the third historical moment of extreme social and political authoritarianism in Chile, whose mission was to reinstitute national and Western values (order, family, and nation) and secure a capitalist mode of production. The Popular Unity front led by Salvador Allende's socialist presidency (1970–73) attempted to move away from this social model through "the Chilean way to Socialism." Allende's attempt was violently halted with the military coup and the dictatorial regime led by Pinochet for seventeen years. This violent period exposed the antidemocratic prerogatives of the Right and the Christian Democrats who supported the coup as well as the brutal ways in which the elite salvaged its privileges. The systematic repression of the opposition and the violation of human rights with the disappeared and the tortured were the price paid by those who supported Allende and the working class. The curtailing of civil and political liberties and the latest version of capitalism through a neoliberal economy, designed by the economist Milton Friedman at the University of Chicago, ruled Chile with the support of the dictatorship. However, when democracy was regained in 1990, the authoritarian legacy and neoliberalism were still in place, as *Los vigilantes* poignantly highlights. The market remained the main regulator while the state disciplined citizens with their own compliance. The dismantling of the welfare state and the defeat of progressive forces are today historical facts.

In Eltit's hostile and nightmarish representation there is a police state that controls through vigilante justice, making social change an individual matter. In this context, women's bodies are doubly exploited to serve the patriarchal ideology and the dictatorship and postdictatorship as labor hand. Margarita's plight shows the reign of an economic rationalization in which order and efficiency rule social productivity with a police state that criminalizes the underprivileged.

The recurrent mention of the son's expulsion and his mother's conduct discloses the role of education in the regulation of citizens in the public and private domains. Margarita, rather than instilling patriotic values, is criticized as a negative influence on the child:

> Si bien entendí tu reciente carta, te altera el que yo quiera promover en tu hijo un pensamiento que te parece opuesto a tus creencias, dices también que soy yo la que intento apartar a tu hijo de una correcta educación y hasta llegas a afirmar que es mi propia conducta la que te inspira desconfianza, pues ya más de un vecino te ha descrito mis curiosos movimientos. (33)

> [If I rightly understood your recent letter, you are disturbed that I want to foster in your son's thinking what seems opposed to your beliefs. You also say that I'm the one trying to lead your son away from a proper education, and you even go so far as to assert that it's my own conduct that arouses your distrust, since more than one neighbor has described my curious movements to you.] (25–26)

This passage depicts upbringing (particularly the area related to moral character) as inextricably linked to the mother and her moral and sexual reputation. Her teachings are expected to mold the ideal citizen and impress on the child the national values. Again, the political ideals of the nation are instilled and disseminated through the traditional heterosexual family and the role of the wife/mother in it. The accusations against the narrator point to her incompetence as inculcator of social and national ideals. Her oppositional teachings question the core values of the nation's project. Instead of a traditional mother, the narrator embodies a desacralized Virgin who sides with the poor, the weak, and the downtrodden to find her own demise. Furthermore, her struggle to feed and keep alive her son, even when it is against the law, underscores the politicization of the maternal figure and the female body. Symbolically, the maternal body here is inscribed with the living memory of the oppressed and shows, as they do, the signs of its degradation. Desperately, Margarita attempts to survive, selling all the furniture first and later going out into the streets, restoring the relation between nature and civilization. Eltit retakes these two metaphors and coincides with Brunet in finding the kernel of negativity in the project of modernity. In the trial that is held against her, Margarita represents "el animal escapado de su madriguera" (55) (the animal escaped from its burrow) (43) who is caught by an illegitimate legal and social system.

Eltit examines a disenfranchised gendered subjectivity against the triumphant national image of postdictatorial times, only to find an insurmountable cultural and social disintegration.[40] The perversion of the social order is expressed in interpersonal relations that become forms of domination. The historian José Bengoa has shown how Chilean culture has been defined by violence, masculine violence in particular. Social domination has been accompanied by sexual domination in a culture in which the state has been conceived as an act of force, reproducing what happens in daily life. During the dictatorship the traditional system of domination with sexual bonds gave way to violence as the foundation of the political. The state is thus stripped of the feminine, without solidarity or community.[41] *Los vigilantes* strikingly presents the embodiment of this authoritarian power in the husband, the mother-in-law, and the elite residents of the city. The latter's ideology coincides with the cultural restoration of traditional values led by the Catholic Church in postdictatorial Chile, which has been instrumental in the present political compact.[42] Olga Grau has written about the hyperrepresentation of the family in contemporary Chilean culture as a result of the progressive weakening of the state and its withdrawal from the public sphere. In public discourse the family replaces the state in providing social unity. In this way there is a seamless connection between the family and the state, which is reinforced by religious discourse. The Catholic Church defines a family as the indissoluble union between a man and a woman through the sacrament of marriage, which forms a community with their children.[43] The political Right and the church, as Susan Franceschet demonstrates, have maintained a "nonnegotiable stance on abortion," and Chile took almost fourteen years and three legislative attempts to legalize divorce. Franceschet concludes that the process of democratization has been incomplete, making it especially difficult for women to have equal citizenship, which has been limited by cultural practices and a dominant political discourse that links politics with masculine activities (in labor and party politics).[44]

In this novel the laws and regulations that favor the neighbors and their social and economic interests are geared to contain the movement and curb the rights of street dwellers as well as other nonprivileged sectors. The homeless are present but made invisible by the citizens who honor the West and its moral code (65). In contrast, the narrator, her child, and the *desamparados* become, what in *El cuarto mundo* (*The Fourth World*) was the fourth world, the multitude condemned to poverty and disempowerment. Their lack of political and social rights is reiterated in *Los vigilantes* through the power of rumors, which streamline the process of rationalization under increasing and multiple mechanisms of surveillance.

Rumors constitute a form of social control used by the neighbors in the text to contain and limit practices and knowledge. The narrator's struggle against them highlights their power to constitute reality and undermine the character's credibility and reputation. The accusations against Margarita begin as rumors with sexual overtones that men have been going to her house. One of the letters discloses how her sexual behavior is publicly challenged by the neighbors' comments and her husband's beliefs:

> Aseguras que mi comportamiento genital origina los más vergonzosos comentarios que traerán graves consecuencias para el futuro de tu hijo. Dices que me atrevo a hacer de mi casa un espacio abierto a la lujuria que atemoriza y empalidece aún más a tu hijo. Afirmas que los vecinos están estupefactos por lo que consideran mis desmanes. (73)

> [You declare that my genital conduct gives rise to the most shameful comments that will entail serious consequences for your son's future. You also say that I dare to make my house into a space open to the lechery that intimidates your son and turns him pale. You assert that the neighbors are stupefied by what they regard as my outrages.] (57)

As this passage shows, the narrator is charged with unrestrained sexuality that disallows her role as mother. The husband's dichotomous and binary gender perspective shows an essentialization of motherhood, on the one hand, and a devaluation of the female body, on the other. Since fatherland and family are inextricably bound in the husband's ideology, he promotes a moral code that desexualizes Margarita and subjects her to his rule. His moral condemnation is linked to a defense of conservative values pertaining to female sexuality and family responsibilities. His position echoes the most conservative political and social views prevalent in public social discourses in Chilean culture in the 90s. Grau claims that various political agencies and state documents have made the family the protagonist of the changes brought about by modernization and globalization. With the progressive weakening of the social fabric and an ongoing cultural dispersion, the family was used in lieu of the state for the preservation of Christian values and social cohesion.[45]

The impossibility of an agreement between the husband and the narrator relates to an ideology that conceives the family as an institution that regulates authority and position in the private realm. Raquel Olea has pointed out that the traditional family in Chile is a space of conflicting powers that are arbitrarily exercised. The fact that the family refers to a private and intimate space allows for an emotional excess that is not accepted in other social spaces.[46] Margarita's letters disclose the duplicity of a relationship that maintains subordination through the family structure and a gendered politics in which woman is the negative other. Despite her distress and physical constraints, she answers the absent man's every letter and cannot forgo patriarchal expectations.

Margarita's writing becomes the stage where language (oral, written, filial, and maternal) turns into the place of entrapment. However, since she has to write as demanded by the disciplinary law of her warden, her only way out is also her condemnation.[47] In her own hand she inscribes her sentence: "Tengo la fama que merezco y llevo la vida que llevo" (77) ("I have the reputation I deserve and lead the life I lead") (61), she states, finally accepting her defeat as citizen. Her weak position evidences the gender privilege underlying social and legal structures.[48] From her perspective, power is embodied in the man, who influences every aspect of her existence. The way it operates here, power resonates with Foucault's ever-increasing disciplinary and punishing system that attempts to rule subjectivities across the social field. The woman's interdicted condition and the progressive interiorization of her writing reveal the enclosure imposed on the postdictatorial female citizen. As *Los vigilantes* makes evident, in postdictatorial societies democracy is more the workings of a modernization that reflects the transition to a poststate market economy. In this social context the state is expansionist, disciplinary, and repressive.[49] Margarita is the example of the social constraints confronted by a middle-class mother who has been confined to the house and banned from exercising any kind of autonomy. She cannot go out and is constricted to the domestic realm, without food or heat, as were many during the dictatorship. In this sense, the narrative discourse corresponds to a moment in Chilean history in which the dictatorship negates history and its liberating social and political movements. This may explain also why there are no signs of the women's movements in the novel, but rather a ground zero, as in *El cuarto mundo,* in which women have lost their civil and political rights. Margarita lacks social support in a society that has no response to an oppressive and authoritarian culture that reproduces itself through indoctrination. Her letters are a testimony to this tragic situation in which citizens have been numbed as consumers or discounted as outcasts, as the narrator and the inhabitants of the margins of the city attest. Hers is a written survival in a desperate and urgent call in which the art of writing allows a political way out of dramatically adverse conditions. Similarly to Brunet's character, María Nadie, Margarita finds in the aesthetic realm a political understanding and solution to her predicament. Here literature has the power to democratize through its interventions a highly regimented cultural and public discourse, as Eltit's collaborations with CADA also highlighted. Art may be political without forgoing the aesthetic nor the political realms, as Mary Beth Tierney-Tello's reflection on Eltit's nonfictional writing insightfully shows.[50]

In the narrator's anxious and ever-fearful account, a highly authoritarian order has taken hold of society and its institutions by suppressing and excluding large sectors of the population. In the novel these are the marginal inhabitants on the edges ("los habitantes de las orillas") and the homeless ("los desamparados"), who, as the narrator and her son, have been stripped of their social identities. The partitioned city displays empty spaces, "eriazos," that reveal the decay and fault lines of Latin America as a peripheral modernity.[51] This negative side of development is integral to Eltit's aesthetic, as well as to that of other Chilean artists. Fernando Blanco discusses women's production in the visual arts in Chile and Eltit's texts within it, stressing their use of the city and a belligerent critique through the civic metaphor of recent history.[52]

The view of a dark and ghostly city has been present in Eltit's narrative from the start. The empty plaza and an urban landscape used by a wandering *lumpen* class are part of the modern city.[53] Moreover, in her prologue to *El padre mío* (1989), *Father of Mine,* Eltit claims that these marginal subjects are the social negative of the official and successful image of Santiago conveyed by the neoliberal market ideology.[54] Margarita is part of this same social repertoire of subjectivities that embody all the negative aspects of a masculine modernity guided by a relentless economic rationality.

The woman in *Los vigilantes* is progressively defined as a virtual traitor to the nation and to the child's father. Official discourse here acts as a moral shield that restores traditional family and sexual values. Richard and Hopenhayn have pointed out that the church in Chile allied with the state and the political parties of the transition in a moral campaign aimed at cleansing practices and customs. Paradoxically, this moral fundamentalism acted as a kind of check against the risk and social liberalization promoted by the market that these same conservative sectors support in the economic realm.[55] The mother-in-law and her son embody the contradictions present in the discourse of the dictatorship, which promoted economic modernity in a free-market economy and integrated it with traditional patriotic models. In this way, the dictatorship symbolically controlled the means of production and reproduction of communication and ideology. Its moral and gender discourse combined the conservative views of the middle classes and its antimodern perspective in terms of cultural and moral liberalization. Thus, a better quality of life did not mean a different life in this new mercantile utopia.

In the novel, the narrator contests patriarchal maternal responsibilities and untenable gender demands, giving shape to the written condemnation of a violent order. Throughout the letters, her tone shifts from explanatory to self-defensive and obsessive, permanently on the verge of breakdown in the face of a confining and harassing world. Her ability to contest and argue also attests, however, to her ability to articulate a written document highly elaborated and conscious of the way authority operates. María Inés Lagos calls attention to this aspect of letter writing in the novel, and how it relates to an entire tradition of Latin American women who write to question and disclaim the charges of patriarchy against them.[56]

In her text, dominant cultural discourse is expressed in the patriarchal significations assigned to the female body. Maternal and sexual experiences are expropriated by sociomasculine meanings and values. Eltit successfully undermines the dominant notion of patriarchal motherhood as the only form of legality for women. In the female character's oppositional stance, this concept is a historical practice subject to change and interpretation. It is a social construct that reflects the proliferation and heterogeneity of experience, on the one hand, and the struggle for interpretative authority, on the other. The narrator's fight to write against all odds reveals her desire to locate a gendered perspective against a monolithic power. She contests the man's "monolithic letter" throughout the multiple moods, doubts, and retractions that shape her writing in eccentric and contradictory ways.[57] Her letters display phobias, desire, and paranoia in an endless and yet futile attempt to establish her innocence and validation.

Mother and child are progressively displaced from the social order, living on the margins of what is considered acceptable. In this repressive atmosphere, this primary relationship becomes a political enclave of sorts that resists a social pact founded on their neutralization, if not the outright elimination of "those who stand in the way of progress."[58] In the narrator's letters, the hungry and homeless wander the streets while the prosperous citizens stay at home, lock their doors, and let the homeless freeze to death on their doorsteps:

> Los desamparados, al decir de los habitantes de las orillas, sucumbieron ante la falta de abrigo y muy cerca del fin, se dirigieron hasta las casas a solicitar ayuda. Las noticias dicen que los vecinos mantuvieron sus puertas cerradas a pesar de las súplicas y que algunos de los desamparados murieron congelados apoyados contra los portones. (66)[59]

> [The homeless, according to the people who live at the city's fringe, succumbed for lack of shelter, and near the end they headed toward private homes, seeking help. Word has it that the neighbors kept their doors locked in spite of the pleas, and that some of the homeless froze to death, propped against front doors.] (51)

The homeless are part of the anonymous crowd that is excluded from the rights of citizenship. As this passage shows, the neighbors view the homeless as criminals, who have no rights or status as citizens. Their mistreated bodies evoke the existence of another city that lives mostly by night, rejected and criminalized by public discourse. These night walkers take to the streets and light bonfires at specific points, suggesting a new form of tribal band in a disintegrating urban space. The neighbors' harsh indifference allegorically encapsulates the climate prevalent in social attitudes toward unprotected sectors of the population.

The dismantling of referents and political alliances within the marginalized is here highlighted by the behavior of a citizenry that conceives the other as absolute negation.[60] The frantic market scene that ended *El cuarto mundo* and initiated the beginnings of a new world in *Los vigilantes* has given birth to a citizenry that establishes policed boundaries to safeguard its territory. The citizens appear to be brainwashed by a political consensus that reinstates homogeneity (of class, ethnicity, and sexuality) as a universal ideal. As Moulian has shown, white-washing the past was the way the political transition in Chile glossed over contradictions, and politics stopped being a fight for alternatives. In the new democracy, politics is defined as a history of small adjustments and variations that do not compromise the global dynamic.[61] Richard has also pointed out that the advent of democracy in Chile was achieved by neutralizing the past and minimizing the signs of violence that make memory a disputed territory. Not only is memory (of the tortured and disappeared) whitewashed, but the victims are also made insignificant and their pasts irrelevant.[62] Erasure of the past attempts to establish a new nation where conflict is nonexistent and differences are absorbed into religious and conservative morality. The *vigilantes* in Eltit's text are the watchdogs of such hegemony, which reproduces capitalism and its values as the only paradigm. The classic concept of *communitas,* understood in this text, as the sense of community proper to a neighborhood that provides support, protection, and recognition to the citizens, has been completely erased by these accomplices. There is actually no neighborhood as such but rather individuals who have become instruments of state control and intimidation, among whom the *sapo* or *soplón* is the dominating figure.[63] In this way, the group of self-appointed *vigilantes* in the story imposes norms, becoming the guardians of a limitless order. This form of structure operates in the same way as Hardt and Negri's concept of biopolitical power. Taking Foucault's notion of biopower, Hardt and Negri apply it to the new forms of authority and the multiple mechanisms of coercion that are expressed in subjectivity and biology not only through the law, but also through individuals who become informal paramilitary forces. In their neo-Marxist analysis, these authors demonstrate how empire and capital need to create a specific kind of space for capitalist reproduction where the city is transformed into a hostile place defined by a state of exception within the logic of a war, as Eltit depicts in *Los vigilantes.* The birth of parastate structures that manage violence through a legitimated juridical and globalized model demonstrates the extent and borderless reach of global capitalism. It permeates the biopolitical sphere and its production of life in order to regulate and contain not only consciousness but also bodies.[64]

The narrator in *Los vigilantes* is among the few who shelter the homeless, providing them with "un lugar de asilo" (66). This is the term given by the homeless to her house, symbolically restoring the political meanings that asylum had in Chile during the dictatorship. However, for the neighbors, Margarita's house is a place of suspicious activity. They are informants and spies who report the neighborhood's daily events to the law. This behavior recalls the ways informants and infiltrators worked for the secret police during dictatorial times. The narrator, in contrast to her neighbors, provides a safe place for the persecuted, sheltering and feeding entire families. In a highly individualistic economic system, Margarita's solidarity makes her a suspect to the state, her mother-in-law, the husband, and the neighbors. As the letters progressively reveal, her actions are criminalized and branded as insubordination to the law.

The suffocating atmosphere and orchestrated harassment increase as the narrator's attempts to establish a relationship with the outside fail. Her fear of being put on trial for aiding the homeless shows how the legal system is an integral arm of the police state. The use of public surveillance also points to the mechanisms used to contain a socially and culturally stratified society rife with inequity.

Margarita's twenty-ninth letter presents the image of a bleeding and abandoned woman, depicting the narrator's bodily vulnerability and the fate of her writing. The reiteration of the image of blood reinstates the excess of the feminine in similar ways to those claimed by Luce Irigaray in her essay "Volumen without Contours." Here Irigaray proposes a different topology of jouissance that opposes phallogocentrism. In it, excess and overflow become primary features of a feminine jouisssance that is based on the self-knowledge of a sex that is not one.[65]

In Eltit's symbolic repertoire, blood becomes inextricably bound to a feminine imaginary in which the limits of the body and consciousness are blurred. It mobilizes new significations around the female body and its paradoxical place between life and death. In other novels by Eltit, female blood is also central to the alteration of patriarchal meanings that have trapped the signifier, making it a carrier of gender degradation and subordination. In contrast, in Eltit's novels blood becomes essential to a ritual of the female body in which the vital fluid is attached to words that reinstate female power. In *Vaca sagrada* (1991) (*Sacred Cow*), for instance, Francisca bleeds throughout the novel and makes menstruation the source of her sexual difference. In this protagonist, blood is a sign of transgression for its ability to subvert the limits between self and other, masculine and feminine, and the constitution of the subject. The presence of blood thus changes everything it contacts.

In the novel *Los vigilantes,* Margarita's survival through a written and denunciatory account echoes Eltit's own narrative project and its place in a cultural milieu where economic considerations predominate.[66] Both women writers, Margarita and Eltit, share the margins of a tradition that has been established around patriarchal and authoritarian aesthetic and political programs. Thus, the fight of this writing subject may also be linked to the fate of critical writings that demand reflection from the readers, rather than easy and complacent consumption.

At the end of the novel, the narrator is found guilty of all charges. As a consequence, she leaves her last resistant bastion and abandons the house. Margarita and her child go out into the unhomely streets, guided by the bonfires. The hybrid and formless figure that fuses mother and son into a grotesque being[67] displays their complete dehumanization by Western culture. When the mother is about to collapse, their subjectivities fuse, blurring the distinctions between humans and dogs, beginnings and endings. In the end, mother and child undergo a metamorphosis that turns them into howling dogs that have lost their language. This dispossession of their humanity recalls the literary images of dogs in Chilean literature and in Spanish letters. Cervantes's exemplary novel, *El coloquio de los perros (The Colloquium of the Dogs)* (1613), is also a baroque literary precedent for Eltit's novel.

The at once tragic and monstrous image of street dogs with which *Los vigilantes* ends transforms the alienated mother into the babbling son, and vice versa. She becomes identical to the son who was the drooling and dumb one. She takes his place in the street, drooling and unable to write, laughing and biting him as he used to bite her in the beginning (131–32). The end repeats the beginning of the novel by inverting positions in which the same words and images reappear. One transforms into the other and in the process becomes the same, with the final separation of the son from the mother. There are no differences between humans and animals once language has disappeared. Throughout the novel, Margarita faced the impossibility of symbolizing herself through language. Once she loses her cause, the trial, and her rights as well as the ability to write, the state of war governs the world without contestation.

This grand and strange finale of a howling pair of dogs declares the end of human identity within the prevalent authoritarian and patriarchal modernity. The organic and resisting energy emanating from this organism fuses aesthetics and politics in a last attempt to fight being devoured by a mercantilist system. We witness the sacrifice of these subjectivities as the hegemonic and technocratic modernity advances through the city. This catastrophic impasse ends the existence of the human realm, equating the son and the mother with dogs and a biological destiny. By losing language, they also lose consciousness, which is here substituted by the empty yet loud bark of the animals.

Conclusion

DESPITE THE GENERATIONAL AND HISTORICAL DISTANCES AMONG Marta Brunet, María Luisa Bombal, and Diamela Eltit, their literary works show an imaginary continuum that reiterates not only themes and gender concerns but a critique of patriarchal ideology and Western epistemology. Their writings dwell on the persistence of discriminatory patterns of class, gender, and sexuality that cut across symbolic discourses within a patriarchal and authoritarian modernity governed by the law of the state and the church. Women's resistance literature and their challenge to the patriarchal literary canon can be traced back to the 1920s mainly in poetry but can also be found in the women's movement throughout the twentieth century in Chile.

In the literary context, the incorporation of women authors in the canon had been warranted as long as they resorted to hegemonic literary genres such as poetry, considered the most appropriate for females. By choosing prose, Brunet and Bombal put themselves outside what had been defined as the female literary domain and explored a realm that up until then had been almost exclusively male. In addition, the reception of their works by a very reduced yet highly powerful group of male critics responded to the pacts about reading demanded by the patriarchal canon with its specific standards and values. This is why traditional readings of women's narratives have dismissed gender and sexuality as analytic categories, together with the critique of the marriage contract and the family that is frequently present in these texts. Instead, they have been read in relation to the national literary canon, its linear narration, and the realist representational paradigm.

Brunet's writing develops in conjunction with the women's movement and the existence of a hierarchical model of social and cultural development that is embodied in the disparity between the countryside and the city, as site of urban culture. Her literary contribution textualizes women's plight across classes and regional contexts through a language that defamiliarizes what ap-

211

pears to be transparent on the surface. Bombal, on the other hand, creates an uncanny landscape in which zombielike female creatures live secluded from historical time and social reality. She shows that what women have gained in the cosmopolitan cities has not been shared by women of the landowning class who have been objectified to the point of being virtually dead. The real and the fantastic blur to the point where it does not matter until a crisis shatters any possibility of meaning. Life for the landowner's wife is meaningless, and only death allows the telling of her story and the final dismantling of a world of silence and isolation.

With their narrative literary projects, Brunet and Bombal are the first writers who explicitly question the operations of gender ideology and the kinds of feminine subjectivities it engenders through the discourse of modernity, women's rights, and the public and private sphere division proper to modern rationalization. Their writings' challenge to the canon is also a challenge to the specific modality of Latin American modernity, which is progressively understood as economic and technical modernization led by the imitative values of a progressively transnational elite. In these novels, as we have seen, the project of a Catholic authoritarian modernity is intertwined with a Eurocentric/Anglo paradigm that collides with heterogeneous and local traditions that resist the imposition of one version of reality. The writings disclose a cultural heterogeneity through their linguistic and symbolic representations, unfolding the contradictions and extreme vulnerability that the dynamic of modernity/modernization entails particularly for women's rights in a culture still deeply rooted in *marianismo* yet attempting to be modern at any price.

A cultural reading of gender is distinctly different from other readings of modernity that have been used to understand Latin American (hybrid, peripheral, transcultural, etc.) reality. In my analysis a patriarchal modernity and its repertoire of identifications have produced myriad positions of subjectivity for women. Some are more systemic than others; some have more agency or are more radical. Whatever the case, we still find *pícaras* that take advantage of what the system has to offer to them while the *marimachas* know that they have to give up something in order to enter the public sphere. The new woman's plight is acutely embodied by María Nadie, who displays the contradictions and ambivalences that modernity means for an unattached and independent woman. Despite being autonomous and financially independent, she feels alienated and unfulfilled. Her awareness of mass culture and alienation in a capitalist system grows with the discovery that happiness and meaningfulness are not guaranteed by a job. In my view, these feminine subjectivities produce a more complex and multilayered psychic universe that fractures the universal male subject of the modernist project.

Within a culturally and economically dependent society, these writings expose institutions such as marriage and the family as hindering and stifling identity in a social order bound by Catholic ideology and state capitalism. The official blissful view of woman as the "queen of the house" is substituted with the alienation and self-destruction of females as primarily wives and mothers. In this social context, gender identity is acquired exclusively through a vicious rite of passage from father to husband in which the woman becomes a commodity that is exchanged among males. In this patriarchal order, the family is a closed and reproductive structure that maintains endogamous bonds that are not only social but also sexual. Women's lives appear fully scripted and restricted to fit the Catholic identity model that tradition has preserved in alliance with the nation-state in order to maintain and reproduce the patriarchal family through the marriage contract. This explains that females who are able to topple these restraints are those who are single, unbound by husband or father. Only consensual relationships and singleness in Brunet's world allow for female autonomy. Bombal's characters, on the other hand, are only free in their fantasy or in death but rarely in their daily existence under the marriage contract. Moreover, Bombal agrees with Brunet that marriage enslaves wives rather than protecting them or fulfilling their expectations. Eltit also agrees with this view and takes it a step further in that alienation and exploitation are incommensurable inside and outside the household of the patriarchal family. For Eltit, autonomy today is almost impossible since the social structures and the market contaminate and control every aspect of human life. Social life thus has been reduced to a struggle to survive for workers and citizens who have lost their rights. Language and the ability to integrate experience into a social and political discourse are the only ways resistance can be kept alive in a global system whose voracity destroys humanity.

The seigniorial structure and culture of the hacienda governing rural areas in Brunet and Bombal's imaginary put women's lives in the hands of fathers and husbands across social classes. Brunet's most radical females, however, have cultural agency and are able to empower themselves; they take many shapes and expressive qualities as well as displaying multiple forms of identities.

Brunet is fundamentally interested in presenting the experience of each of her female characters in an aesthetic operation in which women constantly negotiate the exclusion they encounter. This is indeed a different operation from that of Bombal, who deploys a lettered confession of the untold stories of what can be called "the feminine mystique." Eltit, on the other hand, takes this critique much further and accuses not only husbands and fathers but also the dictator and the modernization paradigm of being in complicity with globalization. Brunet and Eltit give agency to women within the family; however, Eltit's females have no chance of succeeding in contrast to those of Brunet, who only begins to perceive this failure with María Nadie. Brunet's literature does not reach the level of absolute exploitation of bodies that is common in Eltit. Petaca, for example, as a *marimacha* has a heavy body that embodies a physical presence and power. For her, motherhood is still a point of symbolic support and identity. In Eltit's world, in contrast, everything has exploded; the material, symbolic, and natural realms have been perverted and contaminated by the force of capitalism over the entire economy of the sign.

Denationalization and a real and symbolic despoiling of Chilean society, as in the rest of Latin America, are the result of the neoliberal modernization, a model particularly embodied and pushed by the United States not only in the Americas but in the rest of the world. Thus, Eltit points out that this economic model not only has commodified every aspect of society but is also responsible for social genocide. Eltit's critique encompasses the cultural and sociopolitical spheres together with the role that the patriarchal literary canon has played in perpetuating them. Her perspective links patriarchal ideology and Western epistemology, disclosing the mechanisms of domination that the political colonial and postcolonial liberal conception of the state has entailed in Latin American women's and workers' bodies. In this view, the dictatorship and postdictatorship coincide in creating a public sphere in which citizens have turned into exploited laborers and consumers stripped of their rights and demands. Both periods ally in implementing a free-market economy governed by market fundamentalism in which the state became a policing force (dictatorship) and a manager (postdictatorship). The main goal, however, was to protect a social and economic model in line with the dictates of the International Monetary Fund (IMF) and the central world economies at the expense of many citizens.

In the narrative projects I have analyzed, women are part of the many marginalized from the project of modernity. They are kept inside the house, which is alternately household, brothel, and prison in constricting circumstances that limit autonomy and shatter identity. Whether they belong to the oligarchy, the peasantry, the middle or the working class, their stories say that the official discourse on women idealizes or condemns them while their historical experience is silenced. Resistance women's literature, in this way, tells the other history, that of the oppressed and those who have been made invisible within public discourse. In my discussion, I have focused on the changes that modernization has produced materially and in terms of subjectivities for women. These material changes (earning money and having purchasing power) have had a symbolic impact on females in general that takes precedence over the advancement of a lettered modernity in which education is essential.

Within philosophy as in other public discourses, passion has been condemned as disease or perversion. However, the works of the Italian philosopher Giambattista Vico (1668–1744) concur with Marilena Chaui in her reflection on the philosophy of language. While Chaui undertakes a political analysis of philosophical tradition through the concept of passion, Vico confronts the logocentrism of Aristotelian-Thomist philosophy in order to preserve the rhetorical tradition of the tropos in language. For Vico, language is founded on the various associations of multiple experiences and words. The imaginative worlds of Brunet, Bombal, and Eltit are characterized by metaphorical thinking rather than logical reasoning. Their myth-making writings find resonance in Vico's thoughts about the poetic function of language, particularly in his notion of metaphor as the origin of culture. As a consequence, in his paradigm the products of imagination are seen as the ones that sustain the entire structure of cognition. The modernist project holds a linear idea of progress as well as development in which passion is absent. What these writers do is to reintroduce the passions through writings in which desire becomes the signature of an individual and her historical experience.

Furthermore, in all three writings we find the dismantling of the myths governing Western masculinist culture. The authors emphasize different aspects of Western mythology, particularly gender, which is a socially produced and reproduced system of power that may become the basis for marginalization for many while benefiting a few.

Looking back to the diverse discursive modalities used in Brunet and Bombal, the emergence of a new and complex gendered subjectivity is evidently at odds with the literary canon and the domestic ideology advanced by the patriarchal welfare state and later by global neoliberalism. These writings question the definitions of national identity and its gruesome exclusions by resorting to and perverting traditional aesthetic models and confronting the authoritarian and masculinist literary canon and culture at large. By subverting this patriarchal paradigm, these writers define alterations and breaks within the literary canon and its dominant forms of representation. The texts present the domestic realm and traditional female roles of wife, mother, housekeeper, daughter, and grandmother as constraints and conflicted territories of identity disputes, unraveling what a modernity means from a cultural and gendered perspective.

My feminist reading has insisted on the repoliticization of these texts by linking their aesthetic paradigms to their ability to subvert the canon and its patriarchal/national logic. The incorporation of these works in the Chilean canon has occurred hand in hand with the silencing of their political potential by fitting them in the preexisting literary-genre/gender system. This dominant reading has resulted in the domestication of their work, particularly in the case of Brunet and Bombal, making it resonate with the same issues and literary concerns as their male counterparts'. In Eltit's case, the criticism of a "cryptic" and "theoretical" language has served to keep her reception restricted to academics and professional readers. This explicit bias against a literary language that is not realistic or referential has also involved sexist and personal attacks against the author. This masculinist reading has not only slighted Eltit's writing but reduced it to being cerebral and overtly complex. Ironically, these same attributes have been considered evidence of talent in the case of many male authors, thus revealing the discriminatory practices that shape the assessment of creativity and literary quality when the author is female. Brunet's writing, in contrast, was praised by the literary male establishment for possessing masculine qualities and showing strength and defiance. In her particular case, this travesty of sorts served to neutralize and depoliticize the subverting potential of her language and stories in which a decentering perspective is always at play. Bombal's reception shows the opposite side of this same patriarchal argument for literature written by women. Her writing was considered delicate, feminine, and poetic to the point that it became the epitome of female creativity. In this way, the political strength of Bombal's writing was neutralized through domestication and feminization.

In all three instances, as we have seen, the reading pact endorsed by the patriarchal canon has veiled the politics of this passionate literature, which unfolds throughout its metaphorical system. Logical language, in contrast, proves its inadequacy in apprehending reality and truth since neither may be reduced to the logos. In opposition to rationalization, writing shows that the imaginary realm and symbolization join metaphors and the passions to create new fields of significations. Politically, the word here reinstitutes female identity through the resymbolization of its absences and lack as well as through new meanings of the body that liberate it from the constraint of sexual morality and gender imperatives.

The ways in which a female subject and other subordinate groups enter modernity is at the core of the narratives written by Brunet, Bombal, and Eltit. Their works present the multiple and sometimes opaque forms of oppression through a kaleidoscopic view in which symbolic constructions are modified or undermined.

Female attempts to resist the hegemonic and colonizing thrust are also narrated through a series of extreme experiences. Amid dreams, sickness, pleasure, and pain, a precarious modern feminine subjectivity appears wrought by estrangement and uncertainty. Men, alternatively, are displayed as agents of power who enforce the social law in their roles as husbands and fathers. They tend to be presented as omnipotent masters who control through either coldness or aggression. Lacking complex and multifaceted profiles in most cases, they are cultural stereotypes that confirm themselves by performative acts (mostly forceful and abusive) over those who depend on them. Men in this context are forced to enact their virility, understood as their reproductive, social, and sexual ability, as well as the right to exert violence. The exaltation of masculinity for males is linked to a sense of social obligation that demands distinction in the public sphere. Virility is an eminently relational concept that is constructed for other men and against femininity, which is threatening, as Pierre Bourdieu points out. Furthermore, the majority of the female characters in these narratives are antisystemic, according to the way the modern economic and political system is organized from Adam Smith onward.

In the city, metonym of modernity and modernization, Eltit shows the prevalence of unjust social structures and discriminatory cultural patterns, as Brunet did in the rural areas and against Bombal's class model. Their protagonists explore different forms of self-defense to find themselves in the end socially and culturally defeated with few notable exceptions. In fact, victimization is so great that even bodies have been expropriated. Through a sophisticated theoretical discourse intertwined with stark images of tormented bodies, Eltit reveals the difficulties of female empowerment and the forms of violence perpetuated by a neoliberal economy within global capitalism. Her mito-tragic heroines give testimony to the spoils of humanity and the world.

In contrast, Brunet highlights the strategies of the weak through which rural women may survive and at times defeat their oppressor. It is interesting to note some coincidences between her characters and the picaresque as it developed in Spain and later in Latin America. Brunet's females have learned to survive under adverse circumstances and fiercely defend what they value. In her second writing period, women characters metamorphosed from *pícaras* and astute countrywomen to antiheroines who have been raised and taught by a lettered modernity. In this phase of her literature, Brunet incorporates the experience of middle- and upper-class women whose independent economic power redefines their subjectivity. These women are divided between those who identify themselves with the economic structure and its economic rewards and those others who find identity in motherhood. Thus Brunet alters the heteronormative narratives of modernity by masculinizing women and feminizing men, showing that modernization has brought about changes in subjectivity, gender roles, and sexuality.

In an oppressive contemporary setting, females become disenfranchised alongside other marginal groups in Eltit's hostile and nightmarish world in which the husband tends to hold the omnipotent power of father and judge. There is a distinct difference from Bombal's work, where women are represented as being dead yet alive bodies, disembodied minds that are aware that their lives cannot be changed. In this way, Bombal's literature disturbs the canon but without completely abolishing the patriarchal and Catholic ideology that defines it. Her characters tend to sacrifice themselves, with few exceptions, to social arrangements that condemn them and that they can only escape through autoeroticism or sadomasochist relations. Brunet, on the other hand, is closer to Eltit, sharing her social awareness and the ways power works and travels in a stratified society and hierarchical culture. Brunet, as does Eltit, understands power as a continuum that links the household with the community and the state. The level of awareness of the production, circulation, and reception of literary texts that Eltit shows in many of her interviews is something unprecedented that locates her in a new political position. Her thinking regarding symbolic production as a writer and intellectual owes much to poststructuralism and postfeminism.

These three writers produce new and distinct representations of feminine subjectivities, gender identity, and sexuality that challenge the political and historical master narratives of Latin American modernity/modernization and especially the Catholic and authoritarian Chilean version of it. With Eltit's paradigmatic writing, the female writer has reached a new position in that her critique encompasses culture at large and examines how the field of literature and the literary canon work to silence, omit, and include specific voices, reflecting the politics guiding their choices. Eltit shows a political awareness of the power of language and literature in shaping public discourses on subjectivity, sexuality, and the nation. In a mass society dominated by the ideology of consumerism and neoliberalism as the only alternatives, her literary project shows that what is at stake is the power to remember and to tell stories of oppression. In the last analysis, the existence of these narratives is threatened by the new form of colonialism that transnational capitalism reveals in the continent.

Notes

INTRODUCTION

1. It is important to note that the politicization of the social and community-based organizations was led by women and that a "popular feminism" began to take hold, as Susan Franceschet shows (2005). Furthermore, some of the most important human rights organizations were also led by women, such as the Asociación de Familiares de Detenidos Desaparecidos (Group of the Relatives of the Detained-Disappeared). Among the most visible female leaders were Sara Larraín, leader of the ecological movement, and Gladys Marín, secretary of the proscribed Communist Party.

2. Luce Irigaray, "The Power of Discourse and the Subordination of the Feminine," in *Literary Theory: An Anthology,* ed. Julie Rivkin and Michael Ryan, 570–71 (New York: Blackwell, 1998).

3. Marilena Chaui, "Sobre O Medo," in *Sentidos Da Paixao,* ed. Sergio Cardoso et al., 35–75 (São Paulo: Funarte, Companhia Das Letras, 1995).

4. Howard Caygill, "Kant and the Relegation of the Passions," in *Politics and The Passions 1500–1850,* ed. Victoria Kahn, Neil Saccamano, and Daniela Coli, 217–18 (Princeton, N.J.: Princeton University Press, 2006).

5. Chaui, "Sobre O Medo," 43–44.

6. Chaui, "Sobre O Medo," 44.

7. Michel Foucault, *Madness and Civilization: A History of Insanity in the Age of Reason,* trans. Richard Howard (New York: Vintage Books, 1988), 94–95.

8. Chaui, "Sobre O Medo," 45.

9. Luce Irigaray, "Commodities among Themselves," in *Literary Theory: An Anthology,* ed. Julie Rivkin and Michael Ryan, 574 (New York: Blackwell, 1998).

10. Chaui, "Sobre O Medo," 73.

11. Kathya Araujo, "Introducción," in *Sexualidades y sociedades contemporáneas,* ed. Kathya Araujo and Carolina Ibarra, 8–9 (Santiago: Universidad Academia de Humanismo Cristiano, 2003).

12. Claudia Bonan, "Sexualidad, reproducción y reflexividad," in *Sexualidades y sociedades contemporáneas,* ed. Kathya Araujo and Carolina Ibarra, 25–26 (Santiago: Universidad Academia de Humanismo Cristiano, 2003).

13. Marta Lamas, ed., "Introducción," in *El género: La construcción cultural de la diferencia sexual* (México: Universidad Autónoma Nacional de Mexico, 1996), 11.

14. Fernando Blanco, "Secretos y goces en la nación literaria," *Revista Iberoamericana-España-Portugal* 18 (2005): 130.

15. Ibid., 129.

16. Nicolás Casullo, "La modernidad como autoreflexión," in *Itinerarios de la modernidad: Corrientes del pensamiento y tradiciones intelectuales desde la*

Ilustración hasta la posmodernidad, ed. Nicolás Casullo, Ricardo Forster, and Alejandro Kaufman, 13–17 (Buenos Aires: Universidad de Buenos Aires, 1997).

17. Michel Foucault, "What Is Enlightenment?" in *The Foucault Reader,* ed. Paul Rabinow, 37 (New York: Pantheon Books, 1984).

18. Foucault, "What Is Enlightenment?" 47.

19. Mary Ann Caws, "Ladies Shot and Painted: Female Embodiment in Surrealist Art," in *The Female Body in Western Culture: Contemporary Perspectives,* ed. Susan Rubin Suleiman, 267–68 (Cambridge, Mass.: Harvard University Press, 1985).

20. John Berger, *Ways of Seeing* (Middlesex, England: Penguin Books, 1987), 54–55.

21. Rita Felski, *The Gender of Modernity* (Cambridge, Mass.: Harvard University Press, 1995), 16.

22. Ricardo Foster, "La crisis de la racionalidad moderna," in *Itinerarios de la modernidad: Corrientes del pensamiento y tradiciones intelectuales desde la Ilustración hasta la modernidad,* ed. Nicolás Casullo, Ricardo Foster, and Alejandro Krafman, 150 (Buenos Aires: Universidad de Buenos Aires, 1997).

23. Blanco, "Secretos y goces," 132.

24. Rubí Carreño, "Estereotipos e ideologías de género en M. Brunet y M. L. Bombal," *Anales de literatura chilena* 3 (December 2002): 44–45. Her book *Leche amarga: Violencia y erotismo en la narrativa Chilena del siglo XX. Brunet, Bombal, Donoso y Eltit* (2007) also discusses and expands some of these issues.

25. Rubí Carreño, "Eltit y su red local/global de citas: rescates del fundo y el supermercado," in *Letras y proclamas: La estética literaria de Diamela Eltit,* ed. Bernardita Llanos, 164–65 (Santiago: Cuarto Propio, 2006).

26. Judith Butler, *Gender Trouble: Feminism and the Subversion of Identity* (London: Routledge, 1990), 6.

27. Jean Franco, *The Modern Culture of Latin America: Society and the Artist* (Middlesex, England: Penguin Books, 1970), 290–91.

28. Jürgen Habermas, *The Structural Transformation of the Public Sphere: An Inquiry into a Category of Bourgeois Society,* trans. Thomas Burger and Frederick Lawrence (Cambridge, Mass.: MIT Press, 1989).

29. Joan B. Landes, ed., "The Public and the Private Sphere: A Feminist Reconsideration," in *Feminism: The Public and the Private* (Oxford: Oxford University Press, 1998), 139, 142–43.

30. Martín Hopenhayn, "Postmodernism and Neoliberalism in Latin America," in *The Postmodernism Debate in Latin America,* ed. John Beverly, Michael Aronna, and José Oviedo, 102 (Durham, N.C.: Duke University Press, 1995).

31. England and France replaced Spain as cultural sources in the political-economic field (England) and in the cultural realm (France). In this process of building a national identity, as Larraín has argued, the Chilean elite was self-denominated as "the English of South America" (263). Rejection of the past as well as cultural heritage determined the elite's worldview as well as its political project.

32. Vivian Schelling, "Introduction," in *Through the Kaleidoscope: The Experience of Modernity in Latin America,* trans. Lorraine Leu (London: Verso, 2000), 6–7.

33. Jorge Larraín, *Identity and Modernity in Latin America* (Oxford, Mass.: Blackwell, 2000), 136, 204.

34. The critic Bernardo Subercaseaux notes in *Chile ¿Un país moderno?* (Santiago: Ediciones, 1996) that modernity in Chile has oftentimes been defined as an end in itself and predominantly linked to technical and rational universal values. This view sees modernity exclusively in terms of an accomplishment of statistical indicators. Subercaseaux concludes that for a society to be truly modern, its entire population should have access to basic needs (education, health, housing, and culture) (85). The sociologist José Joaquín Brunner further points out that Latin America has a differential and segmented participation in the global market since its colonial insertion in the world order and its subsequent postindependence period. See his book, *Un espejo trizado: Ensayos sobre cultura y políticas culturales* (Santiago: FLACSO, 1988).

35. Schelling, "Introduction," 11–16.

36. Maximiliano Salinas Campos, *"Contrapuntos"* in *Sexualidades y sociedades contemporáneas,* ed. Kathya Araujo and Carolina Ibarra, 93, 94, 99 (Santiago: Universidad Academia de Humanismo Cristiano, 2003).

37. Cited by Mario Lillo Cabezas, "Ensayo chileno e identidad," *Taller de Letras* 27 (November 1999): 25.

38. Asunción Lavrín, ed., "Introducción," in *Sexualidad y matrimonio en la América hispánica: Siglos XVI–XVIII* (México: Grijalbo, 1991), 20–21.

39. Ibid., 31.

40. Sergio Gatica Cortés, "Mujer, matrimonio y poder en Chile colonial: Un enfoque histórico teórico," in *Anuario del Programa Género y Cultura en América Latina* (Santiago: Universidad de Chile, 1996), 21.

41. María Emma Mannarelli, "La domesticación de la sexualidad en las sociedades jerárquicas," in *Sexualidades y sociedades contemporáneas,* ed. Kathya Araujo and Carolina Ibarra, 81–82 (Santiago: Universidad Academia de Humanismo Cristiano, 2003).

42. See www.es.wikipedia.org/wiki/Código_Civil_de_Chile#Fuentes

43. Isabel V. Hull, *Sexuality, State and Civil Society in Germany, 1700–1815* (Ithaca, N.Y.: Cornell University Press, 1996), 371–75.

44. Ibid., 375.

45. Ibid., 371.

46. See "Prólogo," in *Modernidad en otro tono: Escritura de mujeres latinoamericanas: 1920–1950,* ed. Alicia N. Salomone et al., 11 (Santiago: Cuarto Propio, 2004).

47. Grínor Rojo, "Gabriela Mistral en la historia de la mujer latinoamericana," in *Re-leer hoy a Gabriela Mistral: Mujer, historia y sociedad en América Latina,* ed. Gastón Lillo and J. Guillermo Renart, 59–60 (Ottawa and Santiago: University of Ottawa and Universidad de Santiago, 1997). This also explains that in Chile 25 percent of the working class was made up of women, showing the development and increase in female labor. Middle-class women, on the other hand, benefited from the acceptance of teaching as an admissible female occupation. Asunción Lavrín points out that at the beginning of the twentieth century in Chile, 60% of primary school teachers were women and that this percentage increased up to 75% in 1950 (cited by Grínor Rojo, 63).

48. Asunción Lavrín, *Female, Feminine and Feminist: Key Concepts in Understanding Women's History in Twentieth Century Latin America.* Occasional Lecture Series No. 4 (Bristol: University of Bristol, 1988), 5.

49. Asunción Lavrín, *Women, Feminism and Social Change in Argentina, Chile and Uruguay 1840–1940* (Lincoln: University of Nebraska Press, 1995), 194–196.

50. Ibid., 197–214.

51. Patricia Rubio, ed., "Introducción," in *Escritoras chilenas: Tercer volumen. Novela y cuento* (Santiago: Editorial Cuarto Propio, 1999), 21.

52. Carole Pateman, *The Sexual Contract* (Stanford, Calif: Stanford University Press, 1988), 11, 113.

53. In her *A Queer Mother for the Nation: The State and Gabriela Mistral* (Minneapolis: University of Minnesota Press, 2002), Licia Fiol-Mata presents a queer cultural reading of this national image.

54. *Marianismo,* as Evelyn Stevens has shown ("Marianismo: The Other Face of Machismo in Latin America," in *Confronting Change, Challenging Tradition: Women in Latin American History,* ed. Gertrude M. Yeager, 3–17 [Wilmington, Del.: Scholarly Resources, 1994], 9) is a cultural phenomenon that develops most fully in Latin America in comparison to other regions in the Old World cultures, such as Italy and Spain, where it also exists. This ideal for Latin American women enforces pain and submission as feminine virtues. Thus a good woman is symbolically related to the Virgin mother and the mater dolorosa while the bad one, in contrast, is seen as lacking feminine attributes and being masculine. The virginal ideal of *marianismo* in which spiritual strength and moral superiority are central states that these are exclusively feminine characteristics.

55. Sonia Montecino, *Madres y huachos.* Alegorías del mestizaje chileno (Santiago: Cuarto Propio, 1993), 30–32.

56. Cortés, "Mujer, matrimonio y poder," 20–21.

57. Rubí Carreño, "Familia y la crisis de los géneros en los años treinta," *Taller de Letras* 27 (1999): 135–36.

58. Carreño, "Familia y la crisis," 144–45.

59. Amanda Labarca, *Feminismo contemporáneo* (Santiago: Zig Zag, 1947), 46–47.

60. Lavrín, *Women, Feminism, Social Change,* 212.

61. Alejandra Castillo, *La república masculina y la promesa igualitaria* (Santiago: Palinodia, 2005), 93.

62. See my essay "Sobre el retorno y sus fantasmas: Mistral y Tala," in *Más allá de la ciudad letrada. Escritoras de Nuestra América,* ed. Eliana Ortega, 55–64 (Santiago: *ISIS Internacional,* 2001). Mistral reproduces the major pacts of the Catholic imaginary but introduces passion in the same way I have described, as the mother-daughter bond illustrates in her poetry collection, *Tala* (1938).

63. Teresa Valdés, *De lo social a lo político: La acción de las mujeres latinoamericas* (Santiago: LOM, 2000), 20–28.

64. Ibid., 41.

65. Jorge Larraín, *Identidad chilena* (Santiago: LOM, 2001), 226–27.

66. Ibid., 230. Violence against women who do not fit the norm is a prevalent sociocultural issue. Today, marital conflicts, as studies have shown, showcase the prevalence of hostility between spouses and physical violence toward females by males. Domestic violence and sexual abuse within the Chilean family are recurrent practices that have reached not only literary discourse but the media and other public service agencies. The risk of death that wives and sexual partners face at the hands of their husbands or lovers appears to be a real social issue in contemporary Chile, where 38 percent of upper- and middle-class females have suffered some kind of domestic violence according to a study conducted in 2001 by government agencies.

67. Lorena Fries and Verónica Matus, *La ley hace el delito* (Santiago: LOM, La Morada, 2000), 10–11, 36.

68. Ibid., 37–38.

69. Ana Pizarro, "Mistral ¿Qué Modernidad?" in *Re-leer hoy a Gabriela Mistral: Mujer, historia y sociedad en América Latina,* ed. Gastón Lillo and J. Guillermo Renart, 49 (Ottawa and Santiago: University of Ottawa and Universidad de Santiago, 1997).

70. José Joaquín Brunner, "Notes on Modernity and Postmodernity in Latin America," in *The Postmodernism Debate in Latin America,* ed. John Beverly, Michael Aronna, and José Oviedo, 39–40 (Durham, N.C.: Duke University Press, 1995).

71. Ibañez's populist nationalism unexpectedly returned, after a period of exile, with his triumph in the presidential elections of 1952. His "doublespeak," as Simon Collier describes it, allowed him to gain support on both ends of the political spectrum while his right-wing supporters espoused a dictatorship. Ibañez's opportunistic political alliances with the Left and the Right are also reflected in the kind of state capitalism his government implemented for a couple of years, later substituted by an economic liberalization following the recommendations of the International Monetary Fund (IMF). He won the presidency in the fifties (1952–58), mainly with an agenda in which order and presidential strength were strategically positioned against traditional politics and politicians, something that Pinochet would also resort to. Ibañez's appeal to women voters, who actually voted for the first time in this presidential election, also illuminates their support of conservative values and authoritarianism. For more see Tomás Moulian, *Material docente sobre historia de Chile, 1952–1958* (Santiago: FLACSO, 1986), and Simon Collier and William F. Sater, *A History of Chile, 1808–2002* (Cambridge: Cambridge University Press, 2004).

72. Idelber Avelar, *The Untimely Present: Postdictatorial Latin American Fiction and the Task of Mourning* (Durham, N.C.: Duke University Press, 1999), 13.

73. Avelar, *Untimely Present,* 2.

74. See Fernando Blanco, "Figuras chilenas para una memoria en obra," in *Espejos que dejan ver: Artes visuales femeninas en América Latina,* ed. Eliana Ortega y María Elvira Iriarte, 157–82 (Santiago: ISIS Internacional, 2002), and his "Comunicación política y memoria en la escritura de Pedro Lemebel," in *Reinas de otro cielo: Modernidad y autoritarismo en la obra de Pedro Lemebel,* ed. Fernando Blanco, 27–71 (Santiago: LOM, 2004). See also my chapter in this book "Masculinidad, estado y violencia en la ciudad neoliberal," 75–113.

75. Max Horkeimer and Theodor W. Adorno, *Dialectic of Enlightenment,* trans. John Cumming (New York: Continuum, 1986), 3–9.

76. A similarly devastated image of the real may be found in Slavoj Žižek's post-9/11 essay "Welcome to the Desert of the Real," in *Dissent from the Homeland: Essays after September 11,* ed. Stanley Hauver and Frank Letricchia, 137–48 (Durham, N.C.: Duke University Press, 2003). In the neoliberal city, public spaces and collective gathering are proscribed, replaced by neighborhoods under surveillance where the system's ideological matrix is forcefully displayed. The phantoms of Western culture and its definition of modernity travel this narrative and constitute the law in a culture that mimics central powers.

77. The new civil law on marriage (Law 19947), ratified on November 18, 2004, replaced the old one of 1884 that had banned divorce.

78. Olga Grau, "Familia: Un grito de fin de siglo," in *Discurso, Género y*

Poder: Discursos públicos: Chile 1978–1993, ed. Olga Grau et al., 128–35 (Santiago: Arcis, La Morada, 1997).

CHAPTER 1. MARTA BRUNET

1. Literary critic Luis Alberto Mansilla and Brunet's nephew Hugo Montes identify 1897 as the year of Brunet's birth rather than 1901 as others have. See Mansilla's "Prologue" in *Humo hacia el sur* (Santiago: LOM, 1998) 5, and Montes's "Evocación de Marta Brunet," *Atenea* (1992): 293.

2. See *Ercilla* 1373 September 13, 1961, 12–13. For more biographical information on Brunet consult Marjorie Agosín's "Marta Brunet: A Literary Biography," *Revista Interamericana de Bibliografía,* 36 (1986): 452–59.

3. See Sergio Hernández Romero, "Notas biográficas de Marta Brunet," *Theoria* 4 (1995): 112–13.

4. Haydée Ahumada Peña, "Marta Brunet (1901–1967)," in *Escritoras chilenas, Tercer Volumen, Novela y cuento,* ed. Patricia Rubio, 139 (Santiago: Cuarto Propio, 1999).

5. See Interview "Marta Brunet fue calificada como inmoral y hereje . . . ," *Hombres e Ideas* (1-XII-61): 25.

6. Kemy Oyarzún discusses this in relation to the reception of Brunet's literature and its cultural implications. See her "Prólogo" in *Aguas abajo* (Santiago: Cuarto Propio, 1997), 8–12.

7. Cited in Nicomedes Guzmán, "La escritora Marta Brunet en las letras chilenas," *Antología de cuentos* (Santiago: Zig-Zag, 1970), 11.

8. See Berta López, "Recepción crítica de la obra de Marta Brunet," http://www.cervantesvirtual.com/bib_autor/brunet/recritica.shtml.

9. Hernán Díaz Arrieta, *Panorama de la literatura chilena durante el siglo XX* (Santiago: Editorial Nascimento, 1931), 147.

10. Romero, "Notas biográficas de Marta Brunet," 116.

11. Rubí Carreño (unpublished Ph.D. diss., Universidad de Chile, Santiago, 2004).

12. Oscar Guzmán Silva, "90 años de Marta Brunet, Premio Nacional de 1961," *El Mercurio, Antofagasta-Calama,* August 9,1987, 2.

13. Kemy Oyarzún, "Prólogo," *Aguas abajo,* 7–8.

14. Here I am following Gilles Deleuze's discussion on the system of signs as he develops it in *Proust et les Signes* (1964) and in his later work with Felix Guattari, *A Thousand Plateaus: Capitalism and Schizophrenia,* trans. Brian Massumi (Minneapolis: University of Minnesota Press, 1987), particularly chap. 5. When analyzing Brunet's distinctive work the notion of a system or regime of signs aids in understanding the discursive operations she deploys.

15. "La batalla contra la natural barbarie." Cited in José Promis, *La novela chilena actual (Orígenes y desarrollo)* (Argentina: Fernando García Cambeiro, 1977), 24.

16. Hernán Díaz Arrieta, "Prólogo," in *Brunet, Obras completas* (Santiago: Zig-Zag, 1962), 15–16; Fernando Alegría, *Breve historia de la novela hispanoamericana* (México: Editorial Andrea, 1959), 221; and Raúl Silva Castro, *Panorama literario de Chile* (Santiago: Editorial Universitaria,1961), 306–11.

17. Pedro N. Cruz says, "En nuestra literatura, la mujer está compitiendo ventajosamente con el hombre." Cited in Julio Durán Cerda, "Marta Brunet, Puente de plata hacia el sur," AUCH 124, Fourth Trimester (1961): 90.

18. Ibid., 90.

19. Lucía Guerra, "Reflexiones teóricas sobre la novela femenina," *Hispamérica* 28 (1981): 33.

20. Márgara Russotto, *Tópicos de retórica femenina* (Caracas: Monte Avila Editores, 1990), 59.

21. Gabriela Mora, "Una lectura de 'Soledad de la sangre' de Marta Brunet," *Estudios Filológicos* 19 (1984): 81–90, and Marjorie Agosín, "La mimesis de la interioridad: 'Soledad de la sangre' de Marta Brunet y 'El árbol' de María Luisa Bombal," *Neophilologus* 68, no. 3 (July 1984): 380–88, and her "Marta Brunet: A Literary Biography," *Revista Interamericana de Bibliografía* 36 (1986): 452–59.

22. Mora, "Una lectura de 'Soledad de la sangre,' " 82.

23. *Landscapes of a New Land: Short Fiction by Latin American Women,* ed. Marjorie Agosín, trans. Elaine Dorough Johnson, 61–83 (Fredonia, NY: White Pine Press, 1989). "Solitude of Blood" was reprinted in *Changing Lives through Literature,* ed. Robert P. Waxler and Jean R. Trounstine, 59–80 (Notre Dame, Ind,: University of Notre Dame Press, 1999).

24. *What Is Secret: Stories by Chilean Women,* ed. Marjorie Agosín, 142–50 (Fredonia, N.Y.: White Pine Press, 1995).

25. See her article "No me hagas reír" on Brunet's *María Rosa, flor del Quillén* (1929), http://www.letras.s5.com/eltit-b11.htm.

26. Fernando Blanco, "Lecturas enrarecidas: saltos, mariquitas, apollerados y cóndores," *Nomadías* 5, no. 5 (September 2001): 111–14.

27. Juan Pablo Sutherland, *A corazón abierto: Geografía literaria de la homosexualidad en Chile* (Santiago: Sudamericana Planeta, 2001), 25.

28. Angel Rama, "La condición humana de la mujer," in *Soledad de la sangre* (Montevideo: Arca, 1967), 7.

29. Oyarzún, "Prólogo," 30–31.

30. Promis, *La novela chilena actual,* 24.

31. I refer to Kemy Oyarzún, ed., "Piedra callada," in *Aguas abajo,* 35–65 (Santiago: Cuarto Propio, 1997). All the translations are mine unless noted.

32. I quote in Spanish from *Aguas abajo* and from the English translation of this text ("Down River") in Agosín, ed., *What Is Secret,* 142–50.

33. I quote from the Spanish original in *Aguas abajo* and from the English translation ("Solitude of Blood") found in Waxler and Trounstine, eds., *Changing Lives through Literature,* 59–80.

34. Rodrigo Cánovas, *Sexualidad y cultura en la novela hispanoamericana: La alegoría del prostíbulo* (Santiago: LOM, 2003), 21–25.

35. It refers to the right that allowed the feudal lord unrestricted access to the virgins in his estate during their wedding day. Through the hacienda culture this practice was introduced and maintained in rural areas in Chile.

36. Pierre Bourdieu, *La dominación masculina,* trans. Joaquín Jordá (España: Anagrama, 2000), 22.

37. Maritza Carrasco, "La historicidad de lo oculto: La violencia conyugal y la mujer en Chile (Siglos XVIII y la primera mitad del XIX)," in *Perfiles revelados: Historias de mujeres en Chile siglos XVIII–XX,* ed. Diana Veneros Ruiz-Tagle, 121 (Santiago: Editorial Universidad de Santiago, 1997). Carrasco's article gives a comprehensive view of the legacy of violence in the rural family and how it was used to educate children and keep women controlled (encompassing the social, economic, legal, and personal realms).

38. For another discussion on violence and transgression in these stories, see

my article "Transgresión y violencia sexual en Marta Brunet," *Mapocho,* December 2000: 29–37.

39. José Bengoa, "El estado al desnudo: Acerca de la formación de lo masculino en Chile," in *Diálogos sobre el género masculino en Chile,* ed. Sonia Montecino and María Elena Acuña, 73, 75, 76 (Santiago: Bravo y Allende Editores, 1996).

40. See Heidi Tinsman, "Los patrones del hogar: Esposas golpeadas y control sexual en Chile rural, 1958–1988," in *Disciplina y desacato: Construcción de identidad en Chile, Siglos XIX y XX,* ed. Lorena Godoy et al., 119, 125 (Santiago: SUR/CEDEM, 1995).

41. Catalina Arteaga, "Oficios, trabajos y vida," 207–9. Flores Santos in *Bestia dañina* (1926) is the emblematic figure in Brunet's repertoire of the despotic father who exercises his power without regard for his daughters' feelings.

42. Jessica Benjamin, *The Bonds of Love: Psychoanalysis, Feminism, and the Problem of Domination* (New York: Pantheon Books, 1988), 64. Here Benjamin introduces Bataille's discussion on eroticism and its relation to death.

43. Ibid., 52.

44. A similar argument may be found in Rubén Ríos Avila's psychoanalytic cultural analysis of Puerto Rican colonial subjectivity. See his *La raza Cómica del sujeto en Puerto Rico* (Puerto Rico: Ediciones Callejón, 2002), 26–27.

45. For further discussion, see Bourdieu's *La dominación masculina,* 24–25.

46. Susan Griffin, *Rape: The Power of Consciousness* (New York: Harper & Row, 1979), 39.

47. Susan Brownmiller, *Against Our Will: Men, Women and Rape* (New York: Simon & Schuster, 1975), 14–15, 256.

48. Blair Justice and Rita Justice, *The Broken Taboo: Sex in the Family* (New York: Human Science Press, 1979). See particularly chapter 4 for an interesting discussion of different types of incestuous fathers. Bernabé would fit their description of the tyrant father.

49. María Emma Mannarelli, "La domesticación de la sexualidad en las sociedades jerárquicas," in *Sexualidades y sociedades contemporáneas,* ed. Kathya Araujo and Carolina Ibarra, 62–63 (Santiago: Universidad Academia de Humanismo Cristiano, 2003).

50. Oyarzún, "Prólogo," 27. Oyarzún discusses this characteristic of Brunet's short story endings and links it to Cortázar's term.

51. Sigmund Freud, *Totem and Taboo: Resemblances between the Psychic Lives of Savages and Neurotics,* trans. A. A. Brill (Amherst, N.Y.: Prometheus Books, 2000), 55.

52. Claude Lévi-Strauss, *The Elementary Structures of Kinship,* trans. James Harle Bell and John Richard von Sturmer (Boston: Beacon Press, 1969), 12, 18.

53. Sigmund Freud, *Obras completas,* vol. 7, trans. José L. Echeverry (Argentina: Amorrortu Editores, 1975), 203–11.

54. Jessica Benjamin, "The Alienation of Desire: Women's Masochism and Ideal Love," in *Psychoanalysis and Women: Contemporary Reappraisals,* ed. Judith L. Alpert, 12–13 (Hillsdale, N.J.: Analytic Press, 1986).

55. Ibid., 12–27.

56. Tinsman, "Los patrones del hogar," 122.

57. Jean R. Trounstine, "For Discussion," 78–79.

58. Ibid., 66–67. Trounstine calls Brunet's story melodramatic precisely because it is told by a battered wife, who suffers the violence of an arranged marriage and is a victim of a male-dominated culture.

59. Rama, "La condición humana de la mujer," 11.
60. Mora, "Una lectura," 82–83.
61. Ibid., 86.
62. Pierre Grimal, *Dictionary of Classical Mythology,* ed. Stephen Kershaw, trans. A. R. Maxell-Hyslop, 407 (London: Penguin Books, 1990).
63. Julio Durán Cerda, "Puente de plata hacia el sur," *AUCH* 124 (Fourth Quarter 1961): 92.
64. See Ruiz-Tagle, ed., "Continuidad, cambio y reacción 1900–1930," In *Perfiles revelados: Historias de mujeres en Chille siglos XVIII–XX,* 26–27.
65. The protagonist's fate in many ways also resembles that of Bombal's Brígida in "El árbol." Both stories center on the loss of a cherished object (the phonograph here, the tree in "El árbol") as the vehicle of a transformative experience. See Marjorie Agosín, "La mímesis de la interioridad: 'Soledad de la sangre' de Marta Brunet y 'El árbol' de María Luisa Bombal," *Neophilologus* 68, no. 3 (July 1984): 381–83.

CHAPTER 2. *MARIA NADIE*

1. Hugo Montes, "Prólogo," *María Nadie* (Santiago: Pehuén, 1997), 12–13.
2. José Promis, *La novela chilena actual (Orígenes y desarrollo)* (Argentina: Fernando García Gambeiro, 1977), 114–115.
3. Ibid., 87.
4. Berta López Morales, "Recepción crítica de la obra de Marta Brunet," http://www.cervantesvirtual.com/bib_autor/brunet/recritica.shtml.
5. See Promis's *La novela chilena actual,* 24.
6. Cecilia Ojeda in "Hacia una revisión crítica de la narrativa de Brunet: Humo hacia el Sur y María Nadie," *Confluencia* 14, no. (Fall 1998): 18–121.
7. This section has been seen as the "birth of Colloco" rather than the early development of a modernizing process. See "Marta Brunet fue calificada de de inmoral y hereje," Revista *Zig-Zag,* December 1, 1961, 25.
8. See "Crónica Literaria," *El Mercurio,* November 17, 1957, 7.
9. Interestingly, Eltit will also use animal gender markers and animal reactions to profanities to signal the linguistic degradation of females.
10. My reading here is informed by Ann Kaplan's feminist film theory and her critique of patriarchal visual modes of representations as she first argued them in her groundbreaking essay "Is the Gaze Male?" in *Women and Film: Both Sides of the Camera* (New York: 1983), 23–35.
11. Ivonne Cuadra, "(De)formación de la imagen de la virgen María en Isaacs, Brunet y Queiroz," http://www.ucm.es/info/especulo/numero31/deforma.html.
12. Rita Felski, *The Gender of Modernity* (Cambridge, Mass: Harvard University Press, 1995), 3, 9.
13. Even a progressive and feminist women's organization such as MEMCH (founded in 1935) fought for women's equality but did not debate gender. Most women's social and religious organizations were concerned with increasing women's public participation. For more see Corinne Antezanna-Pernet, "El MEMCH en provincia: Movilización femenina y sus obstáculos, 1935–1942," in *Disciplina y Desacato: Construcción de la identidad en Chile, siglos XIX y XX,* ed. Lorena Godoy, et. al. (Santiago: SUR/CEDEM, 1995), 287–329. Also see

Margara Rusotto, *Tópicos de retórica femenina* (Caracas: Monte Avila Editores, 1993), 23–42.

14. Judith Butler, *Antigone's Claim: Kinship between Life and Death* (New York: Columbia University Press, 2000), 34–36.

15. Felski, *Gender of Modernity*, 2.

16. For further discussion on *huachos* and mestizo masculine identity, see Sonia Montecino, *Madres y huachos: Alegorías del mestizaje chileno* (Santiago: Cuarto Propio, 1993), and Jorge Larraín, *Identidad chilena* (Santiago: LOM, 2001).

17. Carolyn Heilbrun, *Writing a Woman's Life* (New York: Ballantine Books, 1989), 37–39.

18. Rita Felski, *Literature after Feminism* (Chicago: University of Chicago Press, 2003), 26–29.

19. Heilbrun, *Writing a Woman's Life*, 51.

20. Ojeda, "Hacia una revisión crítica," 121.

21. Esther Melón de Díaz's *La narrativa de Marta Brunet* (Puerto Rico, España: Editorial Universitaria, 1975), 110–11.

22. For more discussion consult Promis, *La novela chilena actual*, 24.

23. *Marimacha* is Chilean slang for a woman with power who acts like a man in private and in public. This word also refers to a lesbian. *Maricueca*, on the other hand, designates the counterpart, in which a male is identified as powerless, passive, and feminine. This word is also used to identify homosexuals in popular Chilean speech.

24. See also Ojeda, "Hacia una revisión crítica," 113.

25. Diana Veleros, ed. "Continuidad, cambio y reacción 1900–1930," in *Perfiles revelados. Historias de mujeres en Chile. siglos XVIII–XX* (Santiago: Editorial Universidad de Santiago, 1997), 30–39. Consult also the magazine *Familia*, which Brunet directed from 1935 to 1940.

26. Simone de Beauvoir, *El segundo sexo: La experiencia vivida*, trans. Pablo Palant (Buenos Aires: Ediciones de Siglo Veinte, 1987), 471.

27. For more on this consult Promis's article "En torno a la nueva novela hispanoamericana: Reubicación de un concepto," *Chasqui* 7, no. 1 (1977): 16–27.

28. Jessica Benjamin, *The Bonds of Love: Psychoanalysis, Feminism and the Problem of Domination* (New York: Pantheon, 1988), 20, 195.

29. Ibid., 187–88.

30. Ibid., 218.

31. The act of *ningunear* works in this context in a similar way to what Octavio Paz in *El Laberinto de la soledad* (1950) has described for Mexican culture, basically effacing while lowering someone's identity.

32. José Joaquín Brunner, "Tradicionalismo y modernidad," in *Posmodernidad en la periferia: Enfoques latinoamericanos de la nueva teoría cultural*, ed. Hermann Herlinghaus and Monika Walter, 56–57 (Berlin: Langer Verlag, 1994).

33. Brunner, "Tradicionalismo y modernidad," 61–62.

34. Ojeda, "Hacia una revisión crítica," 113, 122.

35. Paulo Antonio Paranaguá, *Tradición y modernidad en el cine de América Latina* (España: Fondo de Cultura Económica, 2003), 20–21.

36. Berta López Morales, *La órbita de Marta Brunet* (Concepción: Edición Universitaria de Concepción, 1997), 54–55.

37. Yvonne Knibiehler, *Historia de las madres y de la maternidad en Occidente*, trans. Paula Mahler (Buenos Aires: Nueva Visión, 2000), 7.

38. See her article "Siglo XX, Cambalache. Breve reseña histórica de los avances de la mujer en Chile," *Investigaciones Red Nacional Universitaria Interdisciplinaria de Estudios de Género* (Santiago: Servicio Nacional de la Mujer, 2001), 106.

39. Sharon Hays, *The Cultural Contradictions of Motherhood* (New Haven, Conn.: Yale University Press, 1996), 3, 18, 49.

40. Ibid., 79.

41. Brunner, "Tradicionalismo y modernidad," According to Brunner 61 percent of the population of Latin America in 1950 was rural and around 26 percent lived in centers with more than 20,000 inhabitants.

CHAPTER 3. MARIA LUISA BOMBAL

1. María Flora Yáñez wrote introspective and sentimental novels and was one of the most productive women writers of her time. As her autobiography, *Historia de mi vida* (Santiago: Nascimento, 1980), reveals, she met Bombal and her family while they were living in Paris in the 1920s and frequented the same circle of Chilean and Argentinian expatriates. See 175.

2. See www.theaterhistory.com/french/artaud001.html.

3. See www.escritores.cl/semblanzas/texto/bombal.htm.

4. See Ana Iris Alvarez Nuñez. In a newspaper article on Bombal she also resorts to the princess image from the title. See her "Princesa de las escritoras," *El día,* La Serena, January 8, 1992, 2.

5. With Geel Bombal represents in Chile a woman writer whose life and passionate actions defied not only conventional morality but also the law. María Carolina Geel (whose real name was Georgina Silva Jiménez) was imprisoned for killing her former lover. Bombal circumvented imprisonment after shooting Eulogio Sánchez because he did not press charges.

6. See Leonidas Morales, *Conversaciones con Diamela Eltit* (Santiago: Cuarto Propio, 1998), 153.

7. Adriana Valdés, "Las novelistas chilenas: Breve visión histórica y reseña crítica," *Aisthesis: Revista chilena de investigaciones estéticas* 3 (1968): 125. For Valdés, Bombal would be the best exponent of this literature: she was the only woman writer who succeeded in transferring a poetic vision to narrative in the Chilean literary tradition of the 1930s. Celeste Kostopulos-Cooperman, in *The Lyrical Vision of Maria Luisa Bombal* (London: Tamesis Books Limited, 1988), also highlights the novel's lyrical and paradoxical language. See especially 7 and her discussion of Bombal's search for a medium that could express an interiorized vision. Amado Alonso also noted this poetic aspiration in his prologue to the second edition of the novel in Chile.

8. Jorge Larraín, *Identity and Modernity in Latin America* (Oxford, Mass.: Blackwell, 2000), 22.

9. My analysis centers on the Spanish novel and does not consider the English version titled *House of Mist* (1947), which Bombal wrote and published in the United States with Farrar Straus. This is really a different text that deviates in significant ways from the original and that merits a study beyond the scope of this one. For more on *House of Mist,* see Patricia Rubio, "*House of Mist,* de María Luisa Bombal: Una novela olvidada," *Literatura y Linguística* 11 (1998):181–204.

10. María Inés Lagos, "Silencio y rebeldía: Hacia una valoración de Maria

Luisa Bombal dentro de la tradición de escritura femenina," in *María Luisa Bombal: Apreciaciones críticas,* ed. Marjorie Agosín, Elena Gascón-Vera and Joy Renjilian-Burgy, 119–35, esp. 126 (Tempe, Ariz.: Bilingual Press/Editorial Bilingue, 1987).

11. Susan Fraiman, *Unbecoming Women* (New York: Columbia University Press, 1993), 6.

12. All references and direct quotations from the novel are from *María Luisa Bombal: Obras completas,* ed. Lucia Guerra (Santiago: Editorial Andrés Bello, 1997). All translations are mine unless noted.

13. Hernán Vidal, *María Luisa Bombal: La femeneidad enajenada* (Gerona, España: Colección Aubi, 1976), 49, 54.

14. Doris Meyer, "Feminine Testimony in the Works of Teresa de la Parra, María Luisa Bombal and Victoria Ocampo," in *Contemporary Women Authors of Latin America,* ed. Doris Meyer and Margarita Fernández Olmos, 3–15, esp. 10 (New York: Brooklyn College Press, 1983).

15. Luce Irigaray, "The Power of Discourse and the Subordination of the Feminine," in *Literary Theory: An Anthology,* ed. Julie Rivkin and Michael Ryan, 572–73 (New York: Blackwell, 1998).

16. Irigaray, "Power of Discourse," 571–72.

17. See her "Revolution in Poetic Language" in *The Kristeva Reader,* ed. Toril Moi, 90–136 (New York: Columbia University Press, 1986).

18. Gilles Deleuze, "Coldness and Cruelty," in *Masochism,* trans. G. Brazilier (New York: Zone Books, 1991); 9–138. esp. 117–18, 120.

19. Gilles Deleuze, "Coldness and Cruelty," 120.

20. See Evelyn Stevens, "Marianismo: The Other Face of Machismo in Latin America," in *Confronting Change, Challenging Tradition: Women in Latin American History,* ed. Gertrude M. Yeager, 3–17 (Wilmington, Del.: Scholarly Resources, 1994); Asunción Lavrín, "The Ideology of Feminism in the Southern Cone, 1900–1940," (working paper of the Latin American Program of the Woodrow Wilson International Center, 169 [1986]): 1–42.

21. Meyer, "Feminine Testimony," 10.

22. Alberto Rábago, "Elementos surrealistas de *La última niebla,*" *Hispania* 64 (March 1981): 68.

23. Rubio, "*House of Mist,* de María Luisa Bombal," 201.

24. Saúl Sosnowski, "El agua, motivo primordial en LUN," *Cuadernos* 277–78 (1973): 371–72.

25. For a further discussion on the connection between transgression and sacrifice, see Georges Bataille, *Erotism, Death and Sensuality,* trans. Mary Dalwood (San Francisco: City Lights Books, 1986), 79–80.

26. See Doré Ripley, "Hunting through Medieval Literature,' www.dead-on websites.com/under%20discount/hunt/med_hunt.htm.

27. Lucía Guerra, ed., "Introducción," *María Luisa Bombal: Obras completas* (Santiago: Editorial Andrés Bello, 1997), esp. 30, 32.

28. Diamela Eltit's narrator in *Los vigilantes (Custody of the Eyes)* reiterates the use of writing as a discourse that protects the subject from a harassing social reality in more acute ways. Interestingly, letter writing, the most private form of writing, becomes an open and public testimony of victimization in both novels.

29. See Soledad Bianchi's "María Luisa Bombal o una difícil travesía," *Atenea (Universidad de Concepción)* 445 (1985): 175–92, esp. 183. Bianchi discusses how Bombal's heroines use their silence and the multiple meanings it

has. Also consult Lagos, "Silencio y rebeldía," 122–23, for a discussion on how silence is used by the female characters in Bombal. See also Sepúlveda, "María Luisa Bombal y el silencio," 230–36.

30. Rubio, *House of Mist,* de María Luisa Bombal," 194.

31. See Phyllis Rodríguez-Peralta, "María Luisa Bombal's Poetic Novels of Estrangement," *Revista de Estudios Hispánicos* 14, no. 1 (1980): 139–55, esp. 142.

32. Consult Margaret Campbell's article "The Vaporous World of María Luisa Bombal," *Hispania* 44 (1961): 415–19, esp. 416. This is a very perceptive analysis of the wraithlike quality of Bombal's texts. Also see Cedomil Goic, "La última niebla," in *La novela chilena: Los mitos degradados* (Santiago: Editorial Universitaria, 1991), 167–86.

33. Esther Nelson, "The Space of Longing: *La última niebla,*" *The American Hispanist,* 3, no. 21 (November 1977): 7–11.

34. See his "La última niebla," 167–69.

35. Gutiérrez Mouat, "Construcción y represión," In *María Luisa Bombal: Apreciaciones críticas,* 103–4.

36. See Cedomil, *"La última niebla,"* 177.

37. See Borinsky, "El paisaje de la apatía," in *María Luisa Bombal: Apreciaciones críticas,* 37. Borinsky shows how this energy is also used by the narrator to become inaccessible to her husband.

38. Helene C. Weldt-Basson, "Women and the City: Sexual Initiation of Female Protagonists in Marta Brunet, María Luisa Bombal, Sandra Cisneros and Rosario Castellanos," *Torre: Revista de la Universidad de Puerto Rico,* 39 (January–March, 2006): 66–69. In Brunet's story, however, the ambivalence of the sexual encounter is expressed in the virtual rape Ruth suffers and how she turns around the potentially destructive effects by becoming the official lover of the stranger while being married.

39. María Luisa Bastos, "Relectura de *La última niebla,* de María Luisa Bombal," *Revista Iberoamericana* 51 (July–December 1985): 560.

40. Deleuze, "Coldness and Cruelty," 119.

41. See Carl Olson, *Zen and the Art of Postmodern Philosophy: Two Paths of Liberation from the Representational Mode of Thinking* (Albany: State University of New York Press, 2000), 93–109. Chapter 5 is especially relevant to the question of the body and the world.

42. Vidal, *María Luisa Bombal: La femeneidad enajenada,* 82–83.

43. Borinsky, "El paisaje de la apatía," 35–36.

44. Rábago, "Elementos surrealistas en *La última niebla,*" 32.

45. Phyllis Rodríguez Peralta, "Bombal' s Novels of Female Estrangement," *Revista de Estudios Hispánicos,* 14, no. 1 (1980): 139–55, esp. 52.

CHAPTER 4. *LA AMORTAJADA*

1. Susana Munnich, *La dulce niebla: Lectura femenina y chilena de María Luisa Bombal* (Santiago: Editorial Universitaria, 1991), 99.

2. Esther W. Nelson, "Un viaje fantástico: ¿Quién habla en *La amortajada?*" in *María Luisa Bombal: Apreciaciones críticas*, ed. Marjorie Agosín, Elena Gascón, and Joy Renjilian-Burgy, 187 (Tempe, Ariz.: Bilingual Press/Editorial Bilingüe, 1987).

3. Adriana Méndez Rodenas, "Narcissus in Bloom: The Desiring Subject in

Modern Latin American Narrative—María Luisa Bombal and Juan Rulfo," in *Latin American Women's Writing: Feminist Readings in Theory and Crisis*, ed. Anny Brooksbank Jones and Catherine Davis, 115 (New York: Oxford University Press, 1996).

4. Colette Soler, "What Does the Unconscious Know about Women?" in *Reading Seminar XX: Lacan's Major Work on Love, Knowledge and Feminine Sexuality*, trans. François Raffoul and David Pettigrew, ed. Suzanne Barnard and Bruce Fink, 102–3 (New York: New York State University Press, 2002).

5. José Bengoa, "El estado desnudo: Acerca de la formación de lo masculino en Chile," in *Diálogos sobre el género masculino en Chile*, ed. María Elena Acuña and Sonia Montecino, 63–81 (Santiago: Universidad de Chile, FLACSO, 1996).

6. See Pierre Bourdieu's chap. 1 of *La dominación masculina*, trans. Joaquín Jordá (Barcelona: Anagrama, 2000).

7. See Naomi Lindstrom's "Foreword," in *House of Mist and The Shrouded Woman Novels by María Luisa Bombal* (Austin: University of Texas Press, 1995), vii.

8. Lucía Guerra-Cunningham, *La narrativa de María Luisa Bombal: Una visión de la existencia femenina* (Madrid: Playor, 1980), 81–82.

9. Denis de Rougemont, *Love in the Western World*, trans. Montgomery Belgion (Princeton, N.J.: Princeton University Press, 1983), 45.

10. Jonathan Dollimore, *Death, Desire and Loss in Western Culture* (New York: Routledge 1998), 65.

11. Maria Inés Lagos, *En tono mayor: Relatos de formación de protagonista femenina en Hispanoamérica* (Santiago: Cuarto Propio, 1996), 115.

12. Jessica Benjamin, *The Bonds of Love: Psychoanalysis, Feminism and the Problem of Domination* (New York: Pantheon, 1988), 111.

13. De Rougemont, *Love in the Western World*, 97, 111. The church converts the desire for love and the idealized woman of courtly love by instituting the new worship of the Virgin at the beginning of the twelfth century, providing new titles for Mary such as *Queen* and *Our Lady*.

14. Robert Tobin, "Masochism and Identity," in *One Hundred Years of Masochism: Literary Texts, Social and Cultural Contexts*, ed. Michael C. Finke and Carl Niekerk 49 (Amsterdam: Rodopi, 2001).

15. Laura Riesco, "La Amortajada: Experiencia y conocimiento," in *María Luisa Bombal. Apreciaciones críticas*, 213–15.

16. Walter Benjamin, "The Storyteller," in *Illuminations*, ed. Harry Zohn, 94 (New York: Schocken Books, 1968).

17. Shoshona Felman, "Benjamin's Silence," *Critical Inquiry* 25, no. 2 (Winter 1999): 207.

18. Ibid., 211.

19. Ibid., 207.

20. Celeste Kostopulos-Cooperman, *The Lyrical Vision of María Luisa Bombal* (London: Tamesis Books Ltd., 1988), 25.

21. Walter Benjamin discusses this as part of Moritz Heimann's statement on death and how the meaning of life can only be revealed by death. See pp. 100–1.

22. Michael Hays and Anastasia Nikolopoulou, eds., "Introduction," in *Melodrama: The Cultural Emergence of a Genre* (New York: Saint Martin's Press, 1996), vii.

23. Peter Brooks, *The Melodramatic Imagination: Balzac, Henry James,*

Melodrama, and the Mode of Excess (New York: Columbia University Press, 1985), xi, 2.

24. Agata Gligo, *María Luisa: Biografía de María Luisa Bombal* (Santiago: Editorial Sudamericana, 1996), 102.

25. See María Inés Lagos, *En tono mayor: Relatos de formación de la protagonista femenina en Hispanoamérica* (Santiago: Cuarto Propio, 1996), 45. Also see Paz Gálvez Lira's *María Luisa Bombal: Realidad y fantasía* (Maryland: Scripta Humanística, 1986) for a discussion of women's dissatisfaction and unhappiness in marriage, especially pp. 59–62. Also see Doris Meyer's "Feminine Testimony in the Works of Teresa de la Parra, María Luisa Bombal and Victoria Ocampo," in *Contemporary Women Authors of Latin America,* ed. Doris Meyer and Margarita Fernández Olmos, 3–15 (New York: Brooklyn College Press, 1983). Meyer focuses on the impact of laws that favor male privileges over women's rights. She also discusses the sense of claustrophobia and abnormal behavior displayed by the narrator of *La última niebla,* see especially pp. 9–10.

26. Naomi Lindstrom, "El discurso de La amortajada," 159–69.

27. All of the English quotations are from Bombal's 1948 translation *The Shrouded Woman* in *The House of Mist and The Shrouded Woman: Novels by María Luisa Bombal* (Austin: University of Texas, 1995) 155–259.

28. María Luisa Bastos, "Relectura de *La última niebla,*" *Revista Iberoamericana,* 51, no. 132–33 (July–December 1985): 558.

29. Phyllis Rodríguez-Peralta, "María Luisa Bombal's Poetic Novels of Estrangement," *Revista de Estudios Hispánicos,* 14, no. 1 (1980): 148–49.

30. Riesco, "La Amortajada: Experiencia y conocimiento," 215.

31. Lucía Guerra, ed., "Introducción," in *María Luisa Bombal: Obras completas* (Santiago: Editorial Andrés Bello, 1997), 32.

32. Borinsky, "El paisaje de la apatía," in *María Luisa Bombal: Apreciaciones críticas,* 34.

33. Gligo, *María Luisa,* 120–121.

34. Ibid., 90–91; 142–43, 146, respectively. While Bombal was writing *La última niebla,* she became certain that Eulogio Sánchez Errázuriz did not love her. Her attempt to commit suicide after their breakup further reveals the connection between female identity and powerlessness and self-destruction as an alternative.

35. See Ian Adams, *Three Authors of Alienation: Bombal, Onetti, Carpentier* (Austin: University of Texas Press, Institute of Latin American Studies, 1975), 16.

36. Susan Brownmiller, *Femininity* (New York: Linden Press/Simon & Schuster, 1984), 215

37. Magali Fernández, *El discurso narrativo en la obra de María Luisa Bombal* (Madrid: Editorial Pliegos, 1988), 68. Fernández discusses the surrealist elements as well as the psychic development of the women characters.

38. Nelson, "Un viaje fantástico," 187.

39. Lira, *María Luisa Bombal,* 82.

40. See Marjorie Agosín, "Entrevista con María Luisa Bombal," *The American Hispanist* 3 (November 1977): 6. I have used Lorna V. Williams's translation of Bombal's words from her article "The Shrouded Woman: The Fiction of María Luisa Bombal," *Latin American Literary Review* 10, no. 20 (Spring–Summer 1982): 21.

41. Adriana Valdés in Susana Munnich, *La dulce niebla: Lectura femenina y chilena de María Luisa Bombal, 111* (Santiago: Editorial Universitaria, 1991).

42. Ibid.
43. Guerra, ed., "Introducción," *María Luisa Bombal*, 30.
44. Cunningham, *La narrativa de María Luisa Bombal*, 51.
45. All quotations in English are taken from the translation of the novel by Bombal, *The Shrouded Woman*, in *House of Mist and The Shrouded Woman: Novels by María Luisa Bombal*, ed. Naomi Lindstrom, 155–259 (Austin: University of Texas, 1995).
46. Ricardo Gutiérrez Mouat, "Contrucción y represión del deseo en las novelas de MLB," in *María Luisa Bombal; Apreciaciones críticas*, 109.
47. Ibid.
48. Consult chapter 7 in Doris Sommer's *Foundational Fictions: The National Romance of Latin America* (Berkeley: University of California Press, 1991). Of special interest to my argument here is her analysis of Alberto Blest Gana's *Martín Rivas* (1862) and the success of an interclass marriage that secures personal happiness and national ideals.
49. Sonia Montecino, *Madres y huachos: Alegorías del mestizaje chileno* (Santiago: Cuarto Propio, 1993), 92–93.
50. Tobin, "Masochism and Identity," 50–51.
51. Lorna A. Williams, "The Shrouded Woman: Marriage and its Constraints in the Fiction of María Luisa Bombal," *Latin American Literary Review* 10, no. 20 (Spring–Summer, 1982): 25.
52. Luce Irigaray, "Commodities among Themselves," *Literary Theory: An Anthology*, ed. Julie Rivkin and Michael Ryan, 574 (New York: Blackwell, 1998).
53. De Rougemont, *Love in the Western World*, 244.
54. C. S. Lewis, *The Allegory of Love: A Study in Medieval Tradition* (New York: Oxford University Press, 1960), 36.
55. Borinsky, "El paisaje de la apatía," 42; Rodríguez-Peralta, "María Luisa Bombal's Poetic Novels of Estrangement," 150.
56. Lagos, *En tono mayor*, 37.
57. Ibid.
58. Otto Kernberg, *Love Relations: Normalcy and Pathology* (New Haven, Conn.: Yale University Press, 1995), 127.
59. Tobin, "Masochism and Identity," 34–35, 40–42.
60. Ibid., 42–49.
61. Ibid., 49.
62. Ibid., 41.
63. Francine Masiello's "Melodrama, Sex, and Nation," in *The Places of History: Regionalism Revisited in Latin America*, ed. Doris Sommer, 271–73 (Durham, N.C.: Duke University Press, 1999).
64. Ana María's induced miscarriage seems to be linked to the herbs Zoila gives her. It would take Mercedes Valdieso's publication of *La Brecha* (1961) (*Breakthrough*), a clearly feminist novel, to reinstate this female experience again in Chile, arousing myriad polemics that ended in the novel's censorship. For more discussion see Ivette Malverde Disselkoen, "De *La última niebla* y *La amortajada* a *La Brecha*," *Texto Crítico* 3, no. 4 (1989): 69–77.
65. It is important to note that divorce was legalized only in 2005 and that abortion is still illegal in Chile.
66. Victor E. Taylor, "Contracting Masochism: Pain, Pleasure and the Language of Power," in *One Hundred Years of Masochism: Literary Texts, Social and Cultural Contexts*, ed. Michael C. Finke and Carl Niekerk, 58–60 (Amsterdam: Rodopi, 2000).

67. Ibid., 61–63.
68. Lewis, *Allegory of Love,* 2.
69. Lindstrom, "El discurso de la amortajada," 150.
70. Judith Butler, *Gender Trouble: Feminism and the Subversion of Identity* (New York: Routledge, 1990), and *The Psychic Life of Power* (Stanford, Calif.: Stanford University Press, 1997).
71. Munnich, *La dulce niebla,* 110–11.
72. For further discussion see Jessica Benjamin, "The First Bond," in *The Women and Language Debate: A Source Book,* ed. Camille Roman, Suzanne Juhasz, and Cristanne Miller, 185 (New Brunswick, N.J.: Rutgers University Press, 1994).
73. Benjamin, "First Bond," 185–86.
74. See Gilles Deleuze's *Proust y los signos,* trans. Francisco Monge (Barcelona: Editorial Anagrama, 1972), 24–35.
75. Nelson, "Un viaje fantástico," 193.
76. Guerra, "Introducción," 33–34. Guerra finds these archetypical connections in texts such as *Las islas nuevas* and the author's poetic *Crónica* published in 1940, *Mar, cielo y tierra, Sea, Sky and Earth.*
77. Bombal's mystical discourse shows resemblances with certain forms of Zen philosophy in which individual consciousness is enlightened by detaching from earthly concerns and accessing a higher knowledge that governs the universe. Esther W. Nelson has also noted the resemblance of Ana María's paradise and the Buddhist conception of it as a vital and cosmic principle. Nelson, "Un viaje fantástico," 195.
78. For a Jungian discussion of Bombal's work, see Antonio Aiello, "Arquetipos y estereotipos femeninos en la novelística de María Luisa Bombal," *Divergencias: Revista de Estudios Lingüísticos y Literarios* 5, no. 1 (Spring 2007): 3–13.
79. Laurence G. Boldt, *The Tao of Abundance: Eight Ancient Principles for Abundant Living* (New York: Penguin Compass, 1999), xxvii–xxix. Boldt discusses Indian Maya and Chinese Mother Tao (or "the Self of all things") as an organic pattern or principle from which everything arises in terms very similar to Bombal's .
80. Benjamin, "First Bond," 185.
81. See Olson's discussion in his *Zen and the Art of Postmodern Philosophy,* 112.

CHAPTER 5. DIAMELA ELTIT

1. Robert Neustadt, *Cada Día: La creación de un arte social* (Santiago: Cuarto Propio, 2001), 16–27.
2. Nelly Richard, "Lo político y lo crítico en el arte," *Revista de crítica cultural* 28 (June 2004): 34–35.
3. Idelber Avelar, "La escena de avanzada: Photography and Writing in Postcoup Chile: A Conversation with Nelly Richard," in *Photography and Writing in Latin America: Double Exposure,* ed. Marcy E. Schwartz and Mary Beth Tierney-Tello, 260 (Albuquerque: University of New Mexico Press, 2006).
4. Ibid.
5. Eugenia Brito, "La narrativa de Diamela Eltit: Un nuevo paradigma so-

cioliterario de lectura," in *Campos minados. (Literatura post-golpe en Chile)* (Santiago: Cuarto Propio, 1990), 116.

6. Ibid., 115–17.

7. See Nelly Richard, "The Rhetoric of the Body," *in Margins and Institutions: Art in Chile since 1973* (Victoria, N.Y.: Art and Text, 1986), 71–72; and her essays "Chile, Woman and Dissidence" and "Women's Art Practices and the Critique of Signs," in *Beyond the Fantastic: Contemporary Art Criticism from Latin America,* ed. Gerardo Mosquera, 137–44, 145–53 (London: Institute of International Visual Arts/Cambridge, Mass.: MIT Press, 1996).

8. Anne Cahill, *Rethinking Rape* (Ithaca, N.Y.: Cornell University Press, 2001), 106.

9. Robert Neustadt, "Diamela Eltit: Clearing Space for a Critical Performance," in *(Con)fusing Signs and Postmodern Positions: Spanish American Performance, Experimental Writing, and the Critique of Political Confusion* (New York: Garland, 1999), 64.

10. Carolina Pizarro, "Mujer: Cómo decirlo," in *Novela chilena: Nuevas generaciones: El abordaje de los huérfanos,* ed. Rodrigo Cánovas, 127 (Santiago: Ediciones Universidad Católica, 1996).

11. Adriana Valdés, *Composición de lugar: Escritos sobre cultura* (Santiago: Editorial Universitaria, 1996), 70–71.

12. Ignacio Valente, "El Cuerpo es un horror y es una Gloria" and "Revista de Libros," *El Mercurio* May 21, 1989, 1, 4.

13. For more on Eltit's critical reception in the United States as well as in Chile, see Gwen Kirkpatrick's essay, "El hambre de ciudad de Eltit. Forjando un lenguaje del Sur," in *Letras y proclamas: La estética literaria de Diamela Eltit,* ed. Bernardita Llanos, 33–68 (Santiago: Cuarto propio, 2006).

14. Carolina Alid, "Diamela Eltit: Una autora por descifrar," *El Llanquihue, Suplemento* July 25, 1998, 4–5. Translations are mine unless noted.

15. Ibid.

16. Cánovas, ed. "Una visión panorámica," 45, 47.

17. Juan Carlos Lertora, ed., "Diamela Eltit: Hacia una poética de literatura menor," in *Una poética de literatura menor: La narrativa de Diamela Eltit,* 27–35 (Santiago: Cuatro Propio, 1993). The contributors of this volume underscore the idea of a poetics constructed around the notion of minority, peripheral, and anticanonical gestures. See also Gilles Deleuze and Félix Guattari, "What Is a Minor Literature?" in *Narrative/Theory,* ed. David H. Richter, 273–80 (New York: Longman, 1996).

18. Danilo Santos, "Retóricas marginales, in *Novela chilena: Nuevas generaciones El abordaje del los huérfanos,* ed. Rodrigo Cánovas, 147 (Santiago: Editorial Universidad Catolica, 1996).

19. Eugenia Brito, "Diamela Eltit (1949)" in *Escritoras chilenas: Novela y cuento,* ed. Patricia Rubio, 534 Tercer Volumen (Santiago: Cuarto Propio, 1999).

20. Idelber Avelar, "Introduction," in *The Untimely Present: Postdictatorial Latin American Fiction and the Task of Mourning* (Durham, N.C.: Duke University Press, 1999), 16.

21. Santos, "Retóricas marginales," 145.

22. For more on masculinity and the neoliberal city, see my chapter "Masculinidad, Estado y violencia en la ciudad neoliberal," in *Reinas de otro cielo: Modernidad y autoritarismo en la obra de Pedro Lemebel,* ed. Fernando Blanco, 79 (Santiago: LOM, 2004).

23. Richard, "Lo político y lo crítico en el arte," 33.

24. Soledad Bianchi, "Escribir desde la mujer," in *Cultura, autoritarismo y redemocratización en Chile,* ed. Manuel Garretón, Saúl Sosnowski, and Bernardo Subercaseaux, 109 (Santiago: Fondo de Cultura Económica, 1993). For another view on what this fourth world signifies, see Raymond Williams, "Women Writing in the Americas: New Projects in the 1980s," in *The Novel in the Americas* (Boulder: University Press of Colorado, 1992), 119–31.

25. See Eltit's reference to Lombardo's definition in Leonidas Morales, *Conversaciones con Diamela Eltit* (Santiago: Cuarto Propio, 1998), 69.

26. Brito, "Diamela Eltit (1949)," 535.

27. Gisela Norat, *Marginalities: Diamela Eltit and the Subversion of Mainstream Narrative in Chile* (Newark, Del.: University of Delaware Press, 2002), 125.

28. Kathya Araujo, "Introducción," in *Sexualidades y sociedades contemporáneas,* ed. Kathya Araujo and Carolina Ibarra, 8–9 (Santiago: Universidad Academia de Humanismo Cristiano, 2003).

29. Raquel Olea, "De la épica lumpen al texto sudaca: El proyecto narrativo de Diamela Eltit," in *Lengua víbora: Producciones de lo femenino en la escritura de mujeres chilenas,* 52 (Santiago: Cuarto Propio, 1998).

30. Francine Masiello, *The Art of Transition: Latin American Culture and the Neoliberal Crisis* (Durham, N.C., and London: Duke University Press, 2001), 208.

31. Morales, *Conversaciones con Diamela Eltit,* 69.

32. Julia Kristeva, "Word, Dialogue, and Novel," in *The Kristeva Reader,* ed. Toril Moi, 49 (New York: Columbia University Press, 1986).

33. Norat, *Marginalities,* 141.

34. Ibid.

35. Ibid., 148.

36. Susan Franceschet, *Women and Politics in Chile* (Boulder, Colo.: Lynne Rienner, 2005), 26.

37. Nelly Richard, *Masculino/femenino: Prácticas de la diferencia y cultura democrática* (Santiago: Francisco Zegers Editor, 1993), 42.

38. Franceschet, *Women and Politics in Chile,* 25.

39. Ibid., 60.

40. Dianna Niebylski, "Against Mimesis: Lumpérica Revisited," *Revista Canadiense de Estudios Hispánicos* 24, no. 2 (Winter 2001): 244. Niebylski discusses something very similar in relation to *Lumpérica.*

41. Idelber Avelar, "Overcodification of the Margins: Figures of the Eternal Return and the Apocalypse," in *The Untimely Present: Postdictatorial Latin American Fiction and the Task of Mourning* (Durham, N.C.: Duke University Press, 1999), 164–85.

42. Vivian Schelling, ed., "Introduction: Reflections on the Experience of Modernity in Latin America," in *Through the Kaleidoscope: The Experience of Modernity in Latin America,* trans. Lorraine Leu, 16 (London: Verso, 2000).

43. Néstor García Canclini, *Consumidores y ciudadanos conflictos multiculturales de la globalización* (México: Editorial Grijalbo, 1995), 69–72.

44. Ibid., 13.

45. Diamela Eltit, "La familia XXI," *La Nación* February 5, 2006. See also www.letrass5.com/de100206.htm.

46. Of interest is the collection of essays in Felipe Aguero and Jeffrey Stark, eds., *Fault Lines of Democracy in Post-Tradition Latin America* (Miami: North-South Center Press, University of Miami, 1998).

47. Norat, *Marginalities,* 130.

48. Mary Russo, *The Female Body* (New York and London: Routledge, 1994), 7.

49. For the Spanish all my references are from *El cuarto mundo* (Santiago: Seix Barral, 1996). For the English version, I will be quoting from Dick Gerdes, trans., *The Fourth World* (Lincoln: University of Nebraska Press, 1995). For another analysis on motherhood and the figure of the mother, see Mary Green's chapter 3 in her *Diamela Eltit Reading the Mother* (Suffolk: Taresis, 2007).

50. Pedro Granados, "El cuarto mundo, un arte de amar nuevo," www.letras 5s.com/de030305.

51. Norat, *Marginalities,* 132.

52. Marilyn Yalom, *Historia del pecho,* trans. Antoni Puigròs (Barcelona: Tusquets,1997), 185–86.

53. Magdalena Maíz-Peña, "Hibridez textual y disidencia cultural: Los vigilantes de Diamela Eltit," *South Eastern Latin Americanist* 1–2 (1996): 29.

54. See Eltit's interview in *El Mercurio,* October 1, 1998, C9. "En mi novela la madre mata a sus hijos de otra manera, de un modo más simbólico."

55. Nelly Richard, "Performance of the Chilean Avanzada," in *Corpus Delecti: Performance Art of the Americas,* ed. Coco Fusco, trans. Paul Foss and Juan Dávila, 214–15 (London: Routledge, 2000).

56. Norbert Lechner and Susana Levy, *Notas sobre la vida cotidiana III. El disciplinamiento de la mujer* (Santiago: Flacso, 1984), 3–5.

57. Richard, "Performance of the Chilean Avanzada," 214.

58. Julia Kristeva, "Stabat Mater," in *The Kristeva Reader,* ed. Toril Moi, 182 (New York: Columbia University Press, 1986).

59. For another kitsch aesthetic that parodies the effects of globalization in Santiago's local culture in the visual arts, see my "Si vas para el mall: Objectos, series y remedos del kitsch de Cabezas y Truffa," in *Cabezas + Truffa, Se Vende. Si vas para el Mall* (Santiago: Fondart, 2001), 1–16.

60. Brito, "Diamela Eltit (1949)," 540.

61. Ibid., 536–37.

62. Ibid., 540.

63. Pedro Lemebel, "Los mil nombres de María Camaleón," in *Loco Afán: Crónicas de Sidario* (Santigo: Editorial Anagrama, 1996), 64–65.

64. Olea, "De la épica lumpen al texto sudaca," 62.

65. Ibid., 66. Also see Green's *Diamela Eltit Reading the Mother,* 92.

66. Gisela Norat, "Diálogo fraternal: El cuarto mundo de Diamela Eltit y Cristóbal Nonato de Carlos Fuentes," *Chasqui* 23, no. 2 (November 1994): 77.

67. Julia Kristeva, *Powers of Horror: An Essay on Abjection,* trans. Leon S. Roudiez (New York: Columbia University Press, 1982), 71.

68. Morales, *Conversaciones con Diamela Eltit,* 97.

69. Ibid.

70. Fredric Jameson, "Marxism and Postmodernism," in *The Cultural Turn: Selected Writings on the Postmodern 1983–1998* (London: Verso, 1998), 34–35.

71. Carlos Monsiváis, "Penetración cultural y nacionalismo (el caso mexicano)" in *No Intervención, autodeterminación y democracia en América Latina,* ed. Pablo Gómez Casanova, 77–79 (México: D.F.: Siglo Veintiuno Editores, 1983).

72. Masiello, *Art of Transition,* 215. Masiello also highlights *Los trabajadores de la muerte* as Eltit's "radical rethinking of our own power of purchase and our use of 'ready-made' objects in a visually based culture."

73. María Inés Lagos, "Reflexiones sobre la representación del sujeto en dos textos de Diamela Eltit: Lumpérica y El cuarto mundo," in *Una poética de literatura menor: La narrativa de Diamela Eltit,* ed. Juan Carlos Lértora, 138 (Santiago: Para Textos/Cuarto Propio, 1993).

74. Robert Neustadt, *Cada Día: La creación de un arte social,* 36–37, 156.

75. Brito, "Diamela Eltit (1949)," 536.

76. Neustadt, "Diamela Eltit: Clearing Space for a Critical Performance," 80.

CHAPTER 6. *LOS VIGILANTES*

1. *El Mercurio,* September 24, 1995, E16.

2. Idelber Avelar, "Overcodification of the Margins: Figures of the Eternal Return," in *The Untimely Present: Postdictatorial Latin American Fiction and the Task of Mourning* (Durham, N.C.: Duke University Press, 1999), 186–209.

3. My article "Historia y memoria del cuerpo en la letra: *Los vigilantes* de Diamela Eltit," in *Mujeres y Cambio desde la letra,* ed. Chonin Horno-Delgado and Janet N. Gold, 187–206 (República Dominicana: Secretaría de la Mujer, 2005), discusses many of the ideas I develop in this chapter. Also see my essay "Hibridismo, confusiones y marcas del sujeto sudaca en *El cuarto mundo* de Diamela Eltit," http://www.literateworld.com/Spanish/2002/escritores/sep/w01/test9escritores.html.

4. One can not help thinking of Kafka's *The Trial* (1925), in which Joseph K is arrested one morning without explanation finally to die "like a dog" in a world in which truth does not exist. Leonidas Morales has also noted this connection between the novel and Kafka's works in his *Conversaciones con Diamela Eltit* (Santiago: Cuarto Propio, 1998), 49.

5. Nelly Richard, "Géneros, valores y diferencias," in *Residuos y metáforas (Ensayos de crítica cultural sobre el Chile de la Transición)* (Santiago: Cuarto Propio, 1998), 200–1.

6. Luisa Muraro, *El orden simbólico de la madre,* trans. Beatriz Albertini (Madrid: Horas y Horas, 1994), 42–43.

7. Kirby Farrell, *Post Traumatic Culture: Injury and Interpretation in the Nineties* (Baltimore: John Hopkins University Press, 1998), 5.

8. Susan Ehrlich, ed., "The Institutional Coerciveness of Legal Discourse," in *Representing Rape: Language and Sexual Consent* (London: Routledge, 2001), 4.

9. See this discussion in "Los bordes de la letra," *Casa de las Américas* 230 (January–March 2003): 108–12.

10. Rita Felski, *The Gender of Modernity* (Cambridge, Mass.: Harvard University Press, 1995), 13.

11. Morales, *Conversaciones con Diamela Eltit,* 47. In this section of the interview with Morales, Eltit reflects on the literary referents that shaped the character of the child in this novel.

12. Avelar, "Overcodificatin of the Margins," 180.

13. See also my article "Fugas y gestos del sujeto cautivo en El infarto del alma de Diamela Eltit y Paz Errázuriz," *Confluencia* 19, No. 1 (Fall 2003): 50–58. For a very insightful analysis of "El infarto del alma" and photography in postdictatorial Chile, see Mary Beth Tierney-Tello's "On Making Images Speak: Writing and Photography," in *Photography and Writing in Latin America: Dou-*

ble Exposures, ed. Marcy E. Schwartz and Mary Beth Tierney-Tello, 87–113 (Albuquerque: University of New Mexico Press, 2006).

14. Richard, "Por amor al arte: Rupturas críticas y fugas de imaginarios," 260.

15. Ibid., 261.

16. Avelar, "Overcodification of the Margin," 182–83. For Avelar, the narrator becomes the last survivor and carrier of the letter.

17. Julia Kristeva, *Powers of Horror: An Essay on Abjection* (New York: Columbia University Press, 1982), 3–5.

18. Ibid., 3–4.

19. Judith Butler, *The Psychic Life of Power* (Stanford, Calif.: Stanford University Press, 1997), 8–9.

20. See "Infantile Sexuality," in *Sigmund Freud: Psychological Writings and Letters,* ed. Sander L. Gilman, trans. James Strachey, The German Library, vol. 59 (New York: Continuum, 1995), 88–89.

21. For another discussion on the novel consult my article "Emociones, hablas y fronteras en Los vigilantes," *Casa de las Américas* 230 (January–March 2003): 126–129. For another reading on the mother and the son, see Mary Green, *Diamela Eltit Reading the Mother* (Suffolk: Tarisis, 2007), 113–31.

22. Raquel Olea, "De la épica lumpen al texto sudaca: El proyecto narrativo de Diamela Eltit," in *Lengua víbora: Producciones de lo femenino en la escritura de mujeres chilenas* (Santiago: Cuarto Propio, 1998), 77.

23. Tomás Moulian, *Chile actual: Anatomía de un mito* (Santiago: Arcis, LOM, 1997), 15–20, 49–56.

24. All translations are from *Custody of the Eyes,* trans. Helen Lane and Ronald Christ (Santa Fe, New Mexico: Lumen, 2005).

25. Magdalena Maíz-Peña, "Hibridez textual y disidencia cultural: Los vigilantes de Diamela Eltit," *South Eastern Latin Americanist* 1–2 (1996): 30–31.

26. Avelar, "Overcodification of the Margin," 179.

27. Ibid., 183–84.

28. Robert Neustadt, "Diamela Eltit: Clearing Space for a Critical Performance," in *(Con)fusing Signs and Postmodern Positions: Spanish American Performance, Experimental Writing, and the Critique of Political Confusion* (New York: Garland, 1999), 62–63.

29. Ibid., 62.

30. Christian Parenti, "DC's Virtual Panopticon," *The Nation,* June 3, 2002, 24–26. See also in this issue Amy Bach, "Vigilante Justice," 18–19, who discusses the restructuring of law and order and the new role of the citizenry as snitches in contemporary America. The similarities of local systems reflect another aspect of globalization and its enforcement of panopticism.

31. See "The 'Uncanny,'" in *Sigmund Freud: Psychological Writings and Letters,* 145.

32. Tomás Moulian's insightful analysis discusses Chile today and the capitalist revolution that the Pinochet dictatorship initiated. See his *Chile actual,* 30–34.

33. Pedro Lemebel, in "Anacondas en el parque," sarcastically highlights the city's surveillance by the use of cameras in downtown Santiago to maintain the "scenography of democratic leisure." See Lemebel, *La esquina es mi corazón, Crónica urbana* (Santiago: Cuarto Propio, 1997), 9.

34. Michael Hardt and Antonio Negri, *Empire* (Cambridge, Mass.: Harvard University Press, 2000), 113.

35. For a further discussion on *Mano de obra* and working-class consciousness, consult Fernando Blanco, "Poéticas de alienación y muerte en Mano de obra," in *Letras y proclamas: la estética literaria de Diamela Eltit,* ed. Bernardita Llanos M., 173–201 (Santiago: Cuarto Propio, 2006).

36. Gisela Norat discusses the plight of this mother and the price she and her son pay for leaving a husband who exerts his control not only as spouse, but metaphorically as government and literary canon. See Norat, *Marginalities: Diamela Eltit and the Subversion of Mainstream Literature in Chile* (Newark: University of Delaware Press, 2002), 178.

37. The letters in the novel ground their narration on the perspective of the woman who stays with the offspring after ending a couple's relationship.

38. Waleska Pino-Ojeda, "Diamela Eltit: El letrado y el lumpen," in *Sobre castas y puentes: conversaciones con Elena Poniatowska, Rosario Ferré y Diamela Eltit* (Santiago: Cuarto Propio, 2000), 146. In this conversation, Eltit puts special emphasis on the distinction between an official Santiago and the otherness of an interurban social and cultural landscape.

39. Olea, "De la épica lumpen al texto sudaca," 74.

40. Jean Franco, *Critical Passions: Selected Essays,* ed. Mary Louise Pratt and Kathleen Newman, 105 (Durham, N.C.: Duke University Press, 1999). Franco comments on the representation of a radical experience of dissociation in Eltit's works, particularly the "dissociation of self from body" that can also be seen in *Los vigilantes.*

41. José Bengoa, "El estado al desnudo," in *Diálogos sobre el género masculino en Chile,* ed. Sonia Montecino and María Elena Acuña, 80 (Santiago: Bravo y Allende Editores, 1996).

42. "Olga Grau et al., eds., "Introduction" in *Discurso, género y poder: Discursos públicos: Chile 1978–1993* (Santiago: Arcis, La Morada, LOM, 1997), 35–36.

43. Olga Grau, ed., "Familia: un grito de fin de siglo," in *Discurso, género y poder,"* 129.

44. Susan Franceschet, *Women and Politics in Chile* (Boulder, Colo.: Lynne Rienner, 2005), 31.

45. Grau, "Familia: Un grito de fin de siglo," 132–42.

46. Riet Delsing, "Sobre mitos y relatos," 161.

47. Olea, "De la épica," 76.

48. See Ann J. Cahill, *Rethinking Rape* (Ithaca, N.Y.: Columbia University Press, 2002), 125. Cahill discusses how sexual hierarchization is embedded in the legal system and social structures in general, sustaining difference as sexual victimization for women.

49. Avelar, 58.

50. Mary Beth Tierney-Tello, "Testimonio, ética y estética en Diamela Eltit," in *Letras y proclamas: La estética literaria de Diamela Eltit,* ed. Bernardita Llanos M., 69–102 (Santiago: Cuarto Propio, 2006).

51. Vivian Schelling, ed., "Introduction: Reflections on the Experience of Modernity in Latin America," in *Through the Kaleidoscope: The Experience of Modernity in Latin America,* trans. Lorraine Leu (London: Verso, 2000), 7–8. As Schelling points out, the contemporary Argentian writer Sergio Chejbec also reveals a "sinister face" of Buenos Aires as a nightmarish wasteland; see p. 27.

52. See his "Figuras femeninas chilenas para una memoria en obra," in *Espejos que dejan ver: Mujeres en las artes visuales latinoamericanas,* ed. María Elvira Iriarte and Eliana Ortega, 168–69 (Santiago: ISIS, 2002).

53. See Djalal Kadir's chapter "A Woman's Place: Gendered Histories of the Subatern," in *The Other Writing: Postcolonial Essays in Latin American Writing Culture,* 182–86 (West Lafayette, Ind.: Purdue University Press, 1993). The *lumpen* in this novel is embodied by the nameless and anonymous multitude that is persecuted and threatened by an essentially policing state. García Canclini and Beatriz Sarlo propose other cultural readings of the Latin American postindustrial city today: Garcia Canclini, see *Consumidores y ciudadanos: Conflictos multiculturales de la globalización* (México: Grijalbo, 1995) and Sarlo, *Una modernidad periférica: Buenos Aires, 1920–1930* (Buenos Aires: Ediciones Nueva Visión, 1988).

54. The reiteration of emptiness, ruins, and social abandonment in the city of Santiago is also present in the art of Voluspa Jarpa and Lotty Rosenfeld. Their work, as Eltit's does, reiterates the failure of modernization in Chile, pointing to the lack of meaningful and cohesive social as well as symbolic bonds.

55. See Richard, "Género, valores y diferencia(s)," 204–5, and Martín Hopenhayn, "Moral y secularización en el Chile finisecular: Especulaciones para el debate," *CIEPLAN* 38 December 1993.

56. See María Inés Lagos, ed., "Lenguaje, género y poder en Los vigilantes de Diamela," in *Creación y resistencia: La narrativa de Diamela Eltit: 1983–1998* (Santiago: Cuarto Propio, 2000), 131. Sor Juana Inés de la Cruz's "Respuesta a Sor Filotea" would be a model.

57. The narrator's high and oftentimes dramatic tone echoes the reflections on love and the female voice in *El infarto del alma*. For a further discussion of *El infarto del alma,* see my article "Fugas y gestos del sujeto cautivo de Diamela Eltit y Paz Errázuriz," *Confluencia* 19, No. 1 (Fall 2003): 50–58.

58. Schelling, "Introduction: Reflections on the Experience of Modernity in Latin America," 11. Here she discusses specifically the works of nineteenth-century Latin American writers and their stance toward modernity in relation to cultural and local legacies that conflict. Eltit's text revisits this same process and highlights the manifold ways in which modernity and the idea of progress are tied to authoritarianism and violence.

59. It is interesting to note the contrast of these frozen figures with the monumental ice sculpture that symbolized Chilean cool economic success at Expo 1992 in Seville. Moulian also discusses this iceberg as the new image of Chile where all blood traces and the disappeared have been erased as if the country had just been born. See his *Chile actual,* 35.

60. Michael Hart and Antonio Negri discuss the construction of the colonial subject by European capitalism as an absolute negation of the European self. See particularly p. 124 in *Empire*.

61. Moulian, *Chile actual,* 37–39.

62. Richard, "La cita de la violencia," in *Residuos y metáforas,* 28–32.

63. The figure of the snitch, spy, or informer (*soplón* and *sapo* in Chile) has had a recurrent presence in Chilean literature from the 1980s and 1990s. Two examples that come to mind are the novel *Santiago Cero, Santiago Zero* (1989) by Carlos Franz and the play *Nadie es profeta en su espejo, Nobody Is a Prophet in His Mirror,* (1998) by Jorge Díaz. A contemporary revision of recent history and family ties is present in works of younger female writers' such as Lina Meruane, Andrea Jeftanovich and Nona Fernández. Meruane explores the theme of betrayal and love attachments in her novels *Cercada, Trapped,* (2000) and *Póstuma, Postumus,* (2000). Jeftanovich in her novel *Escenario de guerra, War Scenario,* (2000) revisits childhood and memory. *Cercada* and *Escenario de*

guerra look to the dictatorial past, enfolding the memories and stories that it silenced. Nona Fernandez's *Mapocho* (2003) also denounces the lies & treasons that have shaped official history. Her recent *Av. 10 de Julio. Huamachuco, July 10th, Ave. Huamachuco* (2008), revisits history & recent memory through the students' movement and the role of adolescents as new social and political actors.

64. Hardt and Negri, *Empire,* 27.

65. Luce Irigaray, "Volume without Contours," in *The Irigaray Reader,* trans. David Masey, ed. Margaret Whitford, 53–67 (Oxford, Mass.: Basil Blackwell, 1991).

66. Eltit discusses how dominant sensibilities and the rule of the market are incorporated in editorial politics and the challenges that this segmentation and appropriations place on the writer. See her "Los bordes de la letra," *Casa de las Américas* 230 (January–March, 2003): 112.

67. For a further discussion of this grotesque mother/child figure, see my chapter "Pasiones maternales y carnales," in *Letras y Proclamas: La estética literaria de Diamela Eltit,* ed. Bernardita Llanos M., 103–41 (Santiago: Cuarto Propio, 2006).

Bibliography

Adams, Ian. *Three Authors of Alienation. Bombal, Onetti, Carpentier"* "María Luisa Bombal: Alienation and the Poetic Image," 15–35. Austin: University of Texas Press, Institute of Latin American Studies, 1975.

Agosín, Marjorie. *Desterradas del Paraíso.* New York: Senda Nueva de Ediciones, Inc., 1983.

———. "La mímesis de la interioridad: 'Soledad de la sangre' de Marta Brunet y 'El árbol' de María Luisa Bombal." *Neophilologus* 68, no. 3 (1984): 380–88.

———. "Marta Brunet: A Literary Biography." *Revista Interamericana de Bibliografía* 36, (1986): 452–59.

Agosín, Marjorie, Elena Gascón-Vera, and Joy Renjilian-Burgy, eds. *María Luisa Bombal. Apreciaciones críticas.* Tempe, Ariz.: Bilingual Press/Editorial Bilingüe, 1987.

Aguero, Felipe, et al., eds. *Fault Lines of Democracy in Post-Transition Latin America.* Miami: North-South Center Press at the University of Miami, 1998.

Ahumada Peña, Haydeé. "Marta Brunet (1901–1967)." In *Escritoras chilenas. Tercer Volumen. Novela y cuento.* Edited by Patricia Rubio, 139–50. Santiago: Cuarto Propio, 1999.

Aillo, Antonio. "Los arquetipos y estereotipos femeninos en la novelística de María Luisa Bombal." *Divergencias: Revista de Estudios Linguísticos y Literarios* 5, no. 1 (2007): 3–13.

Alegría, Fernando. *Breve historia de la novela hispanoamericana.* México D.F.: Editorial Andrea, 1959.

Alid, Carolina. "Diamela Eltit: Una autora por decifrar." *El Llanquihue, Suplemento* no. 25 (July 1998): 4–5.

Allen, Martha E. "Dos estilos de novela: Marta Brunet y María Luisa Bombal." *Revista Iberoamericana* 35, (February–December 1956): 63–91.

Alvarez Nuñez, Ana Iris. "Princesa de las escritoras." *El día,* 1992.

Antezanna-Pernet, Corinne. "El MENCH en provincia. Movilización femenina y sus obstáculos, 1935–1942." In *Disciplina y Desacato: Construcción de la identidad en Chile, siglos XIX y XX.* Edited by Lorena Godoy and et al., 287–329. Santiago: SUR/CEDEM, 1995.

Araujo, Kathya. "Introducción." In *Sexualidades y sociedades contemporáneas,* edited by Kathya Araujo and Carolina Ibarra, 7–19. Santiago: Universidad Academia de Humanismo Cristiano, 2003.

Arens, W. *The Original Sin: Incest and Its Meaning.* New York: Oxford University Press, 1986.

Arrieta, Hernán Díaz. *Panorama de la literatura chilena durante el siglo XX.* Santiago: Editorial Nascimento, 1931.

Arteaga, Catalina. "Oficios, trabajos y vida cotidiana de mujeres rurales en San Felipe, 1900–1940: Una reconstrucción a partir de causas criminales del Archivo Judicial de San Felipe." In *Perfiles revelados: Historias de mujeres en Chile, siglos XVIII–XX*. Edited by Diana Veneros Ruiz-Tagle, 199–216. Santiago: Universidad de Santiago, 1997.

Avelar, Idelber. "La escena de avanzada: Photography and Writing in Postcoup Chile: A Conversation with Nelly Richard." In *Photography and Writing in Latin America: Double Exposure*. Edited by Marcy E. Schwartz and Mary Beth Tierney-Tello, 259–69. Albuquerque: University of New Mexico Press, 2006.

———. In "Overcodification of the Margins: Figures of the Eternal Return and the Apocalypse." *The Untimely Present. Postdictatorial Latin American Fiction*. Durham, N.C.: Duke University Press, 1999, 164–85.

Bastos, María Luisa. "Relectura de 'La última niebla,' de María Luisa Bombal." *Revista Iberoamericana* 51, no. 132–33 (July–December, 1985): 557–64.

Bataille, Georges. *Erotism, Death and Sensuality*. Translated by Mary Dalwood. San Francisco: City Lights Books, 1986.

Bengoa, José. "El estado al desnudo: Acerca de la formación de lo masculino en Chile." In *Diálogos sobre el género masculino en Chile*. Edited by Sonia Montecino and María Elena Acuña, 63–81. Santiago: Bravo y Allende Editores, 1996.

Benjamin, Jessica. "The Alienation of Desire: Women's Masochism and Ideal Love." In *Psychoanalysis and Women: Contemporary Reappraisals*, 113–38. Hillsdale, N.J.: Analytic Press, 1986.

———. *The Bonds of Love: Psychoanalysis, Feminism, and the Problem of Domination*. New York: Pantheon, 1988.

———. "The First Bond." In *The Women and Language Debate: A Source Book*. Edited by Camille Roman, Suzanne Juhasz, and Cristanne Miller, 165–98. New Brunswick, N.J.: Rutgers University Press, 1994.

———. *Shadow of the Other: Intersubjectivity and Gender*. New York: Routledge, 1998.

Benjamin, Walter. "The Storyteller." In *Illuminations*. Edited by Hannah Arendt, 83–109. New York: Schoken Books, 1969.

Berger, John. *Ways of Seeing*. Middlesex, England: Penguin Books, 1987.

Bernstein, J. M. "Coldness: The Fundamental Principle of Bourgeois Subjectivity." In *Adorno. Disenchantment and Ethics*. Edited by J. M. Bernstein, 396–414. Cambridge: Cambridge University Press, 2001.

Bianchi, Soledad. "Escribir desde la mujer." In *Cultura, autoritarismo y redemocratización en Chile*. Edited by Manuel Garretón, Saúl Sosnowski, and Bernardo Subercaseaux, 103–12. Santiago: Fondo de Cultura Económica, 1993.

———. "María Luisa Bombal o una difícil travesía (Del amor mediocre al amor pasión)." *Atenea (Universidad de Concepción)* 445 (1985): 175–92.

Blanco, Fernando. "Figuras femeninas chilenas para una memoria en obra." In *Espejos que dejan ver: Mujeres en las artes visuales latinoamericanas*. Edited by María Elvira Iriarte and Eliana Ortega, 157–82. Santiago: ISIS, 2002.

———. "Lecturas enrarecidas: saltos, mariquitas, apollerados y cóndores." *Nomadías* 5, no. 5 (2001): 111–14.

———. "Poéticas de alienación y muerte en 'Mano de obra.'" In *Letras y proclamas: La estética literaria de Diamela Eltit*. Edited by Bernardita Llanos, M., 173–201. Santiago: Cuarto Propio, 2006.

———. "Secretos y goces en la nación literaria." *Revista Iberoamericana-España-Portugal* 18 (2005): 127–44.

Boldt, Laurence G. *The Tao of Abundance: Eight Ancient Principles for Abundant Living*. New York: Penguin Compass, 1999.

Bombal, María Luisa. *House of Mist and The Shrouded Woman. Novels by María Luisa Bombal*. Edited by Naomi Lindstrom. Austin: University of Texas Press, 1995.

———. *María Luisa Bombal: Obras completas*. Edited by Lucía Guerra. Santiago: Editorial Andrés Bello, 1997.

———. *New Islands and Other Stories*. Translated by Richard Cunningham and Lucía Cunningham. New York: Farrar, Straus, Giroux, 1982.

Bonan, Claudia. "Sexualidad, reproducción y reflexividad." In *Sexualidades y sociedades contemporáneas*. Edited by Kathya Araujo and Carolina Ibarra, 21–43. Santiago: Universidad Academia de Humanismo Cristiano, 2003.

Borinsky, Alicia. "El paisaje de la apatía." In *María Luisa Bombal: Apreciaciones críticas*. Edited by Marjorie Agosín, Elena Gascón-Vera, and Joy Renjilian-Burgy, 31–42. Tempe, Ariz.: Bilingual Press/Editorial Bilingüe, 1987.

Bourdieu, Pierre. *La dominación masculina*. Translated by Joaquín Jorda. Barcelona: Anagrama, 2000.

Braidotti, Rossi. *Nomadic Subjects: Embodiment and Sexual Difference in Contemporary Feminist Theory*. New York: Columbia University Press, 1994.

Brito, Eugenia. "La narrativa de Diamela Eltit: Un nuevo paradigma socioliterario de lectura." In *Campos minados (Literatura post-golpe en Chile)*, 167–218. Santiago: Cuarto Propio, 1990.

———. "Roles sexuales: diversas escenas." In *Discurso, género y poder. Discursos públicos: Chile 1978–1993*. Edited by Olga Grau et al., 65–91. Santiago: LOM, ARCIS, 1997.

———. "Diamela Eltit (1949)." In *Escritoras chilenas: Novela y cuento*. Edited by Patricia Rubio, 521–52. Santiago: Cuarto Propio, 1999.

Brooks, Peter. "Melodrama, Body, Revolution." In *Melodrama, Stage, Picture Screen*. Edited by Jacky Bratton, Jim Cook, and Christine Gledhill, 11–24. London: British Film Institute, 1994.

———. *The Melodramatic Imagination: Balzac, Henry James and the Mode of Excess*. New York: Columbia University Press, 1985.

Brownmiller, Susan. *Against Our Will: Men, Women and Rape*. New York: Simon & Schuster, 1975.

———. *Femininity*. New York: Linden Press/Simon & Schuster, 1984.

Brunet, Marta. *Obras completas*. Santiago: Zigzag, 1963.

———. "Down River." In *What Is Secret: Stories of Chilean Women*. Edited by Marjorie Agosín, 142–50. Fredonia, N.Y.: White Pine Press, 1995.

———. *Aguas abajo*. Santiago: Cuarto Propio, 1997.

———. *Montaña adentro*. Santiago: Editorial Universitaria, 1997.

———. *María Nadie*. Santiago: Pehuén, 1997.

———. "Solitude of Blood." In *Changing Lives through Literature*. Edited by Robert P. Waxler and Jean R. Trounstine, 59–80. Notre Dame, Ind.: University of Notre Dame Press, 1999.

———. "Solitude of Blood." In *Landscapes of a New Land*. Edited by Marjorie Agosín, 61–83. Fredonia, N.Y.: White Pine Press, 1989.

Brunner, José Joaquín. *Un espejo trizado: Ensayos sobre cultura y políticas culturales*. Santiago: FLACSO, 1988.

———. "Tradicionalismo y modernidad." In *Posmodernidad en la periferia: Enfoques latinoamericanos de la nueva teoría cultural*. Edited by Hermann Herlinghauss and Monika Walter, 48–82. Berlin: Langer Verlag, 1994.

———. "Notes on Modernity and Postmodernity in Latin America." In *The Postmodernism Debate in Latin America*. Edited by John Beverly, Michael Aronna, and José Oviedo, 34–54. Durham, N.C.: Duke University Press, 1995.

Butler, Judith. *Gender Trouble: Feminism and the Subversion of Identity*. New York: Routledge, 1990.

———. *The Psychic Life of Power: Theories in Subjection*. Stanford, Calif.: Stanford University Press, 1997.

———. *Antigone's Claim: Kinship between Life and Death*. New York: Columbia University Press, 2000.

Cahill, Ann J. *Rethinking Rape*. Ithaca, N.Y.: Cornell University Press, 2001.

Campbell, Margaret. "The Vaporous World of MLB." *Hispania* 44 (1961): 415–19.

Campos, Maximiliano Salinas. *"Contrapuntos."* In *Sexualidad y sociedades contemporáneas*. Edited by Kathya Araujo, Carolina Ibarra, 93, 94, 99. Santiago: Universidad Academia de Humanismo Cristiano, 2003.

Cánovas, Rodrigo. "Una visión panorámica." In *La novela chilena: Nuevas generaciones: El abordaje de los huérfanos*. Edited by Rodrigo Cánovas, 15–103. Santiago: Ediciones Universidad Católica, 1996.

———. *Sexualidad y cultura en la novela hispanoamericana: La alegoría del prostíbulo*. Santiago: LOM, 2003.

Carrasco, Maritza. "La historicidad de lo oculto: La violencia conyugal y la mujer en Chile (siglos XVIII y la primera mitad del XIX)." In *Perfiles revelados: Historias de mujeres en Chile, siglos XVIII–XX*. Edited by Diana Veneros Ruiz-Tagle, 113–39. Santiago: Universidad de Santiago, 1997.

Carreño, Rubí. "Familia y la crisis de los géneros en los años treinta." *Taller de Letras* 27 (1999): 135–48.

———. "Estereotipos e ideologías de género en M. Brunet y M. L. Bombal." *Anales de literatura chilena* 3 (2002): 43–51.

———. *Leche amarga: Violencia y erotismo en la narrativa chilena del siglo XX Bombal, Brunet, Donoso, Eltit*. Santiago: Cuarto Propio, 2007. Unpublished PhD dissertation, Universidad de Chile, 2004.

———. "Eltit y su red local/global de citas: Rescates del fundo y el supermercado." In *Letras y proclamas: La estética literaria de Diamela Eltit*. Edited by Bernardita Llanos, M., 143–71. Santiago: Cuarto Propio, 2006.

———. *Leche amarga: violencia y erotismo en la narrativa chile del siglo XX*. Bombal, Brunet, Donoso, Eltit. Santiago: Cuarto Propio, 2007.

Castillo, Alejandra. *La república masculina y la promesa igualitaria*. Santiago: Palinodia, 2005.

Casullo, Nicolás. "La modernidad como autoreflexión." In *Itinerarios de la modernidad: Corrientes del pensamiento y tradiciones intelectuales desde la Ilustración hasta la posmodernidad*. Edited by Nicolás Casullo, Ricardo Foster, and Alejandro Krafman, 9–22. Buenos Aires: Universidad de Buenos Aires, 1997.

Caws, Mary Ann. "Ladies Shot and Painted: Female Embodiment in Surrealist Art." In *The Female Body in Western Culture: Contemporary Perspectives*. Edited by Susan Rubin Suleiman, 262–87. Cambridge, Mass.: Harvard University Press, 1985.

Caygill, Howard. "Kant and the Relegation of the Passions." In *Politics and the Passions 1500–1850*. Edited by Victoria Kahn, Neil Saccamano, and Daniela Coli, 217–30. Princeton, N.J.: Princeton University Press, 2006.

Chaui, Marilena. "Sobre o medo." In *Os sentidos da paixáo*. Edited by Sergio Cardoso et al., 35–75. São Paulo: Funarte, Companhia Das Letras, 1995.

Collier, Simon, and William F. Sater. *A History of Chile 1808–2002*. Cambridge: Cambridge University Press, 2004.

Correa, Sofía et al., eds. *Historia del siglo XX chileno*. San Francisco: Editorial Sudamericana, 2001.

Cortés, Sergio Gatica. "Mujer, matrimonio y poder en Chile colonial: Un enfogue histórico teorico." In *Anuario del Programa Genéro y cultura en América Latina*. Santiago: Universidad de Chile, 1996.

Cuadra, Ivonne. "(De)formación de la imagen de la virgen María en Isaacs, Brunet y Queiroz." http://www.ucm.es/info/especulo/numero31/deforma.html.

Danesi, Marcel. *Vico, Metaphor, and the Origin of Language*. Bloomington: Indiana University Press, 1993.

David, Catherine. "Arte y políticas curatoriales." *Revista de Crítica Cultural* 17 (1998): 14–17.

De Beauvoir, Simone. *El segundo sexo*. Buenos Aires: Ediciones Siglo Veinte, 1987.

Deleuze, Gilles. *Proust y los signos*. Translated by Francisco Monge. Barcelona: Editorial Anagrama, 1972.

Deleuze, Gilles, and Félix Guattari. *A Thousand Plateaus: Capitalism and Schizophrenia*. Translated by Brian Massumi. Minneapolis: University of Minnesota Press, 1987.

———. "Coldness and Cruelty." In *Masochism*. Translated by G. Brazilier, 9–138. New York: Zone Books, 1991.

———. "What Is Minor Literature?" In *Narrative/Theory*, edited by David H. Richter, 273–80. White Plains, N.Y.: Longman, 1996.

Delsing, Riet. "Sobre mitos y relatos: El discurso sobre la familia." In *Discurso, género y poder: Discursos públicos: Chile 1978–1993*. Edited by Olga Grau et al., 149–64. Santiago: Arcis, La Morada, LOM, 1997.

Díaz Arrieta, Hernán. *Panorama de la literatura chilena durante el siglo XX*. Santiago: Editorial Nascimento, 1931.

Dollimore, Jonathan. *Death, Desire and Loss in Western Culture*. New York: Routledge, 1998.

Domínguez, Nora. "Diamela Eltit, una voz que pulsa las orillas ásperas." *Feminaria Literaria* 12, no. 18 (2003): 66–70.

Durán Cerda, Julio. "Puente de plata hacia el sur." *AUCH* 124, no. 3 (1961): 89–94.

Ehrlich, Susan. "The Institutional Coerciveness of Legal Discourse." In *Repre-*

senting Rape: Language and Sexual Consent. Edited by Susan Ehrlich, 31. London: Routledge, 2001.

Eltit, Diamela. *El padre mío.* Santiago: Francisco Zegers Editor, 1989.

———. *Vaca sagrada.* Buenos Aires: Editorial Planeta, 1991.

Eltit, Diamela, and Paz Errázuriz. *El infarto del alma.* Santiago: Francisco Zegers Editor, 1994.

———. *Sacred Cow.* Translated by Amanda Hopkinson. London and New York: Serpent's Tail, 1995.

———. *The Fourth World.* Translated by Dick Gerdes. Lincoln: University of Nebraska Press, 1995.

———. *El cuarto mundo.* 1st ed. Biblioteca Breve. Santiago: Planeta chilena, 1996.

———. "En mi novela la madre mata a sus hijos de otra manera, de un modo simbólico." *El Mercurio,* October 1, 1998, C9.

———. *Los trabajadores de la muerte.* Santiago: Planeta chilena, 1998.

———. *Lumpérica.* 3rd ed. Santiago: Seix Barral, 1998.

———. *Emergencias: Escritos sobre literatura, arte y política.* San Francisco: Planeta, 2000.

———. *Los vigilantes.* Santiago: Editorial Sudamericana, 2001.

———. *Mano de obra.* Santiago: Planeta, 2002.

———. "Los bordes de la letra." *Casa de las Américas* 230 (January–March 2003): 108–12.

———. "La Biblioteca personal de Diamela Eltit." http://www.letras.s5com/eltit220602.htm

Eltit, Diamela. *Custody of the Eyes.* Translated by Helen Lane and Roland Christ. Santa Fe, N.M.: Lumen, 2005.

———. "La familia XXI." http://www.letrass5.com/del00206.htm.

———. "No me hagas reír." http://www.letras.s5.com/eltit-b11.htm.

Farrell, Kirby. *Post Traumatic Culture: Injury and Interpretation in the Nineties.* Baltimore: John Hopkins University Press, 1998.

Felman, Shoshona. "Benjamin's Silence." *Critical Inquiry* 25 no. 2 (1999): 201–34.

Felski, Rita. *The Gender of Modernity.* Cambridge, Mass., and London: Harvard University Press, 1995.

———. *Literature after Feminism.* Chicago: University of Chicago Press, 2003.

Fernández, Magali. *El discurso narrativo en la obra de María Luisa Bombal.* Madrid: Editorial Pliegos, 1988.

Fiol-Mata, Licia. *A Queer Mother for the Nation: The State and Gabriela Mistral.* Minneapolis: University of Minnesota Press, 2002.

Foster, Ricardo. "La crisis de la racionalidad moderna." In *Itinerarios de la modernidad: Corrientes del pensamiento y tradiciones intelectuales desde la Ilustración hasta la posmodernidad.* Edited by Nicolás Casullo, Ricardo Foster, and Alejandro Krafman, 143–63. Buenos Aires: Universidad de Buenos Aires, 1997.

Foucault, Michel. *The History of Sexuality. Vol. 1, An Introduction.* Translated by Robert Hurley. New York: Vintage Books, 1980.

————. *Madness and Civilization: A History of Insanity in the Age of Reason.* Translated by Richard Howard. New York: Vintage Books, 1988.

————. "What Is Enlightenment?" In *The Foucault Reader.* Edited by Paul Rabinow, 32–50. New York: Pantheon Books, 1984.

Fraiman, Susan. *Unbecoming Women.* New York: Columbia University Press, 1993.

Franceschet, Susan. *Women and Politics in Chile.* Boulder, Colo. and London: Lynne Rienner, 2005.

Franco, Jean. "Afterword: From Romance to Refractory Aesthetic." In *Latin American Women's Writing: Feminist Readings in Theory and Crisis.* Edited by Anny Brooks, Bank Jones, and Catherine Davis, 226–37. Oxford: Clarendon Press, 1996.

————. *Critical Passions: Selected Essays.* Edited by Mary Louise Pratt and Kathleen Newman. Durham, N.C.: Duke University Press, 1999.

————. *The Modern Culture of Latin America: Society and the Artist.* Middlesex, England: Penguin Books, 1970.

Freud, Sigmund. *Obras completas.* Translated by José L. Echeverry. Vol. 7. Buenos Aires Argentina: Amorrortu Editores, 1975.

————. "Infantile Sexuality." In *Sigmund Freud: Psychological Writings and Letters.* Edited by Sander L. Gilman, 80–99. New York: Continuum, 1995.

————. "The Uncanny." In *Sigmund Freud: Psychological Writings and Letters,* edited by Sander L. Gilman, 120–53. New York: Continuum, 1995.

————. *Totem and Taboo: Resemblances between the Psychic Lives of Savages and Neurotics.* Translated by A. A. Brill. Amherst, N.Y.: 2000.

Fríes, Lorena, and Verónica Matus. *La ley hace el delito.* Santiago: LOM, 2000.

Gálvez Lira, Gloria. *María Luisa Bombal: Realidad y fantasía.* Potomac, Md.: Scripta Humanística, 1986.

García Canclini, Néstor. *Consumidores y ciudadanos: Conflictos multiculturales de la globalización.* México: Editorial Grijalbo, 1995.

————. "Contradictory Modernities and Globalization in Latin America." In *Through the Kaleidoscope: The Experience of Modernity in Latin America.* Edited by Vivian Schelling, 37–52. London and New York: Verso, 2000.

Gatica Cortés, Sergio. "Mujer, matrimonio y poder en Chile colonial: Un enfoque histórico teórico." In *Anuario del Programa Género y Cultura en América Latina,* 17–23. Santiago: Universidad de Chile, 1996.

Gligo, Agata. *María Luisa (Biografía de María Luisa Bombal).* Santiago: Editorial Sudamericana, 1996.

Goic, Cedomil. "La novela chilena actual: Tendencias y generaciones." *Anales de la Universidad de Chile* 119 (1960): 250–58.

————. "La última niebla." In *La novela chilena: Los mitos degradados,* 167–86. Santiago: Editorial Universitaria, 1991.

Granados, Pedro. "El cuarto mundo, un arte de amar nuevo." http://www.letras5scom/de030305.

Grau, Olga D. "Familia: Un grito de fin de siglo." In *Discurso, género y poder: Discursos públicos: Chile 1978–1993.* Edited by Olga Grau et al., 127–47. Santiago: Arcis, La Morada, LOM, 1997.

Grau, Olga D. et al. "Introducción." In *Discurso, Género y Poder: Discursos públicos: Chile 1978–1993*. Edited by Olga Grau et al., 95–103. Santiago: Arcis, La Morada, LOM, 1997.

Green, Mary. *Diamela Eltit Reading the Mother*. Suffolk: Tamesis, 2007.

Griffin, Susan. *Rape: The Power of Consciousness*. New York: Harper & Row, 1979.

Grimal, Pierre. *Dictionary of Classical Mythology*. Translated by A. R. Maxell-Hyslop. Edited by Stephen Kershaw. London: Penguin Books, 1990.

Guerra-Cunningham, Lucía. "Algunas reflexiones teóricas sobre la novela femenina." *Hispamérica* 28 (1981): 29–39.

———. "Introducción." In *María Luisa Bombal. Obras completas*. Edited by Lucía Guerra-Cunningham, 42. Santiago: Editorial Andrés Bello, 1997.

———. *La narrativa de María Luisa Bombal: Una visión de la existencia femenina*. Madrid España: Editorial Playor, 1980.

———. "Visión de lo femenino en la narrativa de María Luisa Bombal: Una dualidad contradictoria entre el Ser y el Deber-Ser." In *Texto e ideología en la narrativa chilena*, 151–68. Minnesota: Prisma Institute, 1987.

Gutiérrez Mouat, Ricardo. "Construcción y represión del deseo en las novelas de María Luisa Bombal." In *María Luisa Bombal: Apreciaciones críticas*. Edited by Marjorie Agosín, Elena Gascón-Vera, and Joy Renjilian-Burgy, 99–118. Tempe, Ariz.: Bilingual Press/Editorial Bilingüe, 1987.

Guzmán, Nicomedes. "La escritora Marta Brunet en las letras chilenas." In *Antología de cuentos*, 7–16. Santiago: Zig-Zag, 1970.

Guzmán Silva, Oscar. "90 años de Marta Brunet, Premio Nacional de 1961." *El Mercurio*, Aug. 9th 1987. Antofagasta.

Habermas, Jürgen. *The Structural Transformation of the Public Sphere: An Inquiry into a Category of Bourgeois Society*. Translated by Thomas Burger and Frederick Lawrence. Cambridge, Mass: MIT Press, 1989.

Hart, Michael, and Antonio Negri. *Empire*. Cambridge, Mass.: Harvard University Press, 2000.

Hays, Michael, and Anastasia Nikolopoulou. "Introduction." In *Melodrama: The Cultural Emergence of the Genre*. Edited by Michael Hays and Anastasia Nikolopoulou, vii–xv. New York: Saint Martin's Press, 1996.

Hays, Sharon. *The Cultural Contradictions of Motherhood*. New Haven, Conn.: Yale University Press, 1996.

Heilbrun, Carolyn. *Women's Lives: A View from the Threshold*. Toronto: University of Toronto Press, 1996.

———. *Writing a Woman's Life*. New York: Ballantine Books, 1989.

Hernández Romero, Sergio. "Notas biográficas de Marta Brunet." *Theoria* 4, (1995): 111–21.

Hopenhayn, Martín. "Moral y secularización en el Chile finisecular: Especulaciones para el debate." *CIEPLAN* 3.8, December 1993: 93–154.

———. "Postmodernism and Neoliberalism in Latin America." In *The Postmodernism Debate in Latin America*. Edited by John Beverly, Michael Aronna, and José Oviedo, 93–109. Durham, N.C.: Duke University Press, 1995.

Horkeimer, Max, and Theodor W. Adorno. *Dialectic of Enlightenment*. Translated by John Cumming. New York: Continuum, 1986.

Hull, Isabel V. *Sexuality, State and Civil Society in Germany, 1700–1815*. Ithaca, N.Y.: Cornell University Press, 1996.

Irigaray, Luce. "Commodities among Themselves." In *Literary Theory: An Anthology*. Edited by Julie Rivkin and Michael Ryan, 574–77. New York: Blackwell, 1998.

———. "The Power of Discourse and the Subordination of the Feminine." In *Literary Theory: An Anthology*. Edited by Julie Rivkin and Michael Ryan, 570–73. New York: Blackwell, 1998.

———. *Thinking the Difference: For a Peaceful Revolution*. Translated by Karen Monton. New York: Routledge, 1994.

———. "Volume without Contours." In *The Irigaray Reader*. Edited by Margaret Whitford, 53–67. Oxford, Mass.: Basil Blackwell, 1991.

Jameson, Fredric. "Marxism and Postmodernism." In *The Cultural Turn: Selected Writings on the Postmodern, 1983–1998*," 33–49. London: Verso, 1999.

———. "Postmodernism and Consumer Society." In *The Cultural Turn: Selected Writings on the Postmodern, 1983–1998*," 1–20. London: Verso, 1999.

———. "Theories of the Postmoderm." In *The Cultural Turn: Selected Writings on the Postmodern, 1983–1998*," 21–32. London: Verso, 1999.

Jay, Martin. "In the Empire of the Gaze: Foucault and the Denigration of the Vision in Twentieth-Century French Thought." In *Foucault: A Critical Reader*. Edited by David Couzens Hoy, 175–204. New York: Blackwell, 1986.

Justice, Blair, and Rita Justice. *The Broken Taboo: Sex in the Family*. New York: Human Science Press, 1979.

Kadir, Djelal. "A Woman's Place: Gendered Histories of the Subaltern." In *The Other Writing: Postcolonial Essays in Latin American Writing Culture*, 179–202. West Lafayette, Ind.: Purdue University Press, 1993.

Kaplan, Ann. "'Is the Gaze Male?" In *Women and Film: Both Sides of the Camera*," 23–35. New York: Methuen, 1983.

Kernberg, Otto. *Love Relations: Normalcy and Pathology*. New Haven, Conn.: Yale University Press, 1995.

Knibiehler, Yvonne. *Historia de las madres y de la maternidad en Occidente*. Translated by Paula Mahler. Buenos Aires: Nueva Visión, 2001.

Kostopulos-Cooperman, Celeste. *The Lyrical Vision of María Luisa Bombal*. London: Tamesis Books, 1988.

Kristeva, Julia. *Powers of Horror: An Esssay in Abjection*. New York: Columbia University Press, 1982.

———. "Revolution in Poetic Language." In The *Kristeva Reader*. Edited by Toril Moi, 90–136. New York: Columbia University Press, 1986.

———. "Stabat Mater." In *The Kristeva Reader*. Edited by Toril Moi. 160–86. New York: Columbia University Press, 1986.

———. "Word, Dialogue and Novel." In *The Kristeva Reader*. Edited by Toril Moi," 34–63. New York: Columbia University Press, 1986.

Labarca, Amanda. *Feminismo contemporáneo*. Santiago: Zig Zag, 1947.

Lagos, Ana María. *En tono mayor: Relatos de formación de la protagonista femenina en Hispanoamérica*. Santiago: Cuarto Propio, 1996.

———, ed. "Lenguaje, género y poder en *Los Vigilantes* de Diamela Eltit." In

Creación y resistencia: La narrativa de Diamela Eltit, 1983–1998, 129–47. Santiago: Editorial Cuarto Propio, 2000.

———. "Silencio y rebeldía: Hacia una valoración de María Luisa Bombal dentro de la tradición de escritura femenina." In *María Luisa Bombal: Apreciaciones críticas.* Edited by Marjorie Agosín, Elena Gascón-Vera, and Joy Renjilian-Burgy, 119–35. Tempe, Ariz.: Bilingual Press/Editorial Bilingue, 1987.

Lamas, Marta, ed. "Introducción." In *La construcción cultural de la diferencia sexual,* 9–20. México D.F.: Universidad Autónoma Nacional de México, 1996.

Landes, Joan B., ed. "The Public and Private Sphere: A Feminist Reconsideration." In *Feminism: The Public and the Private,* 135–63. Oxford: Oxford University Press, 1998.

Larraín, Jorge. *Identidad chilena.* Santiago: LOM, 2001.

———. *Identity and Modernity in Latin America.* Oxford, Mass: Blackwell, 2000.

Lavrín, Asunción. "Female, Feminine, and Feminist: Key Concepts in Understanding Women's History in Twentieth Century Latin America." *Occasional Lecture Series* 1988, 1–23.

———. "The Ideology of Feminism in the Southern Cone, 1900–1940." *Working Paper of the Latin American Program of the Woodrow Wilson International Center,* 1986, 1–42.

———. *Women, Feminism and Social Change in Argentina, Chile and Uruguay 1840–1940.* Lincoln: University of Nebraska Press, 1995.

Lavrín, Asunción, ed. "Introducción." In *Sexualidad y matrimonio en la América Hispánica: Siglos XVI–XVIII,* 13–52. México: Grijalbo, 1991.

Lechner, Norbert, and Susana Levy. *Notas sobre la vida cotidiana III: El disciplinamiento de la mujer.* Santiago: FLACSO, 1984.

Lemebel, Pedro. *La esquina es mi corazón: Crónica urbana.* Santiago: Cuarto Propio, 1997.

———. *Loco afán: Crónicas de sidario.* Santiago: Editorial Anagrama, 1996.

Lewis, C. S. *The Allegory of Love: A Study in Medieval Tradition.* New York: Oxford University Press, 1960.

Lillo, Cabezas, Mario. "Ensayo chileno ee identidad." *Taller de Letras* 27 (November 1999): 23–32.

Lindstrom, Naomi. "El Discurso de La Amortajada: Convención Burguesa vs. Conciencia Cuestionadora." In *María Luisa Bombal: Apreciaciones críticas.* Edited by Marjorie Agosín, Elena Gascón-Vera, and Joy Renjilian-Burgy, 147–61. Tempe, Ariz.: Bilingual Press/Editorial Bilingue, 1987.

———. "Foreward." In *House of Mist and the Shrouded Woman: Novels by María Luisa Bombal,"* vii–xii. Austin: University of Texas Press, 1995.

Llanos, Bernardita. "El sujeto explosionado: Eltit y la geografía del discurso del padre." *Lingüística Y Literatura* (1997): 29–42.

———. "Emociones, hablas y fronteras en *Los Vigilantes* de Diamela Eltit." *Casa de Las Américas* 230 (January–March 2003): 126–29.

———. "Fugas y gestos del sujeto cautivo en *El infarto del alma* de Diamela Eltit y Paz Errázuriz." *Confluencia* 19, no 1 (Fall 2003): 50–58.

———. "Hibridismo, confusiones y marcas del sujeto sudaca en *El Cuarto Mundo* de Diamela Eltit." http://www.Literateworld.Com/Spanish/2002/Escritores/Sep/W01.Test9escritores.html.

————. "Historia y memoria del cuerpo en la letra: *Los Vigilantes* de Diamela Eltit." In *Mujeres y cambio desde la letra*. Edited by Chonin Horno-Delgado and Janet N. Gold, 187–206. República Dominicana: Secretaría de la Mujer, 2005.

————. "Masculinidad, estado y violencia en la ciudad neoliberal." In *Reinas de otro cielo: Modernidad y autoritarismo en la obra de Pedro Lemebel*. Edited by Fernando Blanco, 75–113. Santiago: LOM, 2004.

————. "Si vas para el mall: objetos, series y remedos del kitsch de Cabezas y Truffa." In *Cabezas + Truffa, Se Vende: Si vas para el Mall*, 1–16. Santiago: Fondart, 2001.

————. "Sobre el retorno y sus fantasmas: Mistral y *Tala*." In *Más allá de la ciudad letrada: Escritoras de nuestra América*. Edited by Eliana Ortega, 55–64. Santiago: ISIS Internacional, 2001.

————. "Transgresión y violencia sexual en Marta Brunet." *Mapocho* (December 2000): 29–37.

Llanos, M. Bernardita, ed. "Pasiones maternales y carnales en la narrativa de Eltit." *In Letras y proclamas: La estética literaria de Diamela Eltit*, 103–41. Santiago: Cuarto Propio, 2006.

Loveman, Brian. *Chile. The Legacy of Hispanic Capitalism*. New York: Oxford University Press, 1988.

Lértora, Juan Carlos, ed. "Diamela Eltit: Hacia una poética menor." In *Una poética de literatura menor: La narrativa de Diamela Eltit*, 27–35. Santiago: Cuarto Propio, 1993.

Lévi-Strauss, Claude. *The Elementary Structures of Kinship*. Translated by James Harle Bell and John Richard Von Sturmer. Boston: Beacon Press, 1969.

López Moralis, Berta. *Órbita de Marta Brunet*. Concepción: Ediciones Universidad de Concepción, 1997.

————. "Recepción crítica de la obra de Marta Brunet." http://www.Cervant esvirtual.Com/Bib_Autor/Brunet/Recritica.shtml."

Maíz-Peña, Magdalena. "Hibridismo textual y disidencia cultural en *Los Vigilantes* de D. E.*" South Eastern Latin Americanist 40* (1996): 27–34.

Malverde Disselkoen, Ivette. "De La última niebla y La amortajada a La Brecha." *Nuevo Texto Crítico 3* (1989): 69–78.

Mannarelli, María Emma. "La domesticación de la sexualidad en las sociedades jerárquicas." In *Sexualidades y sociedades contemporáneas*. Edited by Kathya Araujo and Carolina Ibarra, 57–83. Santiago: Universidad Academia de Humanismo Cristiano, 2003.

Mansilla, Luis Alberto. "Prólogo." In *Humo hacia el Sur,* 5–13. Santiago: LOM, 1998.

"Marta Brunet fue calificada de inmoral y hereje." *Revista Zig-Zag,* 1961, 25.

Masiello, Francine. *The Art of Transition: Latin American Culture and the Neoliberal Crisis*. Durham, N.C.: Duke University Press, 2001.

————. "Melodrama, Sex and Nation." In *The Places of History: Regionalism Revisited in Latin America*. Edited by Doris Sommer," 269–78. Durham, N.C.: Duke University Press, 1999.

Melón de Díaz, Esther. *La narrativa de Marta Brunet*. Puerto Rico, España: Editorial Universitaria, 1975.

Méndez Rodenas, Adriana. "Narcissus in Bloom: The Desiring Subject in Modern Latin American Narrative—María Luisa Bombal and Juan Rulfo." In *Latin American Women's Writing: Feminist Readings in Theory and Crisis.* Edited by Anny Brooksbank Jones and Catherine Davies," 104–26. New York: Oxford University Press, 1996.

Meyer, Doris. "'Feminine' Testimony in the Works of Teresa de La Parra, María Luisa Bombal and Victoria Ocampo." In *Contemporary Women Authors of Latin America.* Edited by Doris Meyer and Margarite Fernández Olmos," 3–15. New York: Brooklyn College Press, 1983.

Monsiváis, Carlos. "Penetración cultural y nacionalismo (el caso mexicano)." In *No intervención, autodeterminación y democracia en América Latina.* Edited by Pablo Gómez Casanova, 75–89. México: D. F. Siglo Veintiuno Editores, 1983.

Montecino, Sonia. *Madres y huachos: Alegorías del mestizaje chileno.* Santiago: Cuarto Propio, 1993.

Montes, Hugo. "Evocación de Marta Brunet." *Atenea,* 1992, 291–97.

———. "Prólogo." In *María Nadie,* 7–13. Santiago: Pehuén, 1997.

Mora, Gabriela. "Una lectura de 'Soledad de la sangre' de Marta Brunet." *Estudios Filológicos 19"* (1984): 81–90.

Morales, Leonidas. *Conversaciones con Diamela Eltit.* Santiago: Cuarto Propio, 1998.

Moulian, Tomás. *Chile actual: Anatomía de un mito.* Santiago: LOM, 1997.

———. *Material docente sobre historia de Chile.* Santiago: FLACSO, 1986.

Munnich, Susana. *La dulce niebla: Lectura femenina y chilena de María Luisa Bombal.* Santiago: Editorial Universitaria, 1991.

Muraro, Luisa. *El orden smbólico de la madre.* Translated by Beatriz Albertini. Madrid: Horas y Horas, 1994.

Nelson, Esther. "The Space of Longing: *La última niebla." The American Hispanist 3,* no. 21" (November 1977): 7–11.

———. "Un viaje fantástico: Quién habla en *La Amortajada?"* In *María Luisa Bombal: Apreciaciones críticas.* Edited by Marjorie Agosín, Elena Gascón-Vera, and Joy Renjilian-Burgy, 182–200. Tempe, Ariz.: Bilingual Press/Editorial Bilingue, 1987.

Neustadt, Robert. "Diarula Eltit: Clearing Space for a Critical Performance." In *(Con)Fusing Signs and Postmodern Positions: Spanish American Performance, Experimental Writing and the Critique of Political Confusion,* 25–81. New York: Garland, 1999.

———. *Cada día: La creación de un arte social (Zurita, Eltit, Rosenfled).* Santiago: Cuarto Propio, 2002.

Niebylski, Dianna. "Against Mimesis: *Lumpérica* Revisited." *Revista canadiense de estudios hispánicos 24,* no. 2 (Winter 2001): 241–57.

Norat, Gisela. "Diálogo fraternal: *El cuarto mundo* de Diamela Eltit y *Cristóbal Nonato* de Carlos Fuentes." *Chasqui, Revista de literatura latinoamericana 23,* no. 2 (November 1994): 74–85.

———. *Marginalities: Diamela Eltit and the Subversion of Mainstream Narrative in Chile.* Newark, Del.: University of Delaware Press, 2002.

Ojeda, Cecilia. "Hacia una revisión crítica de la narrativa de Marta Brunet: *Humo hacia el Sur* y *María Nadie." Confluencia 14,* no. 1 (Fall 1998): 112–25.

Olea, Raquel. "De la épica lumpen al texto sudaca. El proyecto narrativo de Diamela Eltit." In *Lengua víbora: Producciones de lo femenino en la escritura de mujeres chilenas*, 47–82. Santiago: Cuarto Propio, 1998.

Olson, Carl. *Zen and the Art of Postmodern Philosophy: Two Paths of Liberation from the Representational Mode of Thinking*. Albany: State University of New York Press, 2000.

Orozco Vera, María Jesús. *La narrativa femenina chilena (1923–1980): Escritura y enajenación*. Zaragoza: Anubar Ediciones, 1995.

Ortega, Julio. "Diamela Eltit y el imaginario de la virtualidad." In *Una poética de literatura menor: La narrativa de Diamela Eltit*. Edited by Juan Carlos Lértora, 53–81. Santiago: Cuarto Propio, 1993.

———. "Eltit: Virtualidades." In *Caja de herramientas: Prácticas culturales para el nuevo siglo chileno*, 37–45. Santiago: LOM, 2000.

Oyarzún, Kemy. "Prólogo." In *Aguas abajo*, 7–33. Santiago: Editorial Cuarto Propio, 1997.

———. "Prólogo." In *Montaña adentro*, 15–37. Santiago: Editorial Universitaria, 1997.

Paranaguá, Paulo Antonio. *Tradición y modernidad en el cine de América Latina*. España: Fondo de Cultura Económica, 2003.

Pateman, Carol. *The Sexual Contract*. Stanford, Calif.: Stanford University Press, 1988.

Piña, Juan Andrés, ed. *Conversaciones con la narrativa chilena*. Santiago: Editorial Los Andes, 1991.

Pino-Ojeda, Waleska. "Diamela Eltit: El letrado y el lumpen." In *Sobre castas y puentes: Conversaciones con Elena Poniatowska, Rosario Ferré y Diamela Eltit*, 137–99. Santiago: Cuarto Propio, 2000.

Pizarro, Ana. "Mistral ¿Qué Modernidad?" In *Re-Leer hoy a Gabriela Mistral: Mujer, historia y sociedad en América Latina*. Edited by Gastón Lillo and J. Guillermo Renart," 43–52. Ottawa and Santiago: University of Ottawa and Universidad de Santiago, 1997.

Pizarro, Carolina. "Mujer: ¿Cómo decirlo?" In *Novela chilena: Nuevas generaciones: El abordaje de los huérfanos*. Edited by Rodrigo Cánovas, 123–33. Santiago: Ediciones Universidad Católica, 1996.

Poblete, Hernán. "Guía de lectores." *La Tercera*, April 30, 1978, 13.

Promis, José. "En torno a la nueva novela hispanoamericana: Reubicación de un concepto." *Chasqui*, 7-1 (1977): 16–27.

———. *La novela chilena actual (Orígenes y desarrollo)*. Argentina: F. García Gambeiro, 1977.

———. "LUN en el contexto novelesco de 1930–1935." In *Literatura chilena, creación y crítica*, 2–4. Los Angeles: Ediciones de la Frontera, 1981.

———. "La técnica narrativa de María Luisa Bombal." In *María Luisa Bombal: Apreciaciones críticas*. Edited by Marjorie Agosín, Elena Gascón-Vera and Joy Renjilian-Burgy, 201–10. Tempe, Ariz.: Bilingual Press/Editorial Bilingue, 1987.

Rábago, Alberto. "Elementos surrealistas en LUN." *Hispania* 64 (1981): 31–40.

Rama, Angel. "Marta Brunet: Premio Nacional de literatura." *Marcha*, February 18, 1962, 21–22.

————. "La condición humana de la mujer." In "Soledad de la sangre," 7–14. Montevideo: Arca, 1967.

————. "Literatura y cultura en América Latina." *Revista de crítica literaria latinoamericana*, 1983, 7–35.

Richard, Nelly. *Margins and Institutuions: Art in Chile since 1973*. Victoria: Art and Text, 1986.

————. *Masculino/Femenino: Prácticas de la diferencia y cultura democrática*. Santiago: Francisco Zegers Editor, 1993.

————. "Chile, Woman and Dissidence." In *Beyond the Fantastic: Contemporary Art Criticism from Latin America*. Edited by Gerardo Mosquera, 137–44. London: Institute of International Visual Arts, and Cambridge, Mass.: MIT Press, 1996.

————. "Women's Art Practices and the Critique of Signs." In *Beyond the Fantastic: Contemporary Art Criticism from Latin America*. Edited by Gerardo Mosquera, 145–53. London: Institute of International Visual Arts, and Cambridge, Mass.: MIT Press, 1996.

————. *Residuos y metáforas: Ensayos de crítica cultural sobre la transición*. Santiago: Cuarto Propio, 1998.

————. "Performance of the Chilean Avanzada." In *Corpus Delicti: Performance Art of the Americas*. Edited by Coco Fusco. Translated by Paul Foss and Juan Avila," 203–17. London: Routledge, 2000.

Riesco, Laura. "La Amortajada: Experiencia y conocimiento." In *María Luisa Bombal: Apreciaciones críticas*. Edited by Marjorie Agosín, Elena Gascón-Vera, and Joy Renjilian-Burgy, 211–21. Tempe, Ariz.: Bilingual Press/ Editorial Bilingüe, 1987.

Ríos Avila, Rubén. *La raza cómica del sujeto en Puerto Rico*. Puerto Rico: Ediciones Callejón, 2002.

Ripley, Doré. "Hunting through Medieval Literature." http://www.dead-onwebsites.com/under%20discount/hunt/med_hunt.htm.

Riquelme, Sonia. "Notas sobre el criollismo chileno y el personaje femenino en la narrativa de Marta Brunet." *Discurso literario: Revista de temas hispánicos* (Spring 1987): 613–22.

Rodríguez-Peralta, Phyllis. "María Luisa Bombal's Poetic Novels of Female Estrangement." *Revista de Estudios Hispánicos* (1980): 139–55.

Rojo, Grínor. "Gabriela Mistral en la historia de la mujer latinoamericana." In *Re-leer hoy a Gabriela Mistral: Mujer, historia y sociedad en América Latina*. Edited by Gástón Lillo and J. Guillermo Renart, 53–82. Ottawa and Santiago: University of Ottawa and Universidad de Santiago, 1997.

Romero Hernández, Sergio. "Notas Biográficas de Marta Brunet." *Theoria, Bío Bío* 4 (1995): 111–21.

Rossi, Jorge. "La evasión de la realidad en *La última niebla*." In *María Luisa Bombal: Apreciaciones críticas*. Edited by Marjorie Agosín, Elena Gascón-Vera, and Joy Renjilian-Burgy, 230–36. Tempe, Ariz.: Bilingual Press/Editorial Bilingüe, 1987.

Rougement de, Denis. *Love in the Western World*. Translated by Montgomery Belgion. Princeton, N.J.: Princeton University Press, 1983.

Rubio, Patricia. "*House of Mist*, de María Luisa Bombal: Una novela olvidada." *Literatura y Lingüística*, 1998, 181–204.

————, ed. *Escritoras chilenas: Novela y cuento*. Santiago: Cuarto Propio, 1999.

Russo, Mary. *The Female Grotesque*. New York: Routledge, 1994.

Russotto, Márgara. *Tópicos de retórica femenina*. Caracas: Monte Avila Editores, 1993.

Salomone, Alicia N. et al. *Modernidad en otro tono: Escritura de mujeres latinoamericanas: 1920–1950*. Santiago: Cuarto Propio, 2004.

Santos, Danilo. "Retóricas marginales." In *Novela chilena: Nuevas generaciones: El abordaje de los huérfanos*, edited by Rodrigo Cánovas, 135–53. Santiago: Ediciones Universidad Católica, 1996.

Sarlo, Beatriz. "The Modern City: Buenos Aires, the Peripheral Metropolis." In *Through the Kaleidoscope: The Experience of Modernity in Latin America*. Edited by Vivian Schelling. Translated by Lorraine Leu, 108–23. London: Verso, 2000.

————. *Una modernidad periférica: Buenos Aires, 1920–1930*. Buenos Aires: Ediciones Nueva Visión, 1988.

Schelling, Vivian, ed. "Introduction: Reflections on the Experience of Modernity in Latin America." In *Through the Kaleidoscope: The Experience of Modernity in Latin America*. Translated by Lorraine Leu, 1–36. London: Verso, 2000.

Sepúlveda, Emma. "María Luisa Bombal y el silencio." In *María Luisa Bombal: Apreciaciones críticas*. Edited by Marjorie Agosín, Elena Gascón-Vera, and Joy Renjilian-Burgy, 230–36. Tempe, Ariz.: Bilingual Press/Editorial Bilingüe, 1987.

Silva Castro, Raúl. *Panorama literario de Chile*. Santiago: Editorial Universitaria, 1961.

Soler, Colette. "What Does the Unconscious Know about Women? In *Reading Seminar XX: Lacan's Major Work on Love, Knowledge and Feminine Sexuality*. Translated by François Raffoul and David Pettigrew. Edited by Suzanne Barnard and Bruce Fink, 99–108. Albany: New York State University Press, 2002.

Sosnowski, Saúl. "El agua, motivo primordial en LUN." *Cuadernos* 1973, 277–78, 365–74.

Stevens, Evelyn. "Marianismo: The Other Face of Machismo in Latin America." In *Confronting Change, Challenging Tradition: Women in Latin American History*. Edited by Gertrude M. Yeager, 3–17. Wilmington, Del.: Scholarly Resources, 1994.

Subercaseux, Bernardo. *Chile, ¿Un país moderno?* Santiago: Ediciones B, 1996.

Taylor, Victor E. "Contracting Masochism: Pain, Pleasure and the Language of Power." In *One Hundred Years of Masochism: Literary Texts, Social and Cultural Contexts*. Edited by Michael C. Finke and Carl Niekerk, 53–69. Amsterdam: Rodopi, 2000.

Tierney-Tello, Mary Beth. "On Making Images Speak: Writing and Photography." In *Photography and Writing in Latin America: Double Exposures*. Edited by Marcy E. Schwartz and Mary Beth Tierney-Tello, 87–113. Albuquerque: University of New Mexico Press, 2006.

————. "Testimonio, ética y estética en Diamela Eltit." In *Letras y proclamas: la estética literaria de Diamela Eltit*. Edited by Bernardita Llanos, M., 69–101. Santiago: Cuarto Propio, 2006.

Tinsman, Heidi. "Los patrones del Hogar: Esposas golpeadas y control sexual en Chile rural, 1958–1988." In *Disciplina y desacato: Construcción de la identidad en Chile, siglos XIX y XX*. Edited by Lorena Godoy et al. 111–46. Santiago: SUR/CEDEM, 1995.

Tobin, Robert. "Masochism and Identity." In *One Hundred Years of Masochism: Literary Texts, Social and Cultural Contexts*. Edited by Michael C. Finke and Carl Niekerk, 33–52. Amsterdam: Rodopi, 2000.

Trounstine, Jean R. "For Discussion." In *Changing Lives through Literature*, 78–80. Notre Dame, Ind.: University of Notre Dame Press, 1999.

Valdés, Adriana. "Las novelistas chilenas: Breve visión histórica y reseña crítica." *Aisthesis: Revista chilena de investigaciones estéticas* no 3 (1968): 113–30. (1968): 113–30.

———. "Gestos de fijación, gestos de desplazamiento: Algunos rasgos de la producción cultural reciente en Chile." In *Cultura, autoritarismo y redemocratización en Chile*. Edited by Manuel Garretón, Saúl Sosnowski, and Bernardo Subercaseaux, 135–46. Santiago: Fondo de Cultura Económica, 1993.

———. *Composición de lugar: Escritos sobre cultura*. Santiago: Editorial Universitaria, 1996.

Valdés, Teresa. *De lo social a lo político: La acción de las mujeres latinoamericanas*. Santiago: LOM, 2000.

Valente, Ignacio. "El cuerpo es un horror y es una gloria." *Revista de libros. El Mercurio*, May 21, 1989, 1–4.

Veneros Ruiz-Tagle, Diana, ed. "Continuidad, cambio y reacción 1900–1930." In *Perfiles revelados: Historias de mujeres en Chile siglos XVIII–XX*, 21–39. Santiago: Universidad de Santiago, 1997.

Veneros Ruiz-Tagle, Diana, ed. "Siglo XX: Cambalache: Breve reseña histórica de los avances de la mujer en Chile," 113–21. Investigaciones Red Nacional Universitaria Interdisciplinaria de Estudios de Género, 2001.

Vidal, Hernán. *María Luisa Bombal: La femenidad enajenada*. España: Colección Aubí, 1976.

Ward, Elizabeth. *Father-Daughter Rape*. London: Women's Press, 1984.

Waxler, Robert P., and Jean R. Trounstine. "Solitude of Blood." In *Changing Lives through Literature*. Translated by Elaine Dorough Johnson, 59–80. Notre Dame, Ind.: University of Notre Dame Press, 1999.

Weldt-Basson, Helene C. Torre. "Women and the City: Sexual Initiation of Female Protagonists in Marta Brunet, María Luisa Bombal, Sandra Cisneros and Rosario Castellanos." *Revista de la Universidad de Puerto Rico,* (January–March, 2006): 65–78.

Williams, Lorna. "The Shrouded Woman: Marriage and Its Constraints in the Fiction of María Luisa Bombal." *Latin American Literary Review,* (Spring–Summer 1977): 21–30.

Williams, Raymond, ed. "Truth Claims, Postmodernism and the Latin American Novel." *Profession* no 92 (1992): 6–9.

———. "Women Writing in the Americas: New Projects in the 1980s." In *The Novel in the Americas,* 119–31. Boulder: University Press of Colorado, 1992.

Yalom, Marilyn. *La historia del pecho*. Translated by Antoni Puigros. España: Tusquets, 1997.

Yáñez, María Flora. *Historia de mi vida*. Santiago: Nascimento, 1980.

Žižek, Slavoj. *The Metastases of Enjoyment: Six Essays about Women and Causality*. London, New York: Verso, 1994.

———. "Welcome to the Desert of the Real." In *Dissent from the Homeland: Essays after September 11*. Edited by Stanley Hauver and Frank Letricchia, 137–48. Durham, N.C.: Duke University Press, 2003.

Index